What's in a Chinese Character

趣味汉字

TAN HUAY PENG

新世界出版社
NEW WORLD PRESS

©1998 Federal Publicaitons (S) Pte Ltd
Original edition under the title
What's in a Chinese Character
First published 1998 by
Federal Publications (S) Pte Ltd
A member of the Times Publishing Group
Times Centre, 1 New Industrial Road, Singapore 536196

Edited by Li Shujuan
Cover Design by Tang Shaowen

Fourth Printing 2001
ISBN 7 − 80005 − 515 − 9 /G·195

Published by
NEW WORLD PRESS
24 Baiwanzhuang Road, Beijing 100037, China

Distributed by
NEW WORLD PRESS
24 Baiwanzhuang Road, Beijing 100037, China

Printed in the People's Republic of China

前 言

　　中国的汉字至今已有五千多年的历史。尽管汉字不断地发展演变，但基础的汉字书写形式在公元200年就形成了。它不仅生动地反映出中国人生活的一个侧面，同时也标志着人类早期文明的伟大成就。

　　汉字包括各种各样的字体形式，从简单的表形和表意字到复杂的复合字，均由汉字的字根或形声旁发展演变而来。在汉字中共有214个形声旁。有些可以独立作为单独的字而存在，有些则需要与其他的字组合而成。

　　本书以卡通漫画形式表现出形声旁以及与它们相关联的字是如何发展演化的过程，形象地讲述了汉字的起源以及中国人内心深处蕴藏的幽默感。书中详细地介绍了369个常用汉字的起源和发展、它们的各种笔画形式和顺序，以及一些基础的汉字知识。这些都能有效地帮助初学者学习汉字，掌握正确的书写形式。同时，本书的附录还为初学者提供了汉语中有关月份、星期和数字的表达方法。此外，书后按汉语拼音音节顺序编排的索引为读者和初学者查找本书中每个汉字的具体内容提供了极大的方便。

　　本书全部漫画均由陈火平（Tan Huay Peng）绘制。此书的出版得到了新加坡联邦出版有限公司的鼎力协助。本书中的英文原文和漫画均引进新加坡联邦出版有限公司1998年出版的 WHAT'S IN A CHINESE CHARACTER 一书。在此，我们向原出版者和作者表示最诚挚的谢意。我们衷心地祝愿此书的出版能使读者在轻松的阅读中体味汉字的无穷魅力，并且读有所获。

Preface

A Chinese script of one form or another has been in existence for over 5,000 years. Although it has continued to develop, the basic form of the writing was already established by 200 A.D. This makes it not only a very interesting aspect of Chinese life, but also one of mankind's greatest early achievements.

Chinese script consists of characters, which range from simple pictographic representations of objects, to complex compound characters. These are built up from root characters, or radicals. Of the 214 radicals, some can function independently as characters, and are then contracted when they appear in combination.

This set of cartoons illustrates how some of the radicals, and their associated characters, have evolved over the years. They make a useful introduction to the Chinese language and also provide a fascinating insight into the Chinese sense of humour. Useful information and basic knowledge is provided on the origins and development, as well as the types of stroke and stroke sequence of 369 commonly used characters introduced in the book, which will help those learning Chinese characters and their written forms. Also, the Chinese words for numbers, days and months are provided in the Appendix. In addition, the Index, arranged in the order of pinyin (the phonetic transcriptions of Chinese characters) syllables, provides great convenience for finding the meaning of each character for readers.

All the cartoons in the book were drawn by Tan Huay Peng. In publishing this bilingual edition we have received great help from Federal Publications (S) Pte Ltd, Singapore who supplied us with the English text and cartoons published in the book WHAT'S IN A CHINESE CHARACTER in 1998. Therefore, with the publication of this bilingual edition, we express our heartfelt thanks to the author and the original publisher. We sincerely hope that this book will help readers savour the inexhaustible charms of Chinese characters and enjoy the fruits of learning through leisurely reading.

引　言
Introduction

历史背景
Historical Background

　　汉字的起源带有一定的神秘色彩，有各式各样的传说解释它的产生。其中的一个传说讲述了黄帝手下一位名叫仓颉的史官如何观察飞禽走兽的足迹。当他注意到每个动物的足迹都不同，而且具有可分辨性时，受到了启发，于是他把每个物体画成画，并简化了线条的数量。这就是最早出现的被汉朝语言学家许慎称之为的象形字。

The origins of Chinese script are shrouded in mystery, and various legends exist to explain its creation. One such legend tells how Cāng Jié 仓颉, a minister of the Emperor Huáng Dì 黄帝, observed the footprints of birds and animals. He noticed how each one was distinct and recognisable. Inspired by this, Cāng Jié drew pictures of objects, simplifying them by reducing the number of lines. These were the first pictographs, called xiàng xìng 象形 by the Han lexicographer Xǔ Shèn 许慎 (30 A.D.-124 A.D.)

象形字
Pictographs

　　象形字可以很好地表现一个事物，例如：动物、植物、身体的各个部位等等。随着汉字的发展，我们不难看出，现在的汉字已失去了它所反映的事物的原本面目。

Certain items could be represented very well by pictographs, for example: animals; plants; parts of the body etc. As the development of a particular character is traced, we can see that, over time, it tends to lose some of its resemblance to the original.

象形字与现在的汉字对照表：
Examples of Pictographs

⊖	日	rì	sun	川	水	shuǐ	water
月	月	yuè	moon	火	火	huǒ	fire
山	山	shān	mountain	木	木	mù	wood
虎	虎	hǔ	tiger	羊	羊	yáng	sheep
象	象	xiàng	elephant	马	马	mǎ	horse
犬	犬	quǎn	dog	目	目	mù	eye
耳	耳	ěr	ear	手	手	shǒu	hand
口	口	kǒu	mouth				

表意字
Ideographs

这些字表示抽象的概念。汉朝语言学家许慎将它们称为指事。

These are characters which represent abstract concepts. Xŭ Shèn called them zhĭ shì 指事.

例句:

Examples of Ideographs

一	yī	one	上	shàng	up, above
二	èr	two	下	xià	lower, below
三	sān	three			

形声字
Determinative-Phonetic Characters

随着文明的进步，新字的需求逐渐增多。于是，一种新字的形式孕育而生，即形声字。

这些字都具有表形旁以表达其意，同时还有一个表声旁以表示读音。

As civilisation grew, so did the demand for new characters. To this end, a new type of character was invented called determinative-phonetic, or xíng shēng 形声.

These characters have a determinative part, to convey the meaning, and a phonetic part to show pronunciation.

下列是读音相近的形声字:

Examples of Determinative-Phonetic Characters with a Similar Pronunciation

表形字 **Determinative**	表声字 **Phonetic**	复合字 **Compound**
水 shuǐ (water; abbrev. 氵)	+ 其 qǐ (his, her its this, that; originally winnowing basket, now 箕)	→ 淇 qí (the River Qi)
玉 yù (jade; abbrev. 王)	+ 其 qí	→ 琪 qí (a valuable white stone or gem)
木 mù (tree; wood)	+ 其 qí	→ 棋檗 qí (chinese chess)

上述表现了读音相同但写法完全不同的字。"其"不论在复合字或单独使用时都念"qí"，意为"他的、她的、它的"。

This shows how words with the same pronunciation are written completely differently. 其 qí is always a phonetic when it appears in a compound word, although it can function as a character itself, meaning his, her, its etc.

下列是意思相近的形声字:

Examples of Determinative-Phonetic Characters with a Similar Meaning

木 mù (wood) +　　　　　　　　　　→ 杜 dù (the russet pear; to shut out;
土 tǔ (earth; land; ground)　　　　　　　　　to stop; to prevent)

木 mù (wood) +　　　　　　　　　　→ 板 bǎn (board; blocks for printing)
反 fǎn (to turn over; to rebel; to turn back)

　　每个象形字都可以当声旁使用，很少具有形旁的功能。形旁的使用是为了给字典中的字归类。到了清朝，形旁的数量已经减少到现有的 214 个。除了上述介绍的三种形式外，还有一些其他形式。当两个或两个以上的象形字或表意字结合在一起时就形成了一个全新的字。

　　Every pictograph can be used as a phonetic, but only a few function as determinatives. This system of radicals was introduced to enable characters to be classified in a dictionary. By the time of the Qing Dynasty (1644 A.D - 1911 A.D.) the number of radicals had been reduced to its current level of 214. Apart from the three major groups of characters already mentioned, there are also a few others. Associative compounds are formed when two or more pictographs or ideographs are combined to create a completely new character.

e.g.

木	+	木	→	林	means 'a place
mù		mù		lín	overgrown with trees'
wood		wood		forest	(represented by the
					component for 'wood')

手	+	分	+	手	→	掰	means 'to separate
shǒu		fén		shǒu		bāi	something with two
hand		to separate		hand			hands'

　　表声字可以组成另外的字，如：来。原先并没有这个字，因为它很难描述。同一个"来"字还可以表示谷类作物。于是，这个字就这样使用下来了。

　　Phonetic loan characters make up another group. An example of this is the word *lái*, which means come. Originally, no character existed for this as it is difficult to depict. The same word can also mean cereal plant 𡴀 𡋡 來 . So the character for this was used instead.

　　从公元 200 年到 600 年楷书出现后，汉字的字体就没有进一步发展。但是由于使用了可以创造新字形声旁，所以汉字便得以一直继续地发展进化。

　　Following the introduction of *kǎi shū*, or standard script, between 200 A.D. and 600 A.D., there was no further formal development of the script. However, as new characters can be created using the determinative-phonetic system, the language has continued to grow and evolve.

汉字的结构
Structure of Characters

一个汉字由一个或多个部分组成，例如:
A Chinese character is made up of one or more parts, e.g.

one component	日				rì	sun

one component   日   rì   sun

two components   女 ＋ 子 → 好   hǎo   good

three components   亻 ＋ 尔 ＋ 心 → 您   nín   you

汉字是一种方块字，有几个基本结构。
The characters are written within the framework of a square, and there are several basic structures.

基本结构 **Basic structure**	形 式 **Form**	范 例 **Examples**
左－右 Left-right	▮▮	你 nǐ : 亻 尔 你 好 hǎo : 女 子 好 观 guān : 又 见 观 地 dì : 土 也 地
上－下 Top-bottom	▬▬	是 shì : 日 疋 是 要 yào : 西 女 要 星 xīng : 日 生 星
左－中－右 Left-middle-right	▮▮▮	哪 nǎ : 口 月 阝 哪 谢 xiè : 讠 身 寸 谢
上－中－下 Top-middle-bottom	▬▬▬	爱 ài : 爫 冖 友 爱
左右对称 Symmetrical	◆▮	坐 zuò 乘 chéng 爽 shuǎng

相同的部件用在不同的位置可以组成不同的字：
The same components may appear in different positions to form different characters:

口	+	马	→	吗	口	（在左） on the left
囗	+	玉	→	国	囗	（在外） on the outside
女	+	子	→	好	子	（在右） on the right
木	+	子	→	李	子	（在下） at the bottom
日	+	疋	→	是	日	（在上） at the top
日	+	月	→	明	日	（在左） on the left
日	+	月	→	明	月	（在右） on the right
𠂇	+	月	→	有	月	（在下） at the bottom

汉字的笔画种类
Types of Stroke

汉字有九种基本的笔画:
There are 9 basic strokes:

笔 画 Stroke	笔画的名称 Name of stroke	笔画的书写 Writing the stroke	范 例 Example Characters	
一	横 héng　　(the horizontal)	→	不	王
丨	竖 shù　　(the vertical)	↓	工	中
丿	撇 piě　　(the sweep to the left)	╱	八	人
乀	捺 nà　　(the sweep to the right)	╲	大	人
丶	点 diǎn　　(the dot)	╲	们	这
╱	提 tí　　(the upward stroke)	╱	汉	我
亅一乚	钩 gōu　　(the hook)	↓→乚	字	小　民
ㄱ	横折 héngzhé　(the horizontal turn)	┐	口	日
ㄴ	竖折	∟	亡	忙

笔画顺序
Stroke Sequence

书写汉字时必须按照笔画顺序写。只有按照正确的笔序写，才会写出快捷流畅的字来。

There is a particular sequence in which the strokes must be written. If it is followed, the writing can be smooth and fast.

笔画范例
Stroke Sequence Examples

先写横后写竖 A horizontal stroke is written before a vertical stroke.	十 shí 干 gān	一 一	十 二	 干
先写撇后写捺 The sweeping stroke to the left is written before the sweeping stroke to the right.	八 bā 人 rén	ノ ノ	八 人	
先写外后写内 The outside component is written before the inside component.	月 yuè 同 tóng	ノ 丨	冂 冂	月 同
先写中间后写左和右 The central component is written first, next the stoke on the left, and then the stroke on the right.	小 xiǎo 水 shuǐ	ノ 丨	亅 丬	小 水
先写内后封口 The components inside the unsealed box are written before the last stroke that seals the box.	日 rì 国 guó	丨 丨	冂 国 日 冂 国	日 国
先写上后写下 The strokes are written from top to bottom	三 sān 京 jīng	一 亠	二 古	三 京
先写左后写右 The strokes are written from left to right.	儿 ér 川 chuān	ノ ノ	儿 川	 川

连续性的笔画
Continues Strokes

有的字中有些笔画是连续写的，例如：

In some characters a couple of the strokes are written continuously, e.g.

ノ 冂 月 月

上面的字有一个连续的笔画，即横折钩。其余的笔画看似连续的，实际上是分开的。

Here a horizontal turn and a hook are written as one continuous stroke. Other strokes may look continous, but are in fact, separate.

女 nǚ
woman;
girl;
daughter

女儿	nǚ ér	daughter
女工	nǚ gōng	woman worker
女皇	nǚ huáng	empress
女人	nǚ rén	woman
女士	nǚ shì	lady
女王	nǚ wáng	queen
女性	nǚ xìng	the female

女: 在最早的象形文字中，"女"字被描述为一个弓着腰的女子的形象（ ），后来为了书写的方便，"女"字被简化为一个女人谦恭地跪着的样子（ ）。现在所用的"女"字描绘的则是一个站直腰身，大步追赶男人的女性的姿态。

The original pictograph for woman depicted her in a bowing position . Apparently, for ease in writing, man reduced this to a humbler form – a woman kneeling down - but not for long.
The modern version 女 graphically portrays the big stride woman has taken to keep up with man.

く 女 女

子 zǐ
infant;
child;
son

子弹	zǐ dàn	bullet
子弟	zǐ dì	young generations
子女	zǐ nǚ	children
子孙	zǐ sūn	descendants
子夜	zǐ yè	midnight
子音	zǐ yīn	consonant
孩子	hái zi	child

子: "子"字的形状源于一个伸展开四肢的婴儿形象。后来经过演变，最终该字的形象仿佛是一个用襁褓包住双腿的婴儿。显然，对于中国父母来说，养好孩子的一个秘诀就是把孩子的身体包起来，使之一头湿，一头干。

This character for child originated from a representation of an infant with outstretched arms and legs. Eventually it was modified to one with legs swaddled in cloth bands. Evidently, to the Chinese parent, the secret of infant care lies in keeping one end wet and the other end dry.

フ 了 子

1

好

hǎo

good;
right;
excellent

好吃	hǎo chī	delicious
好处	hǎo chù	benefit; advantage
好感	hǎo gǎn	good impression
好汉	hǎo hàn	worthy man
好久	hǎo jiǔ	a long time
好看	hǎo kàn	good looking
好听	hǎo tīng	pleasant to the ear

好: 古人把表示女孩或女儿的"女"字与表示小孩或儿子的"子"合在一起形成一个字来表示友善或优秀的意思。对于一个男人来说，幸福莫过于拥有贤妻孝子。当然，如果他的妻子尽心抚养子女的话也是好的。

Man combined 女 (girl or daughter) with 子 (child or son) to form a character for goodness and excellence. From experience he must have found his greatest happiness in the possession of a wife and a child or a son and a daughter. It is also good that his wife sticks to his child.

乀	夊	女	女ノ	女了	好
1	2	3	4	5	6

安

ān

peace;
contentment

安定	ān dìng	stable
安眠	ān mián	sleep peacefully
安排	ān pái	arrange
安全	ān quán	safe; secure
安慰	ān wèi	comfort; console
安装	ān zhuāng	install; assemble
不安	bù ān	uneasy; worried

安: 汉语中把表示女人的"女"字与象征家的"宀"合在一起表示安宁、平定的意思。经验告诉人们，安宁的日子源于一个男人在自家中最好只养一个女子，并且让她足不出户。

The character for peace and contentment is made up of woman (女) and roof (宀). Man conceived the idea that to attain peace he should have only one woman under the roof or confine her within the house.

丶	丷	宀	宀	安	安
1	2	3	4	5	6

字

zì
written character

字典	zì diǎn	dictionary
字号	zì hào	name of shop
字迹	zì jì	handwriting
字据	zì jù	written receipt
字幕	zì mù	subtitle
字体	zì tǐ	style of calligraphy
写字	xiě zì	writing (words)

字: 古代为防止写在纸上的字因日久而腐烂，人们通常会把这些字刻在捆绑成册的竹片上。如此精心刻下的字如同孩子（子）一般受到珍视，当然也就会被深藏家（宀）中。这就形成了"字"这个字。画中屋檐下的那个富家青年子弟正在通过学写字来提高个人修养，从而避免变得粗野。

To preserve written characters from deterioration man transcribed them on bamboo bound into books. Such precious written words came to be cherished as a child (子) is cherished under a roof (宀). Hence 字: the written character.
Pictured here under the roof is a precious youthful character being preserved from deterioration.

丶	丷	宀	字	宁	字				
1	2	3	4	5	6				

豕

shǐ
pig

猪排	zhū pái	pork ribs
猪肉	zhū ròu	pork
猪油	zhū yóu	lard
猪肝色	zhū gān sè	maroon colour
懒猪	lǎn zhū	lazy pig

豕: 象形文字中用"一"来代表猪头。豕字的左半部分（彑）象征着猪的肚子和蹄子，右半部分（乀）则象征猪的后背及尾巴。猪给人以一种生活富足的感觉，因此有人认为人与猪合在一起就构成了衣食无忧的生活。这种共存关系恰好验证了一句俗话："教师离不开书，穷人离不开猪。"

In this pictograph of a pig the head is replaced by a line (一). On the left are the belly and paws (彑) and on the right the back and tail (乀). The domestic pig might well symbolise prosperity to man, so closely knit and tied together were their lives. This interdependence probably gave rise to the proverbial saying: "The schoolmaster should not leave his books, nor the poor man his pig."

一	一	丁	豕	豕	豕	豕			
1	2	3	4	5	6	7			

家 jiā
house; family

家产	jiā chǎn	family's property
家具	jiā jù	furniture
家庭	jiā tíng	family; home
家务	jiā wù	household chores
家乡	jiā xiāng	native place
家长	jiā zhǎng	parents
家族	jiā zú	clan or the family

家: 猪（豕）呆在屋檐下（宀）就给人以"家"的概念。
通过驯化，猪可以与人共同生活在一起。即使让它在屋内随意走动，
也不会给人带来任何麻烦或不便。

A pig (豕) under the roof (宀) gave man his concept of home (家).
Domesticated, the pig brought man no domestic trouble and was allowed freedom to wander about in the house.

丶 宀 宀 宀 宁 宁 宇 家 家 家
1 2 3 4 5 6 7 8 9 10

嫁 jià
to marry a man

嫁娶	jià qǔ	marriage
嫁人	jià rén	get married
嫁妆	jià zhuāng	trousseau
出嫁	chū jià	be married

嫁: 这个字是由"女"字加上"家"字构成，表示一个女子结婚成
家。该字只适用于到了结婚年龄的女子。她们即将有自己的丈夫、自
己的家及自己的家庭。

This character, derived by adding home (家) to woman (女),
provides an incentive for a girl to marry. It applies only to woman
who, in marriage, adds to her possessions a husband, a home and a
family.

乚 女 女 女 女 妇 妒 妒 娇 嫁 嫁 嫁 嫁
1 2 3 4 5 6 7 8 9 10 11 12 13

妻

qī
wife

妻舅	qī jiù	brother-in-law
妻室	qī shì	legal wife
妻子	qī zi	wife
贤妻	xián qī	good wife

妻：通常结婚后，男人会将一把扫帚（Ψ）交到妻子手中（ㅋ），让她掌管家庭一切事务。这就是"妻"字，一个挥动扫帚打扫房间的女子形象。

When man marries woman he puts a broom Ψ into her hand ㅋ bestowing upon her the rulership of the house. Hence 妻: a wife - one who wields the broom, using it to take care of house and home.

一	ㄱ	ㄹ	ㅋ	丰	妻	妻	妻
1	2	3	4	5	6	7	8

木

mù
tree;
wood

木材	mù cái	timber
木筏	mù fá	wooden raft
木工	mù gōng	carpentry
木瓜	mù guā	papaya
木屐	mù jī	clogs
木匠	mù jiàng	carpenter
木料	mù liào	timber; lumber

This is a pictograph of a tree with its branches (一), trunk (丿) and roots (八). Only the trunk and branches are suggested because 木 also stands for wood. The 木 pictured here didn't stand very long though.

木：树枝（一）树干（丿）和树根（八），这三者合在一起构成了象形文字"木"。它只表现出树干和树枝是因为"木"字也含有木材之意。正如图片上所显示的那样，长成材的大树，就该被人们砍伐掉了。

一	十	才	木
1	2	3	4

5

李

lǐ

plum or plum tree; also a Chinese surname

李树	lǐ shù	plum tree
李子	lǐ zi	plum
行李	xíng li	baggage; luggage

李：李子树以其天然多产且为孩童所喜爱而闻名。在象形文字中，孩子（子）位于树木（木）下，就是"李"字。不过现实中，孩子可并不总是在树下。

Owing to its prolific nature and its popularity with children, the plum tree came to be known as the tree（木）the children（子）are fond of. In this idealistic ideograph children were located under the tree, thus: 李 .
This, unfortunately, has not always been true in life.

一	十	才	木	杢	李	李								
1	2	3	4	5	6	7								

栖

qī

to roost; perch or nest; to live in poverty

栖身	qī shēn	dwell; obtain shelter
栖宿	qī sù	rest for the night
栖息	qī xī	rest

栖：这个字以"木"字为形旁，"妻"字为声旁构成。"木"表示与树木有关，"妻"则是该字的读音，后来人们把"妻"字简化为表示方向的"西"字。

This character is built on tree（木）as radical and wife（妻）as phonetic. The tree provides the base and the wife supplies the sound.
Man simplified it by putting in place of wife, the character for "west"（西）.

一	十	才	木	木	栌	柄	栖	栖	栖					
1	2	3	4	5	6	7	8	9	10					

人 rén

man;
person;
human

人才	rén cái	man of talent
人格	rén gé	personality
人口	rén kǒu	population
人类	rén lèi	mankind
人民	rén mín	people
人生	rén shēng	the life of man
人为	rén wéi	man-made

人：象形字"人"所呈现出的是人体的侧面形态，从"人"字的演变中我们可以看出人进化的痕迹。自从诞生于这个世界，具备了手脚之后，原始人不得不通过徒手耕种（彡）来维持生存。这就促使其直立行走（彡）。在脱离了靠手脚的体力劳动后，人类开始只进行脑力劳动（彡）。今天，人类在激烈的竞争中人连头都丢了，甚至于连脚跟也立不稳了（彡）。

The pictographic profile of a person（人）presents an insight into his evolutionary development. Created from earth and equipped with hands and feet, lowly man eked out an existence from the ground with his hands 彡 to help him stand on his feet 彡. Discarding both hands and feet, he used only his head 彡. Today, in the race of the survival of the fittest, he loses his head completely 彡 and finds himself barely able to keep his feet.

ノ	人										
1	2										

大 dà

big; great

大胆	dà dǎn	daring; bold
大概	dà gài	probably
大家	dà jiā	all (people)
大人	dà rén	adult
大声	dà shēng	loud voice
大厦	dà shà	big building
大学	dà xué	university

大：一个双臂完全伸开的成年人，从正面看就是一个"大"字（大）。体现"大"的概念并不是人们的个头，而是靠人们那种喜形于色的表情。正如我们图中所示的那样，但这其中却不乏一些仅仅为炫耀的人。

The ideographic representation for "big" is simply a front elevation of a full-grown man with arms stretched out to the limit 大. What conveys the idea of "big" is not the size of the man but his demonstrative gesture. Some of the assortment of characters pictured above are trying to show what "big" means. Others are merely trying to show off.

一	ナ	大									
1	2	3									

天 tiān
heaven; sky; day

天才	tiān cái	genius
天空	tiān kōng	sky
天生	tiān shēng	inborn
天下	tiān xià	the whole world
天真	tiān zhēn	naive; innocent
白天	bái tiān	daytime
明天	míng tiān	tomorrow

天: 这个字指的是人站稳脚跟的能力（人），伸展的双臂则代表了人的自负（即"大"）。在人们的双肩之上的部分即为"天"，意为上天，同时也可指代具有权威的人。由于出现在空中的曙光象征着新的一天的开始，所以此字还可以用作指代时间的单位，即"一天"。

This stylised representation shows man's ability to stand on his feet (人), extending his arms egotistically (大). But high above man (人), be he ever so great (大), stretches the heavenly firmament, filling the empty space above his shoulders and directing his footsteps. Hence: 天, meaning heaven - man's rightful and authoritative head. Since the growing light of the sky ushers in the dawn of day, 天 came to mean also "day".

一	二	于	天					
1	2	3	4					

夫 fū
husband; distinguished person

农夫	nóng fū	farmer
懦夫	nuò fū	coward
渔夫	yú fū	fisherman
丈夫	zhàng fū	husband
夫妻	fū qī	husband and wife
夫人	fū rén	wife; madam
大夫	dài fū	medical doctor

夫: 一个年轻人（人），到了20岁成年时（大），要用发夹（一）束发，并且戴上一顶有成年男子（夫）才能带的帽子。获得尊称后，也就意味着成为了一个贵人。同时也具备了成家立业的资格。因此"夫"字所指的是受人尊敬的男子或丈夫。

A youthful person (人), grown big (大) and attaining maturity at 20, used a hairpin (一) and was vested with the virile cap of manhood 夫. Given an honourable name, he was considered a distinguished person, qualified as a prospective husband. Hence 夫 means a distinguished person or husband.

一	二	丰	夫					
1	2	3	4					

太 tài
too; over; excessive

太多	tài duō	too many
太后	tài hòu	empress dowager
太监	tài jiàn	eunuch
太空	tài kōng	outer space; sky
太平	tài píng	peace
太太	tài tái	madam
太阳	tài yáng	sun

太：人们将"大"字下面加一横（一）构成了"太"这个表示最高级意思的词。它的意思是太多了或超越极限了。当一系列喜事来临时，男人们又为他们的妻子冠以了一种近乎于奉承的双音节的称呼即"太太"。后来，人们又把一横改成了小小的一点。

By underscoring "big" (大) with a line (一) man came up with a superlative character (太) meaning too much or over the limit. In the ecstasy of double happiness and the rapture of material bliss that followed, man bestowed upon his wife a flattering title: 太太 a double emphasis. She lived up to it. Man thereafter reduced the underline to a teeny-weeny stroke 太.

一	ナ	大	太									
1	2	3	4									

QUACK QUACK

立 lì
stand; rise up

立场	lì chǎng	standpoint; position
立法	lì fǎ	legislation
立即	lì jí	at once
立刻	lì kè	immediately
立体	lì tǐ	three-dimensional
立足	lì zú	base oneself on
建立	jiàn lì	establish; erect

立：这个字表示一个人站立或起立。（一）表示站在坚实的土地上。起初为（立）字形。后来简化成（企），并最终演变为"立"。图中的这些人，有体强的，有体弱的，从中我们不难得出，站立也不是轻而易举的。

This character, meaning plain standing or rising up, portrays a person standing - not in the abstract, but on firm, stable ground (一). Originally written 立, it was modified to 企 and finally to 立. Illustrated here are some human characters, firm and infirm, trying to stand on stable ground and demonstrating that plain standing is not plain sailing.

丶	二	六	立	立						
1	2	3	4	5						

小 xiǎo
small;
petty;
young

小吃	xiǎo chī	snacks
小丑	xiǎo chǒu	clown
小岛	xiǎo dǎo	small island; islet
小姐	xiǎo jiě	lady; miss
小麦	xiǎo mài	wheat
小时	xiǎo shí	hour
小偷	xiǎo tōu	thief

小: 一竖钩（亅）两边各加一点（八），就表示小。可以理解为一个物体分为两半点就比原来小了。对人们来说，除法运算可以让数字变小，而乘法运算则使数字变大。正如我们图中所显示的那样，指导人们如何减少痛苦争取更大的幸福。

A vertical stroke, (亅), separating two little ones (八) gave man his concept of "small". The idea was also derived from the division (八) of an object (亅) already small by its nature. To man, division (÷) makes small (小) and multiplication (✕) makes big (大) a thing. Our illustration shows how to multiply happiness by dividing sorrow.

| 亅 | 小 | 小 | | | | | | | | | |
| 1 | 2 | 3 | | | | | | | | | |

小 small

大 big

大 → 小 → 少

少 shǎo or shào
less; few;
short of

少量	shǎo liàng	small quantity
少女	shào nǚ	young girl
少数	shǎo shù	minority
少许	shǎo xǔ	little; few
少有	shǎo yǒu	rare; scarce
少年	shào nián	teen-ager
多少	duō shǎo	how many

少: "少"字是由"小"字加上"丿"构成的，把本来就小的东西再变小，就成了"少"。上图中通过形象的手段所表现出的就是从"大"到"小"再到"少"的这一过程。

This character combines 小 with 丿 to form 少. It means to cut smaller or diminish (丿) that which is already small (小), thus making it less (少). To cut short the diminishing process, the method suggested above is an effective shortcut to reduce big (大) to small (小) and small (小) to less (少).

| 丿 | 小 | 小 | 少 | | | | | | | | |
| 1 | 2 | 3 | 4 | | | | | | | | |

尖 jiān
pointed; sharp

尖兵	jiān bīng	vanguard
尖刀	jiān dāo	sharp knife
尖顶	jiān dǐng	peak; apex
尖端	jiān duān	highest point
尖利	jiān lì	sharp
尖锐	jiān ruì	sharp; pointed
尖塔	jiān tǎ	spire

尖：把"小"字摞在"大"字之上，就形成了一个下大上小的锥形象形文字，这就是"尖"字。它表示敏锐的、锐利的或机敏的。但并不是所有下大上小的物体都能像图例中那样表示敏锐或机智的概念。

By placing small (小) on top of big (大) man came up with an ideograph to describe anything that tapers from big to small. Hence: 尖, meaning pointed or sharp or, figuratively, sharp-witted. But not all objects which are small at the top and big at the bottom are sharp or sharp-witted, as the illustrations on the left prove.

丶	八	小	少	尖	尖									
1	2	3	4	5	6									

田 tián
rice field; grain field

田地	tián dì	field ; plight
田鸡	tián jī	frog
田径	tián jìng	track and field
田野	tián yě	open country
田园	tián yuán	fields
耕田	gēng tián	plough

田：人们从早到晚都在田间辛勤的劳作。他们坚信一句俗语："农忙不离田，农闲不离家。"于是象形文字的"田"便是一块有犁沟和田埂的耕地（田）。通过滴撒汗水的辛勤劳作，农民收获了他劳动的果实。但同时，劳动的艰辛不仅将道道沟痕留在田野，也将道道皱纹留在农民的眉间。

From dawn to dusk man toiled in the field, taking to heart the proverbial saying: "Never leave your field in spring or your house in winter." The character he shaped for "field" was a pictograph of ploughed field with furrows and cross-paths: 田. By the sweat of his brow he reaped the fruits of his labour. But all that toil has left its mark of furrows and cross-paths, not only on the field, but also indelibly on his brow.

丨	冂	冃	田	田										
1	2	3	4	5										

力 lì

strength;
force;
power

力量	lì liàng	physical strength; force
力气	lì qì	effort; strength
力求	lì qiú	strive; make every effort
力争	lì zhēng	endeavour; fight for
人力	rén lì	labour force

力:"力"字现在的写法像是一条强壮的胳膊—是身体强健的象征。然而实际上人们更渴求的是道义上的完善。从前相信"力量就是正义"的人,很快将不得不接受这样一个现实:正义才是力量。

最初的"力"字()中间有一条竖线(),并且在顶部弯曲形成一块代表突出的健美的肌肉的小空间,另外一笔()代表的则是皮肤。

The modern version (力) is a powerful graphic impression of the forearm - a symbol of physical strength. Moral strength, however, is more to be desired. And those who go by the rule: "Might is right" will soon have to learn that "Right is might".
In the original form () the long middle line (), curved at the top to take less room, represents the sinew that binds muscle to bone. The other line () pictures the fibrous sheath of the sinew.

1	2									
ㄱ	力									

男 nán

man;
male;
masculine

男孩	nán hái	boy
男女	nán nǚ	men and women
男人	nán rén	man
男声	nán shēng	male voice
男性	nán xìng	male
男装	nán zhuāng	male attire
男子	nán zi	man; male

男:"田"地是要花"力"耕作的。 因此"田"与"力"结合就成了表示男性的"男"字 。这大概是因为"男主外,女主内"的原因吧。 图中所绘的即为男子在田间耕耘,女子在家中操持的景象。

A field (田), where strength (力) is exerted, is the symbol for "masculine" man 男, the male of the human species. This is probably because the home is where the female of the same species exerts her strength. Our picture shows strength being exerted - by the male (男) in field-work, the female (女) in housework, and their offspring (子) in promotional work.

1	2	3	4	5	6	7				
丨	冂	冂	田	田	甼	男				

日

rì
sun;
day

日报	rì bào	daily newspaper
日本	Rì Běn	Japan
日常	rì cháng	daily; usual
日出	rì chū	sunrise
日光	rì guāng	sunshine
日记	rì jì	diary
日历	rì lì	calendar

日："日"字最初的写法是在一个圆圈中点一个点，四面画上表示照耀大地的日光(☒)。后来简化为"☉"，再往后就成了"⊖"，最后定形为"日"。对人来说，从日出到日落就为一天。太阳仿佛是在用一只眼睛看世界，因为它从不给谁多些，或给谁少些。它总是不偏不倚地照到世界上的每一个角落。

The sun was first depicted as a circle with an "eye" or centre and rays extending to the corners of the earth ☒. This was simplified to ☉, then modified: ⊖, and finally squared off: 日. Just as surely as its rising and setting mark the "day" (日) for man, the sun's shining upon the wicked as well as the good demonstrates that it sees the whole world with one eye.

丨 冂 冃 日

月

yuè
moon;
month

月饼	yuè bǐng	moon cake
月份	yuè fèn	month
月光	yuè guāng	moonlight
月经	yuè jīng	menstruation
月亮	yuè liàng	moon
月票	yuè piào	monthly ticket
月球	yuè qiú	the moon

月：人们最早用一轮新月的形状(☽)作为表示月亮或农历月份的"月"字。后来人们用了两种表示由亏变盈的月亮图案来表示"月"，即"☽"和倾斜后的"☽"。其后又将它演化为"月"。月光对置身其中的人来说，有时有着惊人的感染力。图中所绘的便是月亮正向世人倾洒它那具有"魔力"光芒的景象。

To form the character for moon (or lunar month) man chose the crescent ☽. The original pictograph suggested two phases of a waxing new moon ☽. Tilting it: ☽ and then directing it earthwards: 月 exposed man to the influence of moonbeam radiation - with striking consequences. Pictured here is a beaming moon casting its spell on some beaming moon-struck earthlings.

丿 冂 冃 月

明 míng
brilliant;
bright;
enlightened

明白	míng bái	understand; clear
明亮	míng liàng	shining; bright
明朗	míng lǎng	bright and clear
明年	míng nián	next year
明显	míng xiǎn	obvious
明智	míng zhì	wise

明：人们把"日"和"月"结合在一起形成了表示光亮、灿烂或启迪的表意文字。人们称之为"明"。同时人们还将与欧洲黑暗时代同期的中国王朝称为"明朝"。今天，科学技术已经发展到了令人眼花缭乱的太空时代，但随着人类智慧的不断增长，人类的未来却越来越黑暗。

Man combined the sun (日) and the moon (月) to produce an ideograph for bright, brilliant or enlightened. He called it: "ming" (明) and used it also for the brilliant Ming Dynasty of China which came in the wake of the Dark Ages of Europe. Today science and technology has ushered in the dazzling Space Age - with man very much enlightened and the future very much bedarkened.

丨	冂	月	日	日刀	明	明	明					
1	2	3	4	5	6	7	8					

白 bái
clear;
white;
plain

白菜	bái cài	Chinese cabbage
白费	bái fèi	in vain; waste
白喉	bái hóu	diphtheria
白色	bái sè	white colour
白糖	bái táng	white sugar
白兔	bái tù	white rabbit
坦白	tǎn bái	frank; confess

白：当旭日（日）东升，撒下第一缕光辉（丿）之时，长夜的黑暗便被驱散，白天来到了。这就是表示清楚、光亮或指白颜色的"白"字。当人们容易理解某事时，这就是"明白"。不过就如画面所示，许多事都不那么容易弄"明白"。

As the sun (日) peeps above the horizon its very first ray (丿) begins to dispel the shadowy haze of night. Hence 白: the symbol for clear, white or plain. Man easily understands anything that is bright (明) and clear (白), so "bright and clear" means to understand (明白). Apparently, this is not always easily understood as our picture shows.

丿	亻	白	白	白								
1	2	3	4	5								

旦 dàn
dawn; daybreak

旦暮	dàn mù	morning and evening
旦夕	dàn xī	in a short while
花旦	huā dàn	prima dona in an opera
元旦	yuán dàn	New Year's Day
一旦	yī dàn	once; as soon as

旦：每当太阳（日）从地平线（一）上升起时，拂晓（旦）来临了。谈及清晨，谚语中说："早起三天，就等于多活一天。"人们日复一日地重复这句话，但却从不照作。

The daily appearance of the sun (日) above the horizon (一) gave man his concept of dawn. From the sun's early rising rose the proverbial saying: "To get up early for three mornings is equal to one day of time." Man preached this - from the rising of the sun to its setting - but it never dawned on him to practise it.

丨	冂	日	日	旦									
1	2	3	4	5									

甲 jiǎ
first; armour or protective covering

甲板	jiǎ bǎn	deck of a ship
甲虫	jiǎ chóng	beetle
甲克	jiǎ kè	jacket
甲壳	jiǎ qiào	crust
甲鱼	jiǎ yú	soft-shelled turtle
甲骨文	jiǎ gǔ wén	inscriptions on oracle bones

甲：甲（意为第一）在逢十为一循环的"天干"中排在第一位。起初写作"十"，后来又在外面加一方框，成为"田"。为了与"田地"的"田"字区别，于是将中间的一竖向下延长成了"甲"。该字后来又溶入了头盔之意，是因为从字形上看它类似于头盔（甲）。通过字意的延伸，现在的"甲"字泛指一切硬的遮盖物，如铠甲、贝壳、鳞片或指甲等。

The guiding mark 甲 (meaning first) is the first of the "ten stems" - the decimal cycle of time reckoning. Originally written: 十, it was later encased in a square: 田. To differentiate it from 田 (field) the vertical line was extended downwards: 甲. A subsequent modification came to suggest "helmet" because of its resemblance: 甲. By extension, the modern form, 甲 covers a whole range of hard protective coverings like armour, shells, scales and nails.

丨	冂	日	日	甲									
1	2	3	4	5									

早 zǎo
early; morning

早安	zǎo ān	good morning
早班	zǎo bān	morning shift
早餐	zǎo cān	breakfast
早操	zǎo cāo	morning exercise
早晨	zǎo chén	early morning
早春	zǎo chūn	early spring
早婚	zǎo hūn	marrying too early

早：“早”（意为早的或清晨）是指一天中太阳升到与人的头盔（十）高度接近的地方的时间。“十”是最早的“甲”字，指头盔。因为“甲”（十）字同时还具有第一的意思，所以“早”字也可指初升的太阳，即早晨。

早 (meaning early or morning) is the time of the day when the sun (日) has risen to the height of a man's helmet (十). 十 is the old form of 甲, originally meaning helmet. Since another meaning of 甲 (十) is "first", the character: 早 signifies also the first (十) sun (日), that is, the early morning: 早.

丨	冂	冃	日	旦	早						
1	2	3	4	5	6						

休 xiū
rest; cease

休会	xiū huì	adjourn (meeting)
休假	xiū jià	on leave
休息	xiū xi	rest or relax
休闲	xiū xián	lie fallow (land)
休想	xiū xiǎng	don't expect
休业	xiū yè	wind up (business)
休战	xiū zhàn	cease-fire

休：这是一个让人喜欢的字，一个人在树荫下歇息，从字形上看是一个（人或亻）靠在一棵树上（木）。如图中所示，后人靠着前人栽下的树悠闲地乘凉，正如中国的古谚中所说的："前人种树，后人乘凉。"

This is a refreshing character for any person (人) working near a shady tree (木). It literally means "rest" (休) and pictures a person (人 or 亻) leaning against a tree (木). Of the tree the Chinese proverb laments: "One generation plants the trees under whose shade another generation takes its ease." Exemplifying this, we show a character leisurely resting in the shade and leaning himself against a tree planted by an older generation.

丿	亻	仁	什	休	休						
1	2	3	4	5	6						

东 dōng
east

东方	dōng fāng	the east
东风	dōng fēng	east wind
东京	Dōng Jīng	Tokyo
东欧	Dōng Ōu	Eastern Europe
东西	dōng-xī	east and west;
	dōngxi	things

东：当一个人注意到太阳每天都从东方升起时，他便四下环视，想找一个适当的符号来表示他所看到的东方。当一天他看到远处升起的太阳（日）恰好与一棵树（木）重叠时，他有了主意：太阳（日）在树（木）的后面就是（东）。使人感到庆幸的是，此人没有被成功冲昏头脑。否则，他将会一直面对着一个错误的方向。

Man turned his head around, looking for a suitable sign for "east" - the direction he faced when he saw the sun rise every day. He succeeded one morning when he observed the sun (日) through the trees (木). So sun (日) behind tree (木) became east (东). Fortunately, success did not turn man's head, otherwise he would have been left facing the wrong direction.

日 + 木 = 東 = 東

| 一 | 左 | 夻 | 夻 | 东 | | | | | | | | | | |
| 1 | 2 | 3 | 4 | 5 | | | | | | | | | | |

西 xī
west

西边	xī bian	west side
西餐	xī cān	Western-style food
西方	xī fāng	the west
西瓜	xī guā	watermelon
西南	xī nán	southwest
西欧	Xī Ōu	Western Europe
西洋	Xīyáng	the West

西：鸟儿总在夕阳西下时归巢栖息，因此以交线表示的鸟巢（图）便成了"西"字的雏形。后来人们运用丰富的想象力以一只卧在巢中的鸟（图）表示"西"。不久又设计出一种新写法"西"，这一写法最终演化为今天的"西"字。因为万物都存在于东、西之间的空间中，因而把东、西两个字合在一起就成了一个可以泛指一切物体的词。

As the sun settles in the west birds roost in their nests; so a cross-hatched bird's nest provided the cradle for "west", and nest became west 图. Man's fertile imagination conceived a new ideograph - a nest with a brooding bird: 图 hatching up a new form: 西 which finally developed into a full-fledged character for west: 西 . As all "things" exist between east (东) and west (西), the combination east-west, meaning "things", came to be applied to anything from east to west.

| 一 | 厂 | 同 | 丙 | 西 | 西 | | | | | | | | | |
| 1 | 2 | 3 | 4 | 5 | 6 | | | | | | | | | |

上 shàng

up;
above;
ascend

上班	shàng bān	go to work
上辈	shàng bèi	one's elders
上苍	shàng cāng	Heaven; God
上策	shàng cè	the best plan
上层	shàng céng	upper strata
上等	shàng děng	first-class
上当	shàng dàng	cheated

上: 上、下、高、低是相对而言的抽象术语。人们用在地平线（一）上加一笔而成的象形文字来表示"上"。最初时这一笔是一点，即为"⸱"；后来延长为一条线，即"⸗"；继而把第二画竖起来成了"⊥"；又曾经被修饰为"⸀"；最后才定形为"上"。

Since up and down, above and below are relative and abstract terms, man conveyed the ideas graphically by relating a simple stroke to a horizontal foundation line (—). This stroke above the base line was originally a dot: ⸱ extended to a line: ⸗ propped upright: ⊥ embellished: ⸀ and finally stabilised: 上 .

一 卜 上
1 2 3

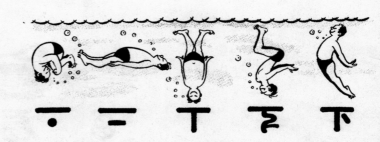

下 xià

down;
below;
descend

下班	xià bān	be off duty
下策	xià cè	bad plan
下层	xià céng	lower level
下场	xià chǎng	end; fate
下沉	xià chén	sink
下等	xià děng	low grade
下级	xià jí	lower level

下: 表达"下"或"低"的概念要涉及地平线。最早是在代表地平线的横线下加一点，即表示"下"，即"⸗"；后变为一横，即"⸗"；为了便于书写又简化为"丅"和"⸀"的形式，最后形成了"下"。

The concept of down and below is clarified in relation to a horizontal line. The stroke below the fundamental line was originally a dot: ⸗ which was extended to a line: ⸗ for ease in writing. The modified forms: 丅 and ⸀ eventually led to the final ideograph: 下 . The characters above, although literally under water, are figuratively above water.

一 丁 下
1 2 3

中 zhōng

centre;
middle;
neutral

中部	zhōng bù	central section
中餐	zhōng cān	Chinese meal
中层	zhōng céng	middle-level
中立	zhōng lì	neutral
中等	zhōng děng	middle-class
中断	zhōng duàn	break off
中间	zhōng jiān	middle

中: 射出一支箭（丨），正中一块方靶（口）的中心，就表示中心的"中"字（甲）。为了起到修饰的作用又加上了二对条纹"甲"，重新调整后变为"甲"，经过简化成了"甲"，最终定形为"中"。"中"又代表了身处中心位置或表示中立。不幸的是，人们在处事中，总是做不到完全中立。

By shooting an arrow: 丨 right into the centre of a square target: 口 man scored a bull's-eye and secured a mark for "centre": 甲. He added a decoration of four stripes: 甲, rearranged them: 甲, stripped them off: 中, and finally hit his mark for simplicity: 中 . The symbol also means standing in the middle or neutrality (中立). Unfortunately, in the application of neutrality, man has completely missed his mark.

丨 冂 口 中

奴 nú

slave;
servant

奴婢	nú bì	female slave
奴才	nú cai	flunkey; lackey
奴化	nú huà	enslave
奴隶	nú lì	slave
奴仆	nú pú	male slave
奴性	nú xìng	servile disposition
奴役	nú yì	slavery

奴:（女）人在主人手下（又） 即为奴隶。从字面上讲，"又"字与"女"字相结合为女仆。但事实上奴隶不分男女。他们被主人所拥有，为主人服务。

A woman 女 under the hand 又 of a master signifies slave. The components 又 and 女 put together literally mean "handmaid" - a female who slaves with her hands. 奴 includes slaves of both sexes who serve their masters hand and foot.

〈 女 女 奴 奴

友 yǒu
friend

友: "友"字最初是由两只向同一方向伸出的象征合作的右手 (ㄑㄑ) 组成的。后演变为友好的两只手(ㄑㄑ)，继而成为互握的双手(ㄑㄑ)。在这个字形上做些小的调整，便成了我们今天所用的"友"字。

The character for "friend" originated, with two right hands acting co-operatively in the same direction ㄑㄑ and later reaching out to clasp each other in friendship ㄑㄑ , placing the hands, one upon the other: ㄑㄑ and, with a little straightening out, man derived the modern reinforced form: 友 .

友爱	yǒu ài	friendly affection
友邦	yǒu bāng	friendly nation
友好	yǒu hǎo	friendly
友情	yǒu qíng	friendship
友人	yǒu rén	friend
友善	yǒu shàn	friendly
友谊	yǒu yì	friendship

| 一 | ナ | 方 | 友 | | | | | | | | | |
| 1 | 2 | 3 | 4 | | | | | | | | | |

手 shǒu
hand

手: 最早的象形文字"手"中特别突出掌纹，因而写作"乎"。后来人们根据实际特点突出了手指的形态，写作"乎"。最后又突出了其中竖写的一笔"乎"而成了今天我们所用的表示五指长短不一的"手"字。正如谚语所言"十指之中，有长有短"。另外"手"还是十分有用的字根。"手"的变种"扌"和"手"是十分常见的形旁。

The earliest pictograph for hand placed undue emphasis on the palm lines as basis 乎. Practical experience, however, put man on the right lines - the fingers 乎. Finally, reinforced with straight lines 乎 the character assumed the modern form 手 with fingers of unequal length. For, as the proverb goes, "Of the ten fingers, some are long and some are short." 手 proved handy as radical for numerous characters with its variants 扌 and 手.

手臂	shǒu bì	arm
手表	shǒu biǎo	wrist-watch
手册	shǒu cè	handbook
手段	shǒu duàn	means; measure
手法	shǒu fǎ	skill; tricks
手工	shǒu gōng	handwork
手铐	shǒu kào	handcuffs

| 一 | 二 | 三 | 手 | | | | | | | | | |
| 1 | 2 | 3 | 4 | | | | | | | | | |

我 wǒ
I; me

我们	wǒ men	we
我爱你	wǒ ài nǐ	I love you
我们的	wǒ men de	our; ours

我:"我"字最早的形状似两把互架的长矛"䇂"。大概是表示双方均在捍卫象征自我的权力,而后又出现了一种新写法"我",像是一只"手"拿着一支长矛(戈)。想必是指当一个人挥动手中的长矛时,他便会有一种唯我独尊的感觉,这就是表示自我的"我"字。

The earliest forms show two spears against each other in direct confrontation: 䇂, presumably symbolising two rights being asserted and, by extension, my right, that is, me. A later transcription projected a new image: 我, a pictograph of a hand 手 grasping a spear 戈, denoting that when man wields in his hand 手 a spear 戈 his ego, the big "I", emerges. Hence 我: I.

| 一 | 二 | 于 | 手 | 扐 | 我 | 我 | | | | | | | |
| 1 | 2 | 3 | 4 | 5 | 6 | 7 | | | | | | | |

你 nǐ
you

你好	nǐ hǎo	how do you do
你们	nǐ men	you (plural)
你们的	nǐ men de	your; yours (plural)

你:"你"字旧写法为对称的"爾"字形,像是一架天平(朩),两边均匀地摆放着四颗砝码(爻爻)。和一个"仒","爾"后来被简化为"尒",最终加上"人"旁而成"你"。

The classical character for "you", an equal, was 爾, a pictograph of a balance 朩 loaded with 爻爻 equally on both sides and topped by a phonetic 仒. 爾 was eventually contracted to 尒. By adding 人 (person) to 尒, man introduced the human element and came up with 你, a person who carries the same weight: you.

| 丿 | 亻 | 仴 | 你 | 你 | 你 | 你 | | | | | | | |
| 1 | 2 | 3 | 4 | 5 | 6 | 7 | | | | | | | |

也 yě
also;
in addition to

也罢	yě bà	let it be
也好	yě hǎo	may as well
也行	yě xíng	all right
也许	yě xǔ	perhaps
也有	yě yǒu	also have

也: "也"字最早象征的是一种古代漏斗，其形同于饮酒的角状容器。人们除拥有属于自己的物品之外，还想要占有这种饮酒器皿。时至今日，酒杯已经变成了人们的所属物。正如图中所示，已经明确表述出人们与酒杯之间的关系。

Original the character 也 was a representation of an ancient drinking horn, shaped like a funnel. In addition to his rightful belongings, man also appropriated this drinking vessel. To this day it has remained in his possession - a pictograph specially horrowed for the conjunction "also", joining man to his drinking horn.

| 冂 | 也 | 也 | | | | | | | | | |
| 1 | 2 | 3 | | | | | | | | | |

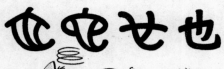

他 tā
he; she

他处	tā chù	elsewhere
他的	tā de	his
他们	tā men	they
他人	tā rén	the other person
他日	tā rì	some other day
他乡	tā xiāng	place far away from home

他: "他"字是由"人"和"也"组合而成。指代第三人称"他"或"她"，意为"那个人也"。

The character 他 is drawn from 人 (person) and 也 (also). By extension it means "that person also" and refers to the other person: he or she.

| 丿 | 亻 | 亻 | 仲 | 他 | | | | | | | |
| 1 | 2 | 3 | 4 | 5 | | | | | | | |

目 mù
eye

目标	mù biāo	aim
目的	mù dì	purpose; aim; goal
目光	mù guāng	sight; vision; view
目见	mù jiàn	see for oneself
目力	mù lì	eyesight
目前	mù qián	at present
目送	mù sòng	watch somebody go

目："目"字最早是由"眼皮"和"眼珠"两部分组成的" "。后写作" "因它容易与" "字混淆，所以人们把它竖起来变成" "，并最终定形为" "。一个人就是眼力再好，也不能用一只眼睛看到另一只眼睛。

In its primitive form the eye was pictured naturally with eyelids and pupil ⬬. When stylised: ⬭ its similarity to ⬭ (four) deceived man's eye; so it was stood on end: ⊟ and finally squared off: 目 . It would seem that even with his very own eyes man could not see eye to eye.

丨	冂	冃	月	目												
1	2	3	4	5												

MY EYE!

见 jiàn
see

见鬼	jiàn guǐ	preposterous
见解	jiàn jiě	opinions
见面	jiàn miàn	meet
见闻	jiàn wén	knowledge
见习	jiàn xí	learn on the job
见效	jiàn xiào	effective
见笑	jiàn xiào	laugh at (me or us)

见：把"目"字写在"人"字之上就成了动词"见"。随着"目"字的变化，人们也将繁体字的" 見 "进行了简化，成为今天的"见"字。

For the verb "to see" the eye 目 was set atop man 人. As the eye grew, man shrank to produce the regular form 見, now simplified to 见.

丨	冂	见	见													
1	2	3	4													

口 **kǒu**
mouth;
opening

口才	kǒu cái	eloquence
口吃	kǒu chī	stutter
口臭	kǒu chòu	bad breath
口袋	kǒu dài	pocket
口福	kǒu fú	gourmet's luck
口供	kǒu gòng	testimony
口号	kǒu hào	slogan

口："口"字在最早的象形文字中是一张张开的嘴"ᗄ"，后来演变成了一张笑开的嘴"ᗑ"，最后变化为"ᗖ"，并被简化为一个方块"口"。"口"字同时还有张开的意思。要小心"祸从口出"。

The character for mouth was originally a pictograph of an open mouth: ᗄ broadening into a smile: ᗑ and eventually stiffening: ᗖ and contracting to a square: 口. 口 also means an opening. But beware: "Mischief comes from much opening of the mouth".

丨	冂	口												
1	2	3												

言 **yán**
words;
speak

言辞	yán cí	one's words
言和	yán hé	make peace
言论	yán lùn	speech
言谈	yán tán	the way one speaks
言行	yán xíng	words and deeds
言语	yán yǔ	spoken language

言：中国有句俗语"言多必失"。这从"言"字自身的结构上就有明确的体现。"言"字最初被写作"ᗱ"，象征着从嘴"ᗄ"中讲出的错话（旧写作"ᡒ"）。为了改正错误，谨慎行事，人们在"口"字上加上了"ᗁ"（代表界限）。由此产生出了表示语言的"言"字。

"In a multitude of words," the Chinese saying goes, "there will certainly be a mistake." This is evident from the character for words itself: 言. Originally written ᗱ, it represented a mouth ᗄ from which issued a mistake ᡒ (an old form of 忷). Apparently, to correct this error, man changed to 言. So today, with great care, his mouth 口 speaks its lines ᗁ, transforming soundwaves into words: 言.

、	亠	亖	言	言	言	言								
1	2	3	4	5	6	7								

24

工 gōng

work;
labour;
skill

工厂	gōng chǎng	factory
工党	Gōng Dǎng	the Labour Party
工地	gōng dì	construction site
工夫	gōng fu	time; effort
工具	gōng jù	tools
工会	gōng huì	trade union
工匠	gōng jiàng	craftsman

工：象形文字"工"代表古代工匠用的尺子。引伸为工人、劳动或技术之意。 早期的"工"字是一把带有三条平行刻度的尺子。人经常为付出的劳动与所得的报酬而产生疑异。因此为了过上好日子，他便改变只知埋头苦干的做法而转为用它作为向雇主争取更多劳资的手段。就如同图中所描绘出的那对主仆一样。

工 is a pictograph of the ancient workman's square or carpenter's ruler. By extension, it means work, labour or skill. An early form: 工 included three parallel lines traced with the square. Man always has problems with work and remuneration. Instead of striving for prosperity through work, he works for prosperity through strife, as our picture of master and servant shows.

一	丁	工						
1	2	3						

左 zuǒ

left;
also a Chinese surname

左边	zuǒ bian	the left side
左面	zuǒ miàn	the left side
左派	zuǒ pài	Leftist; the Left
左倾	zuǒ qīng	left-leaning
左手	zuǒ shǒu	the left hand
左翼	zuǒ yì	left wing
左右	zuǒ yòu	the left and right sides

左："左"字描绘的是一只拿着木工尺（𠂇）的手（工）的形状。手工劳作中，左手通常用来协助右手的技术性工作。例如：当右手画线时，用左手拿尺子。"左"代表左方。

The character for left: 左 depicts the hand 𠂇 that holds the carpenter's square 工, the left. The left hand 𠂇 is meant to help its more skilled correlative member in manual work 工 as, for example, holding the ruler while the right hand draws the line. 左 stands for the direction left.

一	𠂇	𠂋	左	左				
1	2	3	4	5				

右 yòu
right

右边	yòu bian	the right side
右面	yòu miàn	the right side
右派	yòu pài	Rightist; the Right
右倾	yòu qīng	Right deviation
右手	yòu shǒu	the right hand
右翼	yòu yì	right wing
向右	xiàng yòu	turn right

右："右"字是由一只手（ナ）和一张嘴（口）组成的，表示人是用右手吃饭的。"右"代表右方。

The character for right: 右 is simply a hand ナ and a mouth 口, signifying the hand you eat with the right. 右 stands for the direction right.

一	ナ	ナ	右	右									
1	2	3	4	5									

舌 shé
tongue

舌尖	shé jiān	tip of the tongue
舌头	shé tou	tongue
舌音	shé yīn	lingual sounds
舌战	shé zhàn	heated discussion

舌：中国有句谚语说："舌头有如一把杀人不见血的利刃。"因此，早期的"舌"字便如一个伸出口外的叉形舌头（ ）。后来它演变成柔和的" "。最终在" "变得横平竖直之后，就成了今天所用的"舌"字。

"The tongue is like a sharp knife; It kills without drawing blood," so warns the Chinese proverb. Exemplifying this, early forms of the character show a forked tongue thrust viciously out of the mouth: . It skilfully smoothens itself: and finally straightens: into the new form: 舌.

ノ	二	千	千	舌	舌								
1	2	3	4	5	6								

26

话 huà
talk; speech; language

话别	huà bié	say goodbye
话柄	huà bǐng	subject for ridicule
话旧	huà jiù	talk about old time
话剧	huà jù	stage play
话题	huà tí	subject of a talk
笑话	xiào huà	joke

话: 人们把"言"字和"舌"字组合在一起就成了表示语言或交谈的"话"字。中国人用"覆水难收"这个成语来形容出口之言有多重的份量,告诫人们在说话之前要三思,而不可信口开河。

Man combined words 言 and tongue 舌 to produce 话, meaning speech or language. To emphasise the importance of weighing words before delivery and to caution against their indiscriminating proliferation, the Chinese proverb warns: "Water and words are easy to pour out but impossible to recover."

`	讠	讠	讠	讠	话	话	话
1	2	3	4	5	6	7	8

耳 ěr
ear

耳朵	ěr duo	ear
耳光	ěr guāng	a box on the ear
耳环	ěr huán	earring
耳机	ěr jī	earphone
耳孔	ěr kǒng	earhole
耳鸣	ěr míng	tinnitus
耳目	ěr mù	informer

耳: 从远古时期人们就认识到了听觉的好坏也是智慧高低的一种表现,正如谚语中所言:"擅言者不如擅听者。"由此产生了象形文字"ᘿ",随后深化并定形为"耳"。虽然此字是由原先的"ᘿ"演变而来,但已经丝毫看不出原先的形态了。

From time immemorial man discerned the wisdom of listening. He proclaimed from ear to ear the proverbial saying: "A good talker is inferior to a good listener." The pictograph created for the listening ear began with a natural rendition: ᘿ and ended with a stylised form: 耳. His talking about the listening ear began also with a natural rendition, but it doesn't seem like ever ending in any form.

一	丁	丌	丌	耳	耳
1	2	3	4	5	6

取

qǔ

take;
select;
seize

取代	qǔ dài	replace
取道	qǔ dào	by way of; via
取得	qǔ dé	obtain
取缔	qǔ dì	ban; suppress
取决	qǔ jué	be decided by
取巧	qǔ qiǎo	resort to trickery
取消	qǔ xiāo	cancel

取：此字意为抓住（又）某人的耳朵（耳）。含有疏忽、抓紧、抓住之意。图中所示进一步说明"取"字的含意。

To secure a firm hold on a person the hand 又 is laid on the ear 耳. A hand on the ear, then, means to take hold of, to neglect or seize: 取. Pictured here are various characters extending a helping hand to demonstrate what 取 means.

一	丅	厂	F	王	耳	耴	取								
1	2	3	4	5	6	7	8								

兄

xiōng

elder
brother

兄弟	xiōng dì	brothers
兄长	xiōng zhǎng	respectful form of address for an elder brother or a man friend
长兄	zhǎng xiōng	elder brother

兄："兄"这个概念是由"人"字与"口"字组成。"兄"字刻画的是一个人（人）张开大嘴（口）。也指一有权劝戒或管教自己兄弟的兄长。图中所示的是一位兄长在大声训斥他的弟弟或妹妹。此种现象在现实中常见。

The concept of "older brother" is suggested by the ideograph 兄 which combines person 人 with mouth 口. Ideally, 兄 represents a person 人 characterised by a large mouth 口, i.e., one who speaks with authority to exhort or correct a younger brother. Our picture shows what could happen in reality if big mouth of "older brother" went into action.

丶	丨フ	口	尸	兄											
1	2	3	4	5											

八 bā
eight

八仙	Bā Xiān	The Eight Immortals
八月	bā yuè	August
八字	bā zì	Eight Characters (indicating the time of a person's birth, used in fortune telling).

八：从字面上看，"八"字象征划分或分离。它由两个独立的笔划组成一个对称的字形"八"。也许是因为"8"这个数字最容易被多次划分，所以才会以"八"（划分）用来代表阿拉伯数字的"8"。此字最初的篆体写作"㕣"。很凑巧，它正好也是八笔。

In the etymological sense, 八 means to divide or separate. It is made up of two separate strokes, forming a symmetrical symbol 八. Probably because the number 8 can be easily divided and subdivided, 八 (to divide) came to stand for 8, the much-divisible number. The original seal form: 㕣, coincidentally, has 8 lines.

㇒	八										
1	2										

兑 duì
exchange; barter

兑付	duì fù	cash (a cheque, etc)
兑换	duì huàn	exchange
兑现	duì xiàn	pay cash
兑换表	duì huàn biǎo	exchange table

兑："兑"字最初是说话、祈祷或欣喜之意，由代表长兄的"兄"字和"八"字组合而成。指的是哥哥（兄）的训斥（八）会被振奋人心的话语所替代。而今天，在这个金钱为主导的社会中，此字在含义上也产生了变化，指兑换金钱或物品的交换。

The character 兑 originally meant to speak, bless or rejoice. It was derived from older brother's 兄 dissipation of effluent breath 八 into words of encouragement: 兑 involving the exchange of words. With money talking louder than words in man's affluent society, there arose the need to exchange the old meaning, for a new one. Today, 兑 means to exchange money or to barter.

㇔	㇜	㇒	兰	台	尸	兑					
1	2	3	4	5	6	7					

十 shí
ten

十分	shí fēn	very; fully
十万	shí wàn	one hundred thousand
十月	shí yuè	October
十足	shí zú	100 per cent
十二月	shí èr yuè	December
十一月	shí yī yuè	November
十字架	shí zì jià	cross

十："十"字是一种彻头彻尾的象征。 指代的是两种尺度（即"一"和"｜"），含有东、西、南、北、中的意思。同时还是汉字的计数单位，囊括了其它十进位的简单数字。正如图中所示的那样， 它可以用在数字及一定范围之内的事物上来表达一种完整、完全的意义。

十 is a symbol of completeness. It represents extent in two dimensions 十 (一 and ｜) and is formed by joining the five cardinal points: east, west, south, north and centre: 十 .The sign is therefore an appropriate symbol for the numeral 10, a complete number containing all the other simple numbers of decimal numeration. Our picture illustrates the completeness of 10, both in number and extent.

一	十									
1	2									

古 gǔ
old; ancient; also a Chinese surname

古巴	Gǔ Bā	Cuba
古代	gǔ dài	ancient times
古典	gǔ diǎn	classical
古董	gǔ dǒng	antique
古怪	gǔ guài	peculiar; strange
古国	gǔ guó	ancient state
古旧	gǔ jiù	archaic

古："古"这个字用于修饰那些经过"十"代人"口"传的事，包括那些非常陈旧、古老的事或物。 有些是有价值的， 有些价值很低，还有些毫无价值。图中所示的是一件可能有价值的事通过十张嘴流传的一个过程。

This character 古 is applicable to that which has passed through ten 十 mouths 口 ,a tradition dating back ten generations. It includes anything very old, ancient, of antiquity - whether valuable, invaluable or valueless. Our picture illustrates the process of passing through ten mouths something of questionable value.

一	十	十	古	古						
1	2	3	4	5						

心

xīn
heart

心爱	xīn ài	dear
心得	xīn dé	personal insight
心烦	xīn fán	vexed
心理	xīn lǐ	psychology
心目	xīn mù	frame of mind
心情	xīn qíng	state of mind
心思	xīn si	thought; idea

心："心"字最初就是一颗心脏的形状。它的膜囊部分向上张开形成"ㄩ"，在下面再加上一条大动脉就成了"ㄩ"形。经过演变的"ㄩ"则为今天的"心"字提供了雏形。心脏是人体的关键器官。心是用来决定人的善或恶的动机。所以，人们应牢记一句古老的成语："口蜜腹剑"。

The original pictograph was a representation of the physical heart. Its membranous sac was ripped open, exposing it: ㄩ and a delineation of the aorta appended below: ㄩ. A stylisation: ㄩ provided the basis for the modern form: 心. Recognition of this vital organ's role as seat of motivation for both good and evil prompted man to take to heart the ancient saying: "Honey mouth, dagger heart."

1	2	3	4												
丶	心	心	心												

怒

nù
anger;
rage;
passion

怒斥	nù chì	rebuke angrily
怒吼	nù hǒu	howl
怒火	nù huǒ	fury
怒气	nù qì	rage; fury
怒容	nù róng	angry look
怒色	nù sè	angry look
愤怒	fèn nù	angry

怒："怒"这个不吉利的字是由"奴"字和"心"字合在一起组成的，意指生气或愤怒，给人一种警告。这个字提醒人们不要发怒，否则你就会变成"心"的奴隶和女仆"奴"。

The very sinister structure of 怒, meaning anger or passion, constitutes a warning to man, for 怒 was secured by bonding slave 奴 to heart 心. It cautions against giving way to anger or passion and becoming slave and handmaid 奴 to the dictates of the heart 心.

1	2	3	4	5	6	7	8	9					
ㄑ	女	女	如	奴	奴	怒	怒	怒					

怕

pà
fear

怕人	pà rén	terrifying
怕生	pà shēng	shy with strangers
怕死	pà sǐ	fear death
怕羞	pà xiū	bashful; shy
害怕	hài pà	scared
怕事	pà shì	afraid of getting into trouble

怕: 表示恐惧的这个字的形旁是"忄"即"心"字的变形。声旁是"白"字, 由"白"和"心"组成的字就是"怕"。"白色的心"字面意思是害怕或缺乏勇气。有时由于一时害怕会使原本勇敢的人变得特别胆小, 就像图中所示的那样。

The character for fear has, for radical, 忄, a variant of heart 心. The phonetic, sound component 白 (white) collaborates with the radical, 心 (heart) to instil the idea of fear into this character: 怕, which literally means: "white heart", i.e., fear or lack of courage. Sometimes a "white heart" can inspire the bold deeds of a "lion-heart" as our picture shows.

'	ﾉ	忄	忄'	忄'	怕	怕	怕			
1	2	3	4	5	6	7	8			

身

shēn
body

身材	shēn cái	figure (body)
身份	shēn fèn	social status
身价	shēn jià	social status
身躯	shēn qū	body; stature
身世	shēn shì	one's lot
身体	shēn tǐ	body
身心	shēn xīn	body and mind

身: 此字最早的意思为"怀孕", 它描绘的是一个怀孕的妇女挺着肚子, 一条腿跨向前以保持身体平衡, 即"身"。现在的"身"字意指"躯体", 不论男女, 也不论肚子大小都通用。在这里我们画出一对大肚子的夫妇形象——只是肚子大, 可不一定怀孕啊。

This character originally meant "pregnant"; it pictured a human figure with prominent belly and one leg thrust forward to support and balance the body: 身. The modern form: 身 also means "the human body", either male or female, ordinary or outstanding. We show a couple of outstanding ones - outstanding in "body", not in form or figure.

'	ﾉ	勹	甶	身	身	身				
1	2	3	4	5	6	7				

自

zì
self;
oneself

自白	zì bái	self-confession
自动	zì dòng	automatic
自杀	zì shā	commit suicide
自首	zì shǒu	give oneself up
自传	zì zhuàn	autobiography
自己	zì jǐ	oneself
自立	zì lì	independent

自：因为"鼻子"是脸部最突出的器官，所以它被用来代表"自我"。通过象征的手段，鼻子状的象形文字已不再仅是"鼻子"之意，而是表示自己、自我之意。图中所强调的是两人争吵时，鼻子起着决定的作用。

Because the nose sticks out most from the face - sometimes too far out - it characterises the person and symbolises his personality. A pictographic representation of the nose therefore personifies, not the nose, but "self" or "oneself". Our picture emphasises the dominant role of the nose in a confrontation of personalities.

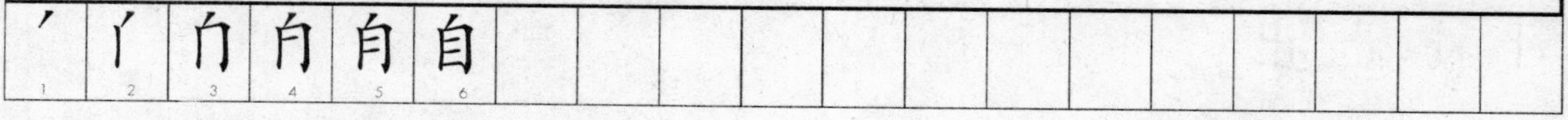

齿

chǐ
teeth

齿轮	chǐ lún	gear-wheel
齿腔	chǐ qiāng	dental cavity
齿痛	chǐ tòng	toothache
齿龈	chǐ yín	the gums
牙齿	yá chǐ	tooth

齿：这个字的演化过程看起来如同人们打了一场败仗。最早的字形是一张布满牙齿的嘴" "。后来，就只剩下了门齿，即" "。后来的牙被削尖，又加上"止"音，就成了"齒"。简化的"齿"字把牙齿减少到只剩下一颗。在这一系列缩减中，唯一让人感到欣慰的是戴着假牙也不影响说真话。

The evolutionary struggle of this character sees man fighting a losing battle. Earliest forms show the mouth filled with teeth: and later only the front teeth: . The regular form: 齒 has the teeth sharpened and capped by the phonetic: 止. The simplified version: 齿 drastically reduces the remaining teeth to one. But, with all that loss, man can still console himself that many a true word is spoken through false teeth.

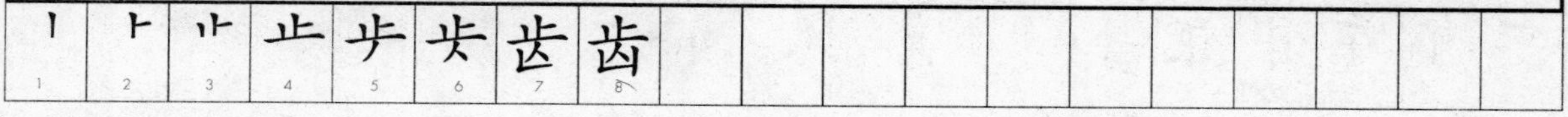

止 zhǐ
halt; stop

止步	zhǐ bù	halt; stop
止境	zhǐ jìng	limit; end
止渴	zhǐ kě	quench thirst
止咳	zhǐ ké	relieve a cough
止痛	zhǐ tòng	allay pains
止血	zhǐ xuè	stop bleeding
停止	tíng zhǐ	halt; stop

止: 虽然这个字的形状像一只只有三个脚趾的脚, 但它并不表示"脚"的意思。它的意思为停顿、停止。图中所示表明了在紧急情况下脚可以十分方便地用来表达停止之意。

Although this character is a crude representation of the motionless foot, with the five toes reduced to three, it does not stand for "foot". Its meanings are derived by extension and include: to halt, stop or stand still. Our illustration shows how, in an emergency, the foot can come in handy to express the idea of "Stop!"

丨	卜	止	止									
1	2	3	4									

正 zhèng
straight; upright; correct; exact

正当	zhèng dàng	proper; rightful
正派	zhèng pài	upright; decent
正确	zhèng què	correct; right
正式	zhèng shì	official
正统	zhèng tǒng	orthodox
正义	zhèng yì	justice
正月	zhēng yuè	January

正: "正"这个字是一只脚"止"(表示"停"的意思)加上一条横线(一)就是"正", 表示在适当的限度(一)内停下来不至于误入歧途。这也是一个表意字, 即一只脚沿着直线走为"正"。引申为直的、适度的、正确的之意。

The character: 正 shows a foot: 止 (meaning "stop") with a straight line above it. It signifies arrival and stopping (止) at the line or proper limit (一) without going astray. It is also an ideograph of a foot walking in a straight line: 正. Hence the extended meanings: straight, upright, proper, correct, exact.

一	丁	下	正	正								
1	2	3	4	5								

是

shì
right; yes;
am; are; is

是的	shì de	yes; right
是非	shì fēi	right and wrong
是否	shì fǒu	whether or not?
是故	shì gù	for this reason
不是	bù shì	not so

是: 这个表意文字是把表示"太阳"的"日"字放在表示"正确的"正"（后修改为"疋"）字上形成的。这个字描绘的是太阳"日"位于子午线上的样子"是"。太阳在这里表示正确的意思。因此，这个字的意思为"对"或"是"。

This ideograph locates the sun: 日 over the character for right or correct: 正 (modified to 疋). It depicts the sun: 日 exactly on the meridian: 是. The sun is here taken as the standard for correctness. Hence the idea of "right, yes, am, are, is."

丶	冂	曰	日	旦	早	早	是	是				
1	2	3	4	5	6	7	8	9				

走

zǒu
walk; run;
hasten;
depart

走动	zǒu dòng	move around
走狗	zǒu gǒu	running dog; lackey
走廊	zǒu láng	corridor
走路	zǒu lù	walk
走私	zǒu sī	smuggling
走失	zǒu shī	be lost

走: 此字最初的篆体为"歪"。上半部分"夭"（或写作"土"），象征一个人。他低着头"大"，快步向前"丿"。下半部分的"止"（或写作"龰"）表示停。"夭"和"止"组成"走"。这个动作同样也解释为在快步行走时脚或脚趾弯曲"夭"（土）。这里画出了一群人物，从中可以看出，止（龰）在此表示走、跑、逃等概念，唯独不当停讲。

In the original seal form: 歪 the upper part: 夭 (or 土) represents a man: 大 bending his head: 丿 forward to walk rapidly. The lower part: 止 (or 龰) means "to stop". This combination of bending and stopping indicates walking. The movement is also suggested by the bending: 夭 (土) of the toes or foot:in swift walking. Pictured here are a host of characters. 止 (龰) walking, running, fleeing - all bending forward but not stopping.

一	十	土	丰	丰	走	走						
1	2	3	4	5	6	7						

土

tǔ

earth;
soil;
ground

土地	tǔ dì	land
土匪	tǔ fěi	bandit
土话	tǔ huà	local dialect
土壤	tǔ rǎng	soil
土人	tǔ rén	native
土质	tǔ zhì	property of soil
泥土	ní tǔ	soil; earth

土：人们依靠土地而生存。对人们来说，土地是由两层（二）构成的，即表土层和底土层—植物就是在这里生根发芽（丨），这就是"土"。所以"土"就是为人们提供生长一切的大地。本图中所绘的便是一些土地的产物。

Man has always been dependent on the ground for subsistence. To him, earth （土） is represented by its two layers （二） - the topsoil and subsoil - from which growing plants sprout （丨）. Hence 土: the good earth that produces all things for man. Pictured here are some such "earthy" provisions.

一	十	土												
1	2	3												

坐

zuò

to sit;
a seat

坐牢	zuò láo	be imprisoned
坐落	zuò luò	locate; situate
坐视	zuò shì	sit by and watch
坐位	zuò wèi	seat
坐下	zuò xià	sit down
请坐	qǐng zuò	please sit down

坐："坐"这个表意字描绘的是两个人面对面"从"坐在地上"土"。虽然偏旁"土"字为这两个人"从"提供了"坐"的地方，但正如图所示的那样，它还可以表示出一种不劳作时的情形。

坐, the ideograph for "sit", depicts two men talking face-to-face （从）, sitting on the ground （土） but not quite down-to-earth. Although the radical 土 (earth) provides the base for the men （从） to "sit" 坐 on, it can prove to be the root of unproductive activity, as illustrated.

丿	人	人丿	从	丛	坐	坐								
1	2	3	4	5	6	7								

出 chū

go out;
issue;
produce

出版	chū bǎn	publish
出产	chū chǎn	produce
出国	chū guó	go abroad
出境	chū jìng	leave a country
出口	chū kǒu	export
出来	chū lái	come out
出卖	chū mài	betray

出:"出"字最初展现的是一株植物(屮)从土地(凵)伸展出来并绽开花朵的样子。这个动词重点用来强调"出去"这个动作。我们图中的施动者与受动者的声音已经对"出"这个概念做出了形象的描述。

Originally, 出 represented a stalk (屮) thrusting itself out of its receptacle (凵) - the ground - and bursting out in full bloom. This verbal character places emphasis on the action "out". Translating this action visually, our picture shows "out" being expressed, not only in the active voice, but also in the passive voice.

乚	凵	屮	出	出										
1	2	3	4	5										

生 shēng

produce;
bear;
grow

生病	shēng bìng	fall ill
生存	shēng cún	survive
生动	shēng dòng	vivid
生活	shēng huó	livelihood
生理	shēng lǐ	physiology
生命	shēng mìng	life
生气	shēng qì	angry

生:"土"地中生长出植物(屮),就形成了"生"字的雏形"㞷"。简化后写作"生",意为生产、出生或生长。人们都是在不同的方式与方向下生长的,我们图中所举的就是三代人的例子。

The earth (土), producing a plant (屮), lays the groundwork for growth (㞷). Hence the modified form: 生, meaning to produce, bear or grow. Man, born imperfect, grows in different ways and directions. Pictured here are examples from three generations.

丿	一	二	牛	生										
1	2	3	4	5										

姓
xìng
surname

姓名	xìng míng	surname and name
姓谱	xìng pǔ	genealogical record; family register
姓氏	xìng shì	surname
百姓	bǎi xìng	common people
贵姓	guì xìng	what is your surname?

姓：“姓”这个字包括“女”字和“生”字两部分，字面意思为“女性所生”。它表示在遥远的远古时代，出生的孩子都要取母姓。所以姓名的“姓”由“女”与“生”组成。图中所示的是远古的一个以李为母姓的家族，但我们已经忘却那微不足道的父姓了。

The character 姓, comprising 女 (woman) and 生 (born), literally means: "born of woman". It suggests that in some remote, forgotten era man, born of woman, got his name from the mother. Hence 姓: "surname". We introduce here Mama Li's（李）family from the remote past, but we've forgotten Papa's insignificant surname.

亅	女	女	女	如	如	姓	姓						
1	2	3	4	5	6	7	8						

贝
bèi
shells; valuables

贝雕	bèi diāo	shell carving
贝壳	bèi ké	shell
贝类	bèi lèi	shellfish
贝玉	bèi yù	valuables; gems
贝子	bèi zi	cowries-used as currency in ancient times

贝：象形文字“贝”表示的是一个珍贵的贝壳。贝壳在封建社会早期被当作货币来使用。它表示“值钱”的意思。“贝”字正规的写法为“貝”，表示的是一个有两只触角活着的贝类动物。但是就像它当初作为钱使用时中间是空的那样，今天所用的简体“贝”字中间也是空的。

This character is a pictograph of the precious cowrie shell. Used in early feudal times as money, it came to mean also "valuables". The regular form（貝）shows a live shell with feelers; but today, like the money it once represented, the shell reveals its hollowness in the simplified form（贝）.

丨	冂	贝	贝									
1	2	3	4									

38

贱 jiàn
low-priced;
cheap;
humble

贱价	jiàn jià	cheap; low-priced
贱卖	jiàn mài	cheap-sale
贫贱	pín jiàn	poor and humble

贱: 两只长矛"戋"捣碎有价值、曾作为货币使用的贝壳"贝",就表示便宜的、不值钱及谦卑的意思。人们用这个字形容那些不值钱的东西。有句俗话说得很明白"便宜没好货,好货不便宜"。有时人们也用这字来自嘲。

Two spears: 戋 shattering and destroying the value of shells: 贝, once used as money, conveys the idea of cheap, worthless, mean or humble. Man applied this word to anything of little value, uttering the proverbial saying: "Cheap things are of little value; valuable things are not cheap". In mock humility, he applied it also to himself.

丨 冂 贝 贝 贝 贝 贱 贱 贱

贵 guì
expensive;
dear;
honourable

贵宾	guì bīn	guest of honour
贵妇	guì fù	noblewoman
贵姓	guì xìng	your name, please
贵重	guì zhòng	valuable; precious
贵族	guì zú	aristocrat; noble
宝贵	bǎo guì	precious

贵: 一个装满珍贵货币"贝"的篮子或容器"虫"(或写作"史")就表示昂贵的意思,引申为高级的或值得尊敬的。在此鄙人(贱)感谢尊敬(贵)的读者阅读此书,并对这本双语读物感兴趣。

A basket or container: 虫 (or 史) filled with precious cowries: 贝 (once used as money) means dear or expensive. By extension, it also means high-class or honourable. In this connection, humble self (贱) thanks honourable readers (贵) for their appreciation and interest in the Bilingual Page.

丶 口 口 中 虫 虫 贵 贵 贵

39

水

shuǐ
water

水彩	shuǐ cǎi	water colour
水池	shuǐ chí	pond; pool
水沟	shuǐ gōu	drain; ditch
水管	shuǐ guǎn	water pipe
水果	shuǐ guǒ	fruit
水库	shuǐ kù	reservoir; dam
水泥	shuǐ ní	cement

水："水"，一种天然的能量源泉，它的象形文字是由涌动的水组成的，包括一条主流和四个漩窝(⺍)。另有一种不同的写法，即只写三个点的"氵"旁。此"氵"作为字根，用于和水相关的许多字。至今仍流传着一句谚语："水能载舟，亦能覆舟。"

Water (水), a natural source of power, is represented by a pictograph of surging waters with a central mainstream and four whirls:⺍. A variant form, using only three drops (氵), operates as radical to induce a flood of "watery" characters. To this day, the proverbial saying is afloat: "Water can support a ship, and water can upset it".

丿	刁	水	水									
1	2	3	4									

永

yǒng
everlasting;
perpetual;
forever

永生	yǒng shēng	eternal life
永别	yǒng bié	part forever
永不	yǒng bù	never
永固	yǒng gù	permanently fixed
永恒	yǒng héng	eternal; everlasting
永久	yǒng jiǔ	permanent

永：人世是随着一代代人的生死轮回而变化的。但是水不同，它总是在不停息的周而复始地流动。水的这种不间断流动的特点形成了表意文字"水"。"永"字是"水"的变种，就是在"水"字上加上气泡和涟漪写作"⺌"。"永字八笔"将使人们永远记住"永"字。

One generation comes and another goes, but water flows on incessantly in a continuous cycle. From this unceasing flow of water came the ideograph for "everlasting": 永 - a variation of water (水), with foams and ripples added: ⺌. 永 will long be remembered as the "everlasting" character that embodies the eight fundamental strokes used in calligraphy.

丶	丁	刁	永	永							
1	2	3	4	5							

冰 **bīng**
ice

冰雹	bīng báo	hailstones
冰川	bīng chuān	glacier
冰岛	Bīng Dǎo	Iceland
冰冻	bīng dòng	freeze
冰块	bīng kuài	ice-cube
冰冷	bīng lěng	ice-cold
冰凉	bīng liáng	ice-cold

冰："冰"字最早写作"仌",指冰表面的裂缝或晶体。"仌"字旁描绘的是滴水成冰的概念。把"冫"字旁加在"水"字旁边,就使"冫"凝结成了"冰"。图中所示是冰的比喻意义,把"冰冷"和"火热"放在一起作了形象的对比。

The character for ice was originally: 仌, representing cracks or crystals on the surface of ice. The radical 冫 depicts water dripping and freezing into an icicle. 冫 was added to 水 (water) to freeze and crystallise it into "frozen water" or ice: 冰. Our illustration applies 冰 figuratively, contrasting icy coldness with fiery passion.

丶	冫	刂	冯	冰	冰						
1	2	3	4	5	6						

雨 **yǔ**
rain

雨点	yǔ diǎn	raindrop
雨季	yǔ jì	rainy season
雨量	yǔ liàng	rainfall
雨伞	yǔ sǎn	umbrella
雨水	yǔ shuǐ	rain water
雨天	yǔ tiān	rainy day
雨衣	yǔ yī	raincoat

雨："雨"这个字是由天空中(一)云层里(冂)垂直(丨)掉下来的雨点(⼆⼆)组成的。不过不是所有的人都像求雨者那么喜欢下雨,正如谚语所言:"农民盼雨天,游客盼晴天。"

雨, the character for rain, is a picture of raindrops (⼆⼆) falling vertically down (丨) from a cloud (冂) in the heavens (一). Not all welcome the rain as showers of blessing from heaven for, as the saying goes, "The farmer hopes for rain, the traveller for fine weather."

一	冂	冂	币	雨	雨	雨	雨				
1	2	3	4	5	6	7	8				

yún
cloud

云彩	yún cǎi	cloud
云层	yún céng	layers of cloud
云雾	yún wù	mist; fog
云霞	yún xiá	rosy clouds
云霄	yún xiāo	the skies
云烟	yún yān	cloud and mist
白云	bái yún	white clouds

云: 当湿热的蒸气（ʒ或ㄥ）上升遇到低温，就会凝结成"云"。把"云"字和"雨"字合在一起就成了繁体字的"雲"。简体字中去掉了其中的"雨"字，把它简化为"云"。

When the humid and warm vapours (ʒ or ㄥ) rise (ㄥ or) and reach the colder regions, they condense and form clouds: 云. Loading the clouds（雲）with rain（雨）produces the regular form: 雲. The simplified version relieves the clouds（雲）of their load, reverting the character to its original form: 云.

一	二	云	云							
1	2	3	4							

xuě
snow

雪白	xuě bái	snow-white
雪崩	xuě bēng	snowslide
雪恨	xuě hèn	avenge
雪花	xuě huā	snowflake
雪茄	xuě jiā	cigar
雪景	xuě jǐng	snow scenery
雪亮	xuě liàng	bright as snow

雪: 此字的篆体是把"雨"和"彗"（扫帚之意）合在一起而成的，即"雪"。今天的"雪"字由"雨"和"彐"（简化的"彗"）组成。这两种字形都很适合用来表示雪，即可以捧在手里（彐）或用扫帚扫（彗）的雨。

The seal character 雪 associates rain 雨 with broom 彗. The modern character 雪 relates rain 雨 to hand 彐 (a contraction of 彗, broom). Both versions fittingly symbolise snow, i.e., rain 雨 which can be taken up in the hand （彐）or swept away by a broom（彗）.

一	厂	戶	币	雨	雨	雫	雪	雪	雪	雪
1	2	3	4	5	6	7	8	9	10	11

电 diàn
lightning; electricity

电报	diàn bào	telegram; cable
电池	diàn chí	battery
电工	diàn gōng	electrician
电话	diàn huà	telephone
电流	diàn liú	electric current
电脑	diàn nǎo	computer
电视	diàn shì	television

电: 一道闪"电"在"雨"中划过就形成了表示闪电的"電"字。闪电是一种可见的放电现象。"電"也可以指一般的电。经过锐减，闪电还是在放电中失去了十三笔中的八笔，成了简体的"电"。

A streak of lightning (电) amidst the falling rain (雨) forged the character for lightning: 電. Lightning being a visible discharge of electricity, 電 came to mean also electricity. 電 takes the path of least resistance, discharging eight of its thirteen strokes to transform itself into the simplified form: 电.

一	冂	日	日	电							
1	2	3	4	5							

雷 léi
thunder

雷达	léi dá	radar
雷鸣	léi míng	thunderous
雷声	léi shēng	thunderclap
雷雨	léi yǔ	thunderstorm
打雷	dǎ léi	to thunder
地雷	dì léi	land-mine
水雷	shuǐ léi	sea-mine

雷: 经验告诉人们，当一块雨云(雨)位于田地(田)上空的时候，闪电的吼声－"雷"就要响起来。最初的"雷"字有三个或者四个田字(畾)组合起来表现雷声的回荡，对人们来说，雷声是靠闪电使人印象深刻的。

From experience, man knows that rain clouds (雨) over his fields (田) means thunder: 雷, the voice of lightning. The original version of 雷 has three or four fields (畾) incorporated in a graphic pattern to express the reverberation of thunder. To man, thunder is impressive, but it is lightning that does the work.

一	冂	厂	中	巿	雨	雨	雫	雫	雫	雫	雷	雷
1	2	3	4	5	6	7	8	9	10	11	12	13

伞

sǎn
umbrella

伞兵	sǎn bīng	paratroop; parachuter
雨伞	yǔ sǎn	umbrella
降落伞	jiàng luò sǎn	parachute

伞: 此字为象形文字, 即"伞", 象征着伞下所避藏的四个人。但作为部首的"人"字与此字的原形 (即"伞") 没有任何关系。正如谚语所说的: "天晴需备伞, 肚饱需备粮。"

伞 is a pictograph of an umbrella. Its radical: 人 (man) has nothing to do with the original character: 傘. Nevertheless, the regular form: 傘 seems to be harbouring four persons (众) not included in the simplified version: 伞. Under cover of the umbrella, man counsels for the rainy day: "When the sky is clear, carry an umbrella; though your stomach is full, carry provisions."

丿 人 仐 伞 伞 伞
1　2　3　4　5　6

川

chuān
river; stream

川资	chuān zī	travelling expenses
四川	Sì Chuān	Sichuan, China

川: "大川" 从不拒绝小河的汇入。当河流蜿蜒流过干旱的土地时, 会给田野注入生命力, 使土地不断的受到滋润。河川被恰当地描述为小溪合并成的支流"《《"。现在的"川"字使用一种不同的写法"《《"来作为其它字的字根。

"The great river does not reject little stream." As the river meanders through arid land, infusing life into the fields, it is continually fed by little streams. Fittingly, the river is portrayed as flowing water formed by the union of little streams, upon which it vitally depends: 《《. The modern independent form: 川 uses a variant: 《《 to serve as source for other related characters.

丿 川 川
1　2　3

山 shān
mountain; hill

山顶	shān dǐng	mountain top
山歌	shān gē	folk song
山谷	shān gǔ	valley
山脉	shān mài	mountain range
山坡	shān pō	hill slope
山头	shān tóu	hilltop
山崖	shān yá	cliff

山：一座有三个高峰的山脉，提供了表示山脉或山坡的象形文字"山"的雏形。从一个至高点，人们可以轻易地看到低谷中容易被忽视的事物。正如谚语中所说的："不登高山，不知天下之大也。"

A mountain range, with three towering peaks, provides the structure for this pictograph of mountain or hill: 山. From a high point of vantage, man is able to oversee what is easily overlooked on a lowland. Hence the proverb: "If you don't climb the high mountain, you can't view the plain."

丨	山	山										
1	2	3										

鸟 niǎo
bird

鸟巢	niǎo cháo	bird's nest
鸟瞰	niǎo kàn	bird's eye view
鸟类	niǎo lèi	birds
鸟笼	niǎo lóng	bird cage
鸟爪	niǎo zhǎo	bird's claws
鸟兽	niǎo shòu	birds and animals
小鸟	xiǎo niǎo	small bird

鸟：繁体字"鳥"指的是一种长尾的鸟。它洋洋得意地炫耀自己的美丽和自由自在。不幸的是，漂亮对鸟来说并不总是一种资本。俗话说："漂亮之鸟笼中养。"以今天简体的鸟字来看，可怜的鸟儿已经褪去了它的羽毛，最终成了"鸟"字。

The regular form: 鳥 is a representation of a long-tailed bird, flaunting its beauty and revelling in its freedom. Unfortunately, beauty has not always been an asset to the bird for, as the saying goes, "It's the beautiful bird that we put in the cage." Tragically, the simplified form sees the poor bird stripped of its plumage: 鸟.

'	勹	勺	鸟	鸟						
1	2	3	4	5						

岛

dǎo
island

岛国	dǎo guó	island state
岛屿	dǎo yǔ	islands
半岛	bàn dǎo	peninsula
群岛	qún dǎo	archipelago

岛：海鸟总是在海中耸立的礁石上筑巢，因此把"鳥"字写在"山"字上就表示"岛"的概念。古代的岛字展现的是一只伸着爪子盘旋于山上的鸟"鸟"。现在的"岛"字表明一只收回了脚的鸟在山上安了家。它大概是在孕育简体的"岛"字吧。

Sea-birds often nest on mountainous rocks that emerge from the sea. Hence a bird（鳥）over a mountain（山）gave the concept for island: 岛. The ancient form shows a bird hovering over a mountain, with feet visible: 鸟. The modern version has the bird settling on it, with feet hidden: 岛, probably hatching the simplified character: 岛.

´	ㄅ	ㄅ	鸟	鸟	岛	岛						
1	2	3	4	5	6	7						

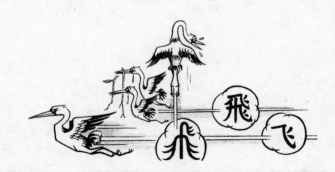

飞

fēi
fly

飞行员	fēi xíng yuán	pilot
飞禽走兽	fēi qín zǒu shòu	birds and beasts

飞：创造这个字的灵感来源于鹤的迁徙飞行。它的长脖子将自身弯成"飞"型。后来这个字由九划的繁体"飛"简化为三划的"飞"字。

This character draws its inspiration from the migratory flight of the crane - with the long neck of the bird folded on itself: 飛. The flight is speeded up by simplifying the regular form: 飛, lightening its load of strokes from nine to three: 飞.

乁	飞	飞										
1	2	3										

羽

yǔ
feathers;
wings

| 羽毛 | yǔ máo | feather |
| 羽毛球 | yǔ máo qiú | badminton |

羽：此字指鸟类艳丽的羽毛，由一对翅膀组成。羽字的写法历来没有多大的变化。从最初的"羿"到"羿"，再到最终的"羽"字，猛一看上去它们都差不多。我们举出了一些近看鸟羽的图案以确认这一点。

Feathers - the showy plumage of birds - are represented by a pair of wings. Like human nature, feathers have changed little in character through the ages. From the original 羿 to 羿 and finally 羽, all look alike at a glance. To confirm this, our illustration takes a closer look at some birds of a feather.

丁	丁	习	羽	羽	羽									
1	2	3	4	5	6									

习

xí
practise

习惯	xí guàn	habit
习气	xí qì	bad habit
习俗	xí sú	custom; tradition
习题	xí tí	exercise (of school work)
习性	xí xìng	habits and characteristics

习：这个表意文字是由"羽"字与"白"（后缩写为"白"）字组成。使人联想起一只正在自学飞翔的鸟。其引申为练习的意思。像鸟学飞一样，人们也在试着加快简化"習"字复杂结构的过程，用一只翅膀来表示"习"。如果鸟学人只用一支翅膀来飞，那就惨了。

This ideograph combines wings (羽) with self (白, contraction of 白), suggesting a young bird learning to fly by itself; by extension, to practise: 習. Copying the bird, man also tries to fly by speeding up the simplification of the original intricate character: 習, using only one wing for "practice": 习. Woe betide the bird that copies man!

丁	习	习												
1	2	3												

扇

shàn
fan

扇动	shān dòng	fan; flap
扇惑	shān huò	incite; agitate
扇形	shàn xíng	fan-shaped
扇子	shàn zi	fan
一扇门	yī shàn mén	a door

扇: 这个表意文字由代表翅膀的"羽"字和代表大门的"户"字组合而成。因这两个物体都可以像扇子一样展开，所以用这两部分来强调"扇"字是最合适不过了。另外，人们所用于装饰的物品很多也是用"羽"来制作的。

In this ideograph, a wing (羽) is likened to the leaf of a door (户) in that its attachment is at the end, and both are capable of vibrating and spreading out like a fan: 扇. The combination of these two related components enforces the idea of "fan" (扇), a useful and decorative device often made of feathers (羽).

丶	宀	冖	户	庐	庐	肩	扇	扇	扇						
1	2	3	4	5	6	7	8	9	10						

鱼

yú
fish

鱼饵	yú ěr	fish-bait
鱼钩	yú gōu	fish-hook
鱼雷	yú léi	torpedo
鱼鳞	yú lín	fish-scales
鱼群	yú qún	shoal of fish
鱼网	yú wǎng	fishing net
鱼肝油	yú gān yóu	cod-liver oil

鱼: "鱼"字为象形文字。鱼吃鱼的生活习性给于人们启迪，正所谓: "大鱼吃小鱼，小鱼吃虾米，虾米吃污泥。""鱼"字的尾巴原是"火"字。大概是因为鱼一般被人用火烤熟了吃的原故吧。

鱼 is a pictograph of the fish, whose predatory habits prompt man to snap at his own fishy way of life: "Big fish eat small fish; small fish eat water insects; water insects eat weeds and mud." The tail of the fish: proves to be its fiery end, being a form of fire (火), presumably kindled as man prepares to eat big fish.

丿	夕	夕	皃	皃	角	鱼	鱼								
1	2	3	4	5	6	7	8								

渔

yú
fishing

渔村	yú cūn	fishing-village
渔夫	yú fū	fisherman
渔港	yú gǎng	fishing port
渔歌	yú gē	fisherman's song
渔民	yú mín	fisherman
渔业	yú yè	fishery
渔舟	yú zhōu	fishing boat

渔："鱼"和"水"（氵）是钓鱼（渔）所必不可少的两个条件。古代的"渔"字所展现出的是大量的水和鱼"燎"。简化后鱼与水的数量均只剩一，可能是因为已经把鱼钓上来了吧。这里再透露一种"钓鱼"的方法—不需要水和鱼。不过看起来不太可能。

Fish (鱼) and water (氵) are requisites for fishing (渔). The ancient form for fishing reveals water teeming with fishes: 燎. The modified form sees the number reduced to one, probably due to success in fishing: 燎. Disclosed here is yet another form of fishing - without fish or water - but it doesn't look too successful.

`	`	氵	氵	氵	氵	泊	泊	渔	渔	渔		
1	2	3	4	5	6	7	8	9	10	11		

鲁

lǔ
stupid;
simple

鲁钝	lǔ dùn	stupid
鲁莽	lǔ mǎng	reckless; careless

鲁：为了表示单纯或愚蠢之意，人们创造了这个字，把一个表示鼻子的"自"（后简化为："日"）字放在一个"鱼"字之下。这样 拼凑的结果就是一条没有嗅觉和感觉的大鼻子哑巴鱼"鲁"。而傻人恰恰就像只看到鱼饵而看不见鱼钩的傻鱼一样笨。

In his eagerness to acquire an ideograph for simple or stupid, man literally acted the part. He appended to fish (鱼) a representation of a nose (自) which was later corrupted to 日 (speak).The tragic result: a "dumb" fish unable to speak and a "nosey" one, without scent or sense: 鲁. Simple man, like stupid fish, sees the bait, not the hook.

′	″	⺈	⺈	刍	角	鱼	鱼	鲁	鲁	鲁	鲁	
1	2	3	4	5	6	7	8	9	10	11	12	

羊

yáng
sheep; goat

羊角	yáng jiǎo	ram's horn
羊毛	yáng máo	sheep's wool
羊排	yáng pái	mutton chop
羊皮	yáng pí	sheep skin
羊群	yáng qún	flock of sheep
羊肉	yáng ròu	mutton

羊: 因为天性温顺驯服, 所以 "羊" 是一个很恰当的表示温和的符号。它的象形文字呈现出很平衡的结构。早期的 "羊" 字展现的是一个从正面看的羊头的形状。后来经过修改加入了犄角、耳朵、腿和尾巴几部分。当加入这几部分后, 羊尾巴便被削去成 "羊"。

Because of its mild and gentle nature, the sheep (羊) is a fitting symbol for meekness. Its pictographic representations take on well-balanced forms. Early versions show frontal views of the head; later modifications fill in the horns, ears, legs and tail. When combined with other components, the tail is often left out: 羊.

`	゛	丷	兰	兰	羊								
1	2	3	4	5	6								

鲜

xiān
fresh

鲜果	xiān guǒ	fresh fruit
鲜红	xiān hóng	bright red
鲜花	xiān huā	fresh flower
鲜美	xiān měi	delicious; tasty
鲜明	xiān míng	vividness
鲜奶	xiān nǎi	fresh milk
鲜血	xiān xuè	blood

鲜: 这个字是由 "鱼" 肉和 "羊" 肉两部分组成。尽管肉类可以通过腌制、烘干或薰制来保存, 古人仍首选吃新鲜的羊肉或鱼肉。因此, "鱼" 字与 "羊" 字一起就成了表示新鲜的 "鲜" 字。换句话说, 肉已经变得等同于鲜了。

This character combines two types of flesh: fish (鱼) and sheep (羊). Although meat was usually preserved by salting, drying or smoking, ancient man preferred to eat the flesh of fish and sheep fresh. Hence, fish (鱼) and sheep (羊) put together means "fresh": 鲜. In other words, "flesh" becomes "fresh".

⁄	⼓	⼓	乌	刍	角	甶	鱼	鱼	鱼	鲜	鲜	鲜	鲜
1	2	3	4	5	6	7	8	9	10	11	12	13	14

美

měi
beautiful;
pretty;
very satisfactory

美观	měi guān	nice looking
美好	měi hǎo	fine; glorious
美化	měi huà	beautiful
美景	měi jǐng	beautiful scenery
美丽	měi lì	beautiful
美梦	měi mèng	fond dream
美妙	měi miào	splendid

美：这个结构比例优美的字是由"羊"字加上"大"字而组成。"大"本指一个人长大；"羊"是一种性情温顺，为人所喜爱的动物。这个象形文字表示一个如同羊一般温顺的成年人即被认为是受人尊敬的人，是美的。

This beautifully proportioned character is shaped from 羊 (sheep) and 大 (big). 大 originally represented a person grown big; 羊 is an animal admired for its peace-loving virtue. Ideographically, a mature person (大) who has the mild and gentle disposition of a sheep (羊) regarded as beautiful, admirable: 美.

、	٠٠	٣٣	٣	羊	羊	羊	羊	美
1	2	3	4	5	6	7	8	9

义

yì
justice;
righteousness

义愤	yì fèn	indignation
义务	yì wù	obligation; duty
义演	yì yǎn	benefit performance
意义	yì yì	meaning
正义	zhèng yì	justice

义：当正义成风时，好斗的"我"（"手"中握着长矛"戈"）就会变得屈服得如同一只驯服、温和的羊。因此"义"字证明了它代表的是正确的行为。后来，"义"字被简化到了只剩三划，使它成为一个表示简单、完美及公平正义的"义"字。

When justice (義) prevails, the aggressive "I": 我 (with spear 戈 in hand 手) becomes subdued like a docile and gentle sheep (羊). Hence 義 justifies itself as a symbol for right conduct. For the sake of righteousness the regular form is now slashed to three strokes, transforming it into a simplified and perfectly balanced justice: 义.

丿	乂	义						
1	2	3						

洋

yáng
ocean;
foreign

洋葱	yáng cōng	onion
洋行	yáng háng	foreign firm
洋化	yáng huà	westernized
洋灰	yáng huī	cement
洋人	yáng rén	foreigner
洋溢	yáng yì	fill with
海洋	hǎi yáng	ocean

洋: 虽然 "羊" 字是声旁, 但它也对强调 "洋" 字的意思起作用。羊是生长在内陆的动物, 在远离大洋的草原上放牧。因此, 远离 "羊" 的 "水" (氵) 就表示海洋的 "洋"。洋字还引申为外国, 即大洋彼岸之意。

Although 羊 is a phonetic, it also serves to emphasise the meaning of this character for ocean: 洋. Sheep, being inland animals, graze on land away from the ocean; so water (氵) far away from the sheep (羊) came to mean ocean: 洋. By extension, 洋 also means "foreign", i.e., far away beyond the ocean.

丶	冫	氵	氵	汸	浐	洋	洋	洋						
1	2	3	4	5	6	7	8	9						

火

huǒ
fire

火柴	huǒ chái	match
火车	huǒ chē	train
火光	huǒ guāng	flame; blaze
火海	huǒ hǎi	sea of fire
火花	huǒ huā	sparks
火化	huǒ huà	cremate
火箭	huǒ jiàn	rocket

火: 两块石头磨擦就产生了象形文字 "火"。这是一种摄人的自然力量, 它给人们带来安逸的同时也带来了一定的灾难。燃烧的火光总是会照亮人们的生活。但火终究是易点而不易控制的, 正如俗语所说的: "纸包不住火。"

火 is a pictograph of fire, produced by rubbing stones together. A terrifying force of nature, it brings both calamity and comfort to man. Like burning issues that often flare up in life, fire is easy to kindle, but difficult to handle, as the proverb warns: "You can't use paper to wrap up fire."

丶	丷	少	火											
1	2	3	4											

炎 yán
blaze; flame

炎凉	yán liáng	cold-shoulder
炎热	yán rè	burning (or scorching) hot
炎夏	yán xià	hot summer
炎炎	yán yán	sweltering
炎症	yán zhèng	inflammation

炎："炎"字是由两个"火"字叠加而成的。因其天然具有易煽动性，所以像野火一样，蔓延得很快，使它周围的人遭受烘烤。

The character for flame (炎) itself was formed from two fires (火), one atop the other. Because of its inflammatory nature, it may well spread like wildfire and the people around it would suffer.

、	` ``	丷	火	火	火	炏	炎				
1	2	3	4	5	6	7	8				

灾 zāi
calamity

灾害	zāi hài	calamity; disaster
灾患	zāi huàn	calamity
灾荒	zāi huāng	famine
灾祸	zāi huò	disaster
灾情	zāi qíng	condition of a disaster
灾区	zāi qū	disaster area

灾：人类经常遭受水灾（巛）和火灾（火）的威胁，因而一度将这些不可预知的灾害称为天灾（灾）。现在的"灾"字实际就是把"火"字写在"宀"下，即把发生的灾害归咎于人。

Man, plagued by floods (巛, stream) and fire (火), once regarded these unforeseen calamities as divine judgement: (灾). The modern simplified character for calamity: 灾, however, sets matters straight by locating fire (火) under roof (宀) pinning the responsibility onto man himself.

、	八	宀	宀	宀	灾	灾					
1	2	3	4	5	6	7					

黑

hēi
black

黑暗	hēi àn	dark
黑白	hēi bái	black and white
黑板	hēi bǎn	blackboard
黑人	hēi rén	black people
黑色	hēi sè	black
黑市	hēi shì	black market
黑夜	hēi yè	dark night

黑：“黑”字最初的篆体是火焰（炎）冒出的烟把烟窗（囱）薰黑（黑）的景象。后来烟窗的形状化作“罒”，把炉火简化为“灬”，就成了我们今天表示黑色的“黑”字。

The original seal form depicted a flame (炎) under a smoke vent or window (囱), blackening it (黑) with soot. Squaring the window: 罒 and modifying the flame: 灬, produced the modern character: 黑, meaning black.

墨

mò
ink;
Chinese ink

墨迹	mò jì	ink mark
墨水	mò shuǐ	ink
墨砚	mò yàn	inkstone
墨鱼	mò yú	inkfish; cuttlefish
墨汁	mò zhī	prepared Chinese ink
墨水笔	mò shuǐ bǐ	fountain pen

墨：中国的“墨”最早是由烟灰（黑）胶质和“土”混合而成的。把这种混合物浇铸成固体墨，以备用水来研磨成墨汁。俗话说：“好记性不如烂笔头”。这充分表现了“墨”的重要性。另外中国有句俗语：“近墨者黑。”

Chinese ink: 墨 was first made by mixing smoke-soot (黑) with gum to produce and earthy (土) substance. The mixture was then moulded and hardened into a solid stick, ready to be ground with water to form live ink. Even though a little ink is better than a good memory, man apparently prefers to heed the proverb: "He who is near ink gets black," committing it to memory.

英 yīng
brave;
heroic

英镑	yīng bàng	pound sterling
英豪	yīng háo	hero
英俊	yīng jùn	handsome
英明	yīng míng	brilliant
英名	yīng míng	illustrious name
英雄	yīng xióng	hero
英勇	yīng yǒng	courageous

英: 一个置身于广阔的（冖）茂密丛林（艹）中的成年人（大）的形象，就是英雄形象。"英" 表示勇敢或英明。英雄总是受到人们的尊敬。勇气的来源归根结底是一句话："艺高人胆大。"

A mature man (大) in the midst of a large space (冖) , thick with vegetation (艹) , suggests a brave man in a jungle. Hence: 英 , meaning brave or heroic. Although there will always be a brave man to respond to a high reward, the ancient saying reveals the true source of courage: "Men of principle have courage."

一	十	艹	艿	艻	苁	英	英
1	2	3	4	5	6	7	8

竹 zhú
bamboo

竹竿	zhú gān	bamboo pole
竹林	zhú lín	bamboo grove
竹笋	zhú sǔn	bamboo shoot
竹子	zhú zi	bamboo
山竹	shān zhú	mangosteen
竹叶青	zhú yè qīng	bamboo-leaf-green liqueur

竹: "竹" 最初在象形文字中由两片竹叶组成 "竹"。与不成器的人不同，竹子总是长得高大挺拔而成为有用的栋梁之材。俗话说："不打不成器。" 图中所示的就是怎样 "从下面入手" 来使人成材的。

Originally written: 竹, the character for bamboo is a pictograph of two whorls of bamboo leaves. Unlike a wayward man, the bamboo grows straight and up-right into a useful and decorative plant. "The bamboo stick makes a good child," so says the proverb. Our picture demonstrates how starting right from the bottom.

丿	丿	仁	竹	竹	竹		
1	2	3	4	5	6		

笔

bǐ
pen;
pencil

笔记	bǐ jì	notes
笔迹	bǐ jì	writing
笔尖	bǐ jiān	pen nib
笔名	bǐ míng	pseudonym
笔墨	bǐ mò	pen and ink
笔误	bǐ wù	slip of the pen
笔战	bǐ zhàn	written polemics

笔：一只手（⺕）中握笔（丨），在书板（一）上划下一横（一），这样 构成的字就表示写字用的尖笔（聿）。加上竹字头（⺮）后就成了"筆"。后来把"筆"简化成"⺮"加上一个"毛"字。虽然繁体的"筆"与简体的"笔"不同，都可以用来写作笔。但俗话却说："一笔同时写不出二个字。"

A hand（⺕）holding a stylus（丨）, scratching lines（一）on a tablet（一）, symbolises a writting stylus: 聿. Bamboo（⺮）added to stylus（聿）produces "pen": 筆. Bamboo（⺮）combined with hair 毛 also makes "pen": 笔. Although both the regular 筆 and simplified 筆 can be used to write "pen", the saying goes: "A pen cannot write two words at the same time."

| ノ | ⺊ | ⺥ | ⺮ | ⺮ | 竺 | 竺 | 竺 | 笔 | 笔 |
| 1 | 2 | 3 | 4 | 5 | 6 | 7 | 8 | 9 | 10 |

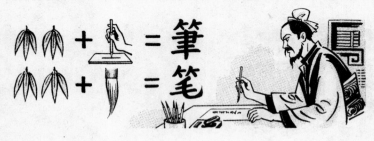

笑

xiào
laugh;
smile

笑话	xiào huà	joke
笑剧	xiào jù	farce
笑脸	xiào liǎn	smiling face
笑料	xiào liào	laughing-stock
笑骂	xiào mà	deride and taunt
笑容	xiào róng	smiling expression

笑："笑"字的由来十分有趣。声旁"夭"描绘的是一个低头（一）大笑的人（大），表示笑得浑身颤动。"⺮"象征仿佛发笑般地在风中摇摆的竹子。笑同时也是一种重要的商业手段，如俗语中所说的："和气生财。"

笑 has an amusing origin. The phonetic element: 夭 depicts a man（大）inclining his head（一）to laugh more easily, suggesting rocking or shaking. The radical component: ⺮ likens such laughter to the swaying of bamboo（⺮）in the breeze. But laughing or smiling is serious business, as implied in the proverb: "A man without a smiling face should not open a shop."

| ノ | ⺊ | ⺥ | ⺮ | ⺮ | 竺 | 竺 | 竺 | 竺 | 笑 |
| 1 | 2 | 3 | 4 | 5 | 6 | 7 | 8 | 9 | 10 |

禾

hé
grain

禾叉	hé chā	pitchfork
禾虫	hé chóng	harvest grub
禾苗	hé miáo	grain seedling
禾黍	hé shǔ	millet
禾穗	hé suì	a ear (of rice grain)

禾：代表谷物的"禾"指的是类似树木的植物（木），由于谷子成熟而垂下了头。谷物不仅可以提供物质食粮，还可以提供精神食粮。因为粮食越多，谷子的头就压得越低。它告诉人们，知道的越多，就应当越谦逊。

禾, the radical for "grain", is a tree（木）with the top bent over to represent the head of a ripened grain. The grain-stalk provides, not only food for the body, but also food for thought: the more grain it bears in the head, the more it bends in humility.

一	二	千	禾	禾								
1	2	3	4	5								

秋

qiū
autumn

秋季	qiū jì	autumn season
秋千	qiū qiān	swing
秋色	qiū sè	autumn scenery
秋收	qiū shōu	autumn harvest
秋水	qiū shuǐ	autumn waters
秋天	qiū tiān	autumn
秋种	qiū zhòng	autumn sowing

秋：秋收时节，在似"火"的骄阳之下谷物（禾）成熟了，这就是秋天的"秋"字。在中国，你可以看到人们打谷子，并把剩下没用的秸秆用"火"焚烧的情景。

During the autumn harvest, the grain（禾）ripens under the fiery heat（火）of the sun. Hence:秋, meaning "autumn". In China, one can see the waste stalks of grain（禾）disposed of by fire（火）after the harvesting and threshing in Autumn.

一	二	千	禾	禾	禾	秋	秋	秋				
1	2	3	4	5	6	7	8	9				

愁

chóu
sad; melancholy

愁苦	chóu kǔ	anxiety; distress
愁眉	chóu méi	knitted brows
愁闷	chóu mèn	feel gloomy
愁容	chóu róng	sorrowful countenance
愁绪	chóu xù	gloomy mood

愁: 当一年即将过去的时候，落叶便开始提醒人们"秋"天来了。于是人们的"心"情便会因怀旧而变得沉重，即"愁"。人们明白自然界不可能不经过春天而一下子从冬天跃到夏天，也不可能不经历秋天而一下子从夏天跃到冬天。"秋"对"心"灵的影响就是愁。

As the year declines, with each falling leaf signalling autumn（秋），man's heart（心）becomes weighed down with a nostalgic melancholy: 愁. He realises nature cannot jump from winter to summer without a spring or from summer to winter without a fall. Hence: 愁, the influence of autumn（秋）on the heart（心）.

′	二	千	禾	禾	禾	禾′	秋	秋	秋	愁	愁	愁
1	2	3	4	5	6	7	8	9	10	11	12	13

税

shuì
tax

税额	shuì é	amount of tax to be paid
税款	shuì kuǎn	tax payment; taxation
税率	shuì lǜ	tax rate
税收	shuì shōu	tax revenue
税制	shuì zhì	tax system

税: 人们把"禾"（谷物）字和兑（交换）字组合在一起构成了表示赋税的"税"字。显然，农民通过以谷物（禾）交纳赋税来换取（兑）他们可以享有的服务和权力。有句俗话说："富人从不为纳税而争执。"他们只是不闻不问地等待勒索。

To justify taxation, man coined税from 禾 (grain) and 兑 (exchange). Evidently farmers paid their taxes in grain（禾）in "exchange"（兑）for services and privileges. The proverb, however, has the last word: "Those who are prospering do not argue about taxes." They just close their eyes, shut their mouths and pay through the nose.

′	二	千	禾	禾	禾	禾′	秒′	秒	秒	秒	税
1	2	3	4	5	6	7	8	9	10	11	12

秃 tū
bald; bare

秃笔	tū bǐ	bald writing brush, (figuratively) poor writing ability
秃顶	tū dǐng	bald
秃山	tū shān	barren hill
秃头	tū tóu	bald-headed
秃子	tū zi	baldhead

秃: 这个象形文字把人的头顶"几"比作收获后的谷（禾）田。这就是表示光秃、赤裸的"秃"字。图中所示是一位年过半百的男子，他的头顶已秃了。

This ideograph likens the top or head of man (几) to a field of grain (禾) after the harvest. Hence: 秃 , meaning bare or bald. The picture shows a man in the autumn of his life - after his very last harvest.

一	二	千	禾	禾	禾	秃							
1	2	3	4	5	6	7							

甘 gān
sweet

甘草	gān cǎo	licorice root
甘苦	gān kǔ	weal and woe
甘露	gān lù	sweet dew
甘心	gān xīn	willingly; readily
甘愿	gān yuàn	readily
甘蔗	gān zhe	sugarcane

甘: 正如谚语所说："饿了吃糠甜如蜜。""甘"字所描绘的是一张嘴（口）咬着一口东西"一"的样子。甜的东西就是"甘"。"甘"字又被引申为指代任何令人感觉美好的东西，如图中所示的那样。

"Sweetness" is handled with taste in the proverb: "All food tastes sweet to those who are hungry." The radical for "sweet" pictures the mouth (口) with something (一) in it worth holding - something sweet: 甘 . 甘 can be extended to include anything pleasing to the senses, as illustrated here.

一	十	廿	廿	甘								
1	2	3	4	5								

牛 niú

ox; cow; bull

牛豆	niú dòu	cowpox
牛角	niú jiǎo	ox-horn
牛劲	niú jìn	great strength
牛奶	niú nǎi	milk
牛排	niú pái	beef steak
牛棚	niú péng	cowshed
牛肉	niú roù	beef

牛: 这是一个牛状的象形文字，有两只竖起来的牛角（Ψ）。作为人生终生的奴隶，牛被广泛用于劳作并提供肉食、牛奶、皮革、胶质、肥料等等。直至今日，"牛"字也没能摆脱失去一角的可怜地位。

The seal form of this character is a pictograph of the ox, characterised by two prominent horns: Ψ. Man's slave for life, the cow or ox has been exploited to the bone for labour, meat, milk, leather, glue, manure, etc. Even the modern form: 牛 does not spare the poor animal its horn.

丿	一	二	牛									
1	2	3	4									

牢 láo

cattle pen; prison

牢固	láo gù	firm; secure
牢记	láo jì	remember well
牢牢	láo láo	firmly; safely
牢骚	láo sāo	grumbling; complaint
牢狱	láo yù	prison; jail
坐牢	zuò láo	be in prison

牢: 此字的篆体描绘的是一个圈（Ω）里圈着一头劳作了一天的"牛"。今天的"牢"字，则是仁慈地给牛棚上加了一个屋顶（宀）。通过字意引申，"牢"还指关押那些社会上需要劳动改造的犯人的监狱。

The seal form: pictures a paddock (Ω) confining an ox (牛) after the day's hard labour. The modern form: 牢 mercifully puts a roof (宀) over the ox (牛). By extension, 牢 represents a prison for the incarceration of "beasts" of human society who are also in for "hard labour".

丶	丷	宀	宀	宓	宔	牢						
1	2	3	4	5	6	7						

半 bàn
half

半岛	bàn dǎo	peninsula
半价	bàn jià	half-price
半票	bàn piào	half-price ticket
半生	bàn shēng	half a lifetime
半数	bàn shù	half the number
半天	bàn tiān	half of the day
半途	bàn tú	half way

半: 这个字源于一个典故: 即屠夫在杀"牛"时要把牛切分(八)成平均的两半, 这样就形成了表示一半的"半"字。虽然一头牛很容易切为两半, 但如谚语所说的: "一头牛不可能有两张皮。"

This character originated from the butcher's practice of dividing(八) an ox(牛) into two halves, in all its length, before cutting up. 牛 was modified to 半 to facilitate exact division. Hence: 半, meaning "half". Even though it is easy to split one ox into two halves, the saying proves true: "you cannot get two skins from one ox."

、	丷	丷	半	半						
1	2	3	4	5						

伴 bàn
companion; associate; mate

伴侣	bàn lǚ	companion; partner
伴随	bàn suí	accompany; follow
伴娘	bàn niáng	bridesmaid; maid-of-honour

伴: "伴"这个表意文字是由"亻"和"半"组成的, 表示一个人只是一对伙伴的一半。为了获得完整的整体, 另一半是必不可少的。这就是"伴"这个字, 表示同志、助手或配偶。在寻找合适的另一半时, 人们应注意: "鹿与虎是永远走不到一起的。"

The ideograph: 伴 is made up of man(亻) and half(半), suggesting that the single man is but half of a pair. To attain "oneness" another half, a complement, is needed. Hence: 伴, meaning companion, associate or mate. In the choice of a better half, let man take heed: "Tiger and deer do not walk together."

丿	亻	亻	仁	仁	伴	伴				
1	2	3	4	5	6	7				

有 yǒu
have

有理	yǒu lǐ	reasonable
有力	yǒu lì	strong; powerful
有效	yǒu xiào	efficacious; valid
有利	yǒu lì	advantageous; favourable
有功	yǒu gōng	have rendered great service

有:"有"字最初描绘的是一只拿着一块肉（🝁）的手（⺕），表示占有或持有之意，即"🝁"。因为"肉"（🝁）字与"月"（🝁）字有类似之处，人们很快便以"月"字代替了"肉"字，并向别人起誓说他希望拥有月亮。今天，在"月"字上方加上代表"手"的"𠂇"，即表示拥有天下万物之意。

Early forms portrayed a hand (⺕) grasping a piece of meat (🝁), signifying to possess or to have: 🝁. Because of the resemblance between meat (🝁) and moon (🝁), man soon lost sight of meat and reached for the moon, promising it to anyone he wishes to possess. Today, with hand (𠂇) on moon (月), he classified 有 under "moon".

一	𠂇	才	冇	有	有								
1	2	3	4	5	6								

来 lái
come

来宾	lái bīn	guest
来到	lái dào	arrive; come
来电	lái diàn	incoming telegram
来访	lái fǎng	come to visit
来回	lái huí	make a round trip
来客	lái kè	guest
来临	lái lín	approach; come

来:"靠天种地"是一个俗语。所以人们就认为粮食的丰收是从天上"来"的。最早此字为象形字，指的是生长中的小麦或大麦。现在的"来"字由代表大米的"米"字和代表树木的"木"字组成，它同样受人欢迎。

"He who sows his grain in the field puts his trust in heaven," so observed the proverb. A bountiful yield of grain was therefore gratefully acknowledged as having "come" from above. Thus 来, originally a pictograph of growing wheat or barley, came to stand for "come". The simplified form grafts rice (米) on to tree (木) to produce 来 - a character no less welcome.

一	一	一	平	平	来	来							
1	2	3	4	5	6	7							

果

guǒ
fruit

果断	guǒ duàn	resolute; decisive
果酱	guǒ jiàng	jam
果皮	guǒ pí	skin of fruit
果品	guǒ pǐn	fruit
果肉	guǒ ròu	flesh of fruit
果实	guǒ shí	fruit; gain
果树	guǒ shù	fruit tree

果:"果"字最早描绘的是一棵结满果实的树（樂）。随着树的茁壮成长，它结出了更多的果实（樂），但这些均不如今天的"果"字好辨认。长熟的果子到哪里去了呢？也许"树高千尺，叶落归根"这句俗语会给我们一些启示。

The earliest form was a stylised tree sporting a showy display of fruit: 樂. As it grew mighty, it boasted of more fruit: 樂 but these are not easily discernible in the modern form: 果. The proverb provides a clue to the missing fruit: "Though a tree grows to a thousand feet, its fruits will fall to earth again."

`	冂	冃	曰	旦	甲	畢	果						
1	2	3	4	5	6	7	8						

课

kè
lesson

课本	kè běn	textbook
课程	kè chéng	course; curriculum
课外	kè wài	outside class
课文	kè wén	text
课余	kè yú	after school
功课	gōng kè	homework
上课	shàng kè	attend class

课:"課"表示"上课"的意思，是以"言"字和"果"字组合而成，上课是通过言语(言)的教导来取得成效，即取得成"果"。为了能接受有益的教诲，就要牢记"忠言逆耳利于行"这句话。

課, meaning "lesson", is based on words (言) and fruit (果). A lesson (課) involves the use of words of instruction (言) to produce results, i.e., bear fruit (果). But, for words to be fruitful, take a lesson from the proverb: bitter words are medicine; sweet words bring illness."

`	讠	讠	讶	讶	评	评	课	课			
1	2	3	4	5	6	7	8	9			

未 wèi

not; not yet

未必	wèi bì	not necessarily
未曾	wèi céng	have not; never
未定	wèi dìng	uncertain; undecided
未婚	wèi hūn	unmarried
未来	wèi lái	future
未完	wèi wán	unfinished

未: "未"这个字要区别于"末"(限制之意)字。它上面的横比"末"字短，这是因为"末"字中强调上面的一划，而在"未"字中，上面一划受到压制，而没有完全展开。不能写长。这就是表示"没有"之意的"未"字。同时此字也告诫有雄心壮志的人必须有耐性，并牢记"没有嫩苗，何来参天的大树"。

This character is to be distinguished from 末 (limit) in that the horizontal stroke across the top is much shorter: 末. In 末 the top line is emphasised; in 未 it is subdued, not fully grown. Hence 未: not yet. Those who have "not yet" attained their end should exercise patience and take heart from the proverb: "A giant tree grows from a tiny bud."

一	二	十	才	未					
1	2	3	4	5					

妹 mèi

younger sister

妹夫	mèi fu	younger sister's husband
妹妹	mèi mei	younger sister
表妹	biǎo mèi	younger female cousin

妹: 声旁"未"是一棵尚未长成但已枝繁叶茂的树，表示"没"的意思。加上"女"字旁，就成了表示妹妹的"妹"字。这就是表示还没（未）成年的女子，即"妹"字。

未, the phonetic, is a tree in full leaf and branch, but not fully mature and means: "not". With the addition of the radical for girl（女）, the character for "younger sister' is formed. Hence 妹: a girl（女）who has not yet（未）reached maturity.

く	女	女	女	女	奸	妷	妹		
1	2	3	4	5	6	7	8		

姐
jiě
elder
sister

姐夫	jiě fu	elder sister's husband
姐姐	jiě jie	elder sister
姐妹	jiě mèi	sisters
表姐	biǎo jiě	elder female cousin

姐: "女"字旁表示女孩或妇女, 声旁"且"是一把放在地上 (一) 的有两条档 (二) 的凳子 (冂), 这里用作表示而且的"且"字。在图中, 凳子并不是区别姐姐和妹妹的唯一事物。

女 is the radical for girl or woman. 且, the phonetic, is a picture of a stool (冂) with two rungs (二), standing on the ground (一), now borrowed for the conjunction: 且 "moreover". In our picture, the stool is not the only thing that distinguishes older sister from younger sister.

く	女	女	奴	如	如	姐	姐						
1	2	3	4	5	6	7	8						

爱
ài
love;
affection

爱国	ài guó	patriotic
爱好	ài hào	interest; hobby
爱护	ài hù	cherish; take good care of
爱怜	ài lián	show tender affection for
爱惜	ài xī	treasure; cherish

爱: 繁体的"愛"字, 是由"爫"(表示吸入)、"心"(表示心脏)和"夂"(表示温柔的动作) 组成的。意指爱情从心中产生并使人们采取亲昵的动作。经过简化后的"爱"字, 主要指代友爱。友 (手"𠂇"拉手"又"的合作) 是一种更现实的爱。不管爱的形式如何, 人们不可能总无私奉献自己的爱心, 因此记住谚语所说的: "要想被人爱, 必须要懂得去爱别人。"

The regular form: 愛 is made up of 爫 (breathe into), 心 (heart) and 夂 (gracious motion), implying that what gives breath to the heart and inspires gracious motion is love - an idealistic love. The simplified form: 爱 highlights the role of friendship: 友 (hand 𠂇 in hand 又 co-operation) - a more realistic love. But whatever form love may take, none can excel the selfless and unselfish love based on the principle extolled in the proverb: "Those who love others will themselves be loved."

一	丶	爫	爫	爫	爫	爫	爫	爱	爱				
1	2	3	4	5	6	7	8	9	10				

想

xiǎng
think;
hope

想到	xiǎng dào	think of; call to mind
想来	xiǎng lái	it may be assumed that
想念	xiǎng niàn	remember with longing; miss
想起	xiǎng qǐ	recall

想: 这个字由"相"（相互之意）和"心"（心脏之意）组成。声旁表示一只眼睛（目）躲在树（木）后观察可能发生的危险情况，象征检查或观察之意。它与表示心脏或心灵之意的"心"字合在一起就成了"想"字，表示在心里观察，即思考、考虑和希望的意思。

This character is composed of 相 (inspect) and 心 (heart). The phonetic: 相 represents an eye (目) behind a tree (木) on the lookout for possible danger, and signifies to examine or inspect. Combination with the radical: 心 (heart, mind) produces 想, meaning to examine or inspect in the heart or mind, i.e., to think, ponder or hope.

一	十	才	木	利	机	相	相	相	相	想	想	想						
1	2	3	4	5	6	7	8	9	10	11	12	13						

忆

yì
recall;
remember;
reflect

回忆	huí yì	recollect
记忆	jì yì	remember
记忆力	jì yì lì	memory

忆: 声旁"意"指"心"灵的声"音"，即意图或想法。在表示思想的"意"上再加上一个心（"忄"旁），则表示再度地想反省或回忆，即"憶"。为了便于记忆，简体字中把"心"（忄）和表示第二之意的"乙"合在一起成为"忆"字。

The phonetic: 意 denotes sound (音) in the heart or mind (心), i.e., intention or thought. The addition of another heart (the radical 忄) to thought (意) suggests to think again - to reflect or remember: 憶. As a mnemonic aid, the simplified form combines heart (忄) with second (乙) producing 忆.

丶	忄	忄	忆															
1	2	3	4															

忘

wàng

forget

忘本	wàng běn	forget one's origin
忘掉	wàng diào	forget
忘怀	wàng huái	forget
忘记	wàng jì	forget
忘情	wàng qíng	be unmoved
忘我	wàng wǒ	selfless
忘形	wàng xíng	be beside oneself

忘："忘"字的声旁"亡"指一个躲进（入）隐藏地（乚）的人，表示不见或毁灭之意，即"亡"。在底部加上"心"字则强化了表示"忘记"或停止思考的意思。这就是表示忘记的"忘"字。

The old form of the phonetic: 亡 represents someone entering (入) a place of concealment(乚), and means to disappear or perish: (亡). The addition of the heart radical: 心 enforces the idea of "lost mind" or a mind that ceases to act; hence, to forget: 忘. Minds should not be lost when it comes to the memorable proverb: "Forget favours given: remember favours received."

丶	亠	亡	亠	忘	忘	忘								
1	2	3	4	5	6	7								

聪

cōng

intelligent; clever

聪慧	cōng huì	bright; intelligent
聪明	cōng míng	intelligent
聪颖	cōng yǐng	bright; clever

聪：这个字通过加入"耳"表示听得很快，想得很快，这就是聪明或聪慧。简体字中灵活地把表示耳朵的"耳"字和表示总和的"总"字合起来，以此表示在聆听或理解事物时机敏的意思，即"聪"。

This character enlarges on 聰 (excitement, haste) by adding the ear radical(耳) to produce, suggesting quickness at hearing or grasping ideas, i.e., intelligent. The simplified form ingeniously combines 耳 (ear) with 總 (general, comprehensive) to convey the idea of cleverness at hearing and comprehending things generally: 聪.

一	丆	丌	丌	耳	耳	耳	耵	耵	聊	聊	聊	聪	聪	聪
1	2	3	4	5	6	7	8	9	10	11	12	13	14	15

慧 huì
wit; wisdom

慧心	huì xīn	wisdom
慧眼	huì yǎn	mental discernment
智慧	zhì huì	wisdom

慧：手中（ヨ）拿着两条长满叶子的树枝（艹）就组成了一把扫帚（彗）。将扫帚（彗）放在"心"上就表示智慧和聪明，这就是"慧"字。一颗打扫干净的心，准备去接受一个格言式的忠告："人们为什么不能像天天梳理头发那样每天清洗他的心灵呢？"

Two leafy branches (艹) held in the hand (ヨ) improvise a broom (彗). Broom (彗) placed over heart (心) clears the way for wit and wisdom. Hence 慧: a heart swept clean, ready to receive the proverbial counsel: "Man combs his hair every morning; why not his heart?"

一	=	三	丰	丰	丰	丰	拌	彗	彗	彗	彗	慧	慧	慧
1	2	3	4	5	6	7	8	9	10	11	12	13	14	15

恶 ě, è or wù
evil

恶毒	è dú	malicious
恶化	è huà	worsen
恶劣	è liè	harsh; abominable
恶习	è xí	bad habits
恶心	ě xīn	nauseating
恶意	è yì	ill-will
可恶	kě wù	hateful

恶：在表示丑的意思的声旁"亚"中，两竖被双写表示不完美的或畸形的意思，水平的两条线（二）表示第二或次等之意。象形文字"二"象征两个面对面的驼背者，指丑陋。"亚"字与"心"字合在一起就成为表示邪恶的"恶"字。请记住这个忠告："不要听，不要看，不要说邪恶的事，也不做邪恶的事。"

In the phonetic: 亚 (ugly), the vertical line is double to indicate imperfection and deformity. The two horizontal lines (二) signify second or inferior. Pictographically, 亚 suggests two hunchbacks facing each other, representing ugliness. 亚 (ugliness) collaborates with the heart (心) to breed evil: 恶, stirring up in the mind the proverbial exhortation: "See no evil; hear no evil; speak no evil; and do no evil."

一	丁	丌	亓	严	亚	亚	恶	恶	恶
1	2	3	4	5	6	7	8	9	10

恩

ēn
mercy;
kindness;
grace

恩爱	ēn ài	conjugal love; loving
恩德	ēn dé	kindness; grace
恩典	ēn diǎn	favour; grace
恩惠	ēn huì	favour; kindness
恩情	ēn qíng	loving-kindness
恩人	ēn rén	benefactor

恩: 为什么一个成年人（大）会被囚禁在一个小牢房（口）中？答案就是表示原因或理由的"因"字。这个被关的人会引起别人心中（心）的同情。如果由于同情心而使关在牢中的人获得解放的话，这就是恩典或怜悯。这也是把"因"字与"心"字合在一起作为 恩典的"恩"字的原因。

Why is a mature man (大) confined in a cell or enclosure (口)? The answer forms the character: 因, meaning cause or reason. The sight of such a confined man may excite pity in the heart (心), and if this feeling leads one to liberate him, that is grace or mercy - the result of tempering reason (因) with sentiment (心).

| 丨 | 冂 | 冂 | 因 | 因 | 因 | 因 | 恩 | 恩 | 恩 | | | | |
| 1 | 2 | 3 | 4 | 5 | 6 | 7 | 8 | 9 | 10 | | | | |

合

hé
unite;
join

合唱	hé chàng	chorus
合法	hé fǎ	legal; lawful
合格	hé gé	qualified; up to standard
合伙	hé huǒ	form a partnership
合计	hé jì	add up to; amount to; total

合: 这个字的上半部分是由三笔构成的一个等边三角形"△"组成，下半部分是表示嘴的"口"字。这就是"合"字。三张嘴（口）合（△）在一起，即联合或互相理解。三个人意见一致是很少见的。所以，俗话说："三人齐心，土能变金。"

The upper portion of this character is made up of three lines joined together to form a balanced triangle: △, indicating "together". The lower part is the character for "mouth": 口. Hence 合: three mouths (口) together (△), i.e., unity and understanding - a very rare occurrence, as the saying goes: "If three persons can agree entirely, then the earth can be changed to gold."

| 丿 | 人 | 亼 | 合 | 合 | 合 | | | | | | | |
| 1 | 2 | 3 | 4 | 5 | 6 | | | | | | | |

佥 qiān

unanimous;
all together

佥谋	qiān móu	plan decided by all
佥议	qiān yì	public opinion

佥：“僉”是由表示一起的“亼”和表示嘴的“口口”，和表示人的“从”这三部分组成。“亼”表示合在一起，描述吵闹的声音，“从”指一前一后两个人。因此，“僉”表示一致或一起的意思。巧合的是“僉”字的结构与人脸部的结构很相近，因此加上“月”旁的“僉 ”字就成了“臉”字。

僉 is a coming together (亼) of mouths (口口) and persons (从). 亼 signifies together; indicates the clamour of voices; and 从 represents persons, one following another. 僉 therefore means unanimous or all together. Coincidentally, 僉 bears a striking resemblance to the face in a crowd and, clarified by the flesh radical (月), stands for face: 臉.

丿	人	亼	今	佘	佥	佥
1	2	3	4	5	6	7

今 jīn

now;
present

今后	jīn hòu	from now on
今年	jīn nián	this year
今天	jīn tiān	today
今生	jīn shēng	this life
今昔	jīn xī	the present and the past

今：这个有关时间的字是由“亼”和“フ”（“及”的缩写）组成的。“亼”表现出了时间的连续性，将昨天、今天、明天三者相连。“及”（或“フ”）是一只抓住“人”的手（又），表示联系。这就是我们必须把握的今天的“今”字。

This character, dealing with time, is composed of 亼 and フ (contraction of 及). 亼 shows the continuity of the time and unity of its three elements: past, present and future. 及 (or フ) is a hand (又) holding a person (人), suggesting contact. Hence: 今, the time element we are always in contact with - the present.

丿	人	亼	今
1	2	3	4

念 niàn
read;
recite

念经	niàn jīng	recite or chant scriptures
念头	niàn tou	thought
念珠	niàn zhū	beads; rosary
观念	guān niàn	sense; idea; concept
怀念	huái niàn	cherish

念: 组成"念"字的成份是表示现在的"今"字和表示心脏的"心"字。"念"通过朗读、背诵、吟唱等手段进入人们的心中。它引申的意思包括想、学、回忆、甚至于希望恢复过去。

The components of 念 are 今 (present) and 心 (heart). 念 is to bring the mind the past by means of reading, reciting or chanting. Derived meanings include thinking, studying, remembering and even wishing to revive the past.

贪 tān
covet;
greedy

贪婪	tān lán	avaricious; greedy
贪图	tān tú	covet
贪污	tān wū	corruption
贪心	tān xīn	greedy
贪脏	tān zāng	take bribes; practise graft
贪便宜	tān pián yi	keep on gaining petty advantages

贪: 值钱("贝"一种货币）东西的存在（今）会引起人的贪求或贪婪感，这就是"贪"字。而这种贪欲既能使人得到金钱买不到的东西，也能使人失去用金钱换不来的东西。

The presence (今) of anything precious (贝, cowrie money) arouses the emotion of covetousness or greed. Hence: 贪, to covet. Such greed enables a person to gain the things money can buy and lose the things money cannot buy.

金 jīn
gold; metal

金融	jīn róng	finance
金色	jīn sè	golden
金鱼	jīn yú	goldfish
白金	bái jīn	platinum
黄金	huáng jīn	gold
金字塔	jīn zì tǎ	pyramid

金: 此字 最初写作 "金", 展现的是现在 (今) 埋在 "土" (土) 里的四块金子 (丷). 繁体字中把金块减为两个, 即 "金" 字。在简体字中, 则连这仅剩的两块金子也省略了, 写作 "钅"。但不管怎么减, 总还是像俗话所说的那样: "真金不怕火炼, 只怕贼偷。"

The original seal form: 金 showed the presence (今) of four gold nuggets (丷) hidden in the earth (土). The regular form reveals only two nuggets: 金. In the simplified radical form, even these two remaining nuggets are missing: 钅. However, the proverb reassures us: "True gold fears no fire." Only thieves!

ノ	人	仒	今	全	全	余	金						
1	2	3	4	5	6	7	8						

银 yín
silver

银杯	yín bēi	silver cup; trophy
银币	yín bì	silver coin
银行	yín háng	bank
银河	yín hé	the Milky Way (sky)
银婚	yín hūn	silver wedding
银幕	yín mù	(motion-picture) screen

银: "银" 字是由 "金" (表示金子) 字和 "艮" (表示艰难) 两部分组成。"艮" 原来是一只眼睛 (目) 突然转过来 (匕) 用挑衅的目光注视着别人的脸, 表示 "固执" 的意思。与金子相比银子比金子 (金) 坚硬 (艮), 比铜钱要值钱得多。俗话说: "即使一个人拥有上万两白银, 但他死时却连半个铜子也带不走。"

Silver is produced by consolidating 金 (gold) with 艮 (hard): 银. 艮, originally the eye (目) turned suddenly around (匕) to look a man full in the face defiantly, means "obstinate". Compared with gold, silver is a hard (艮) metal (金), more precious than common copper. Hence the saying: "Even he who has accumulated 10,000 taels of silver cannot take with him at death half a copper?"

ノ	𠂉	乍	乍	钅	钅	钅	钅	铟	银	银		
1	2	3	4	5	6	7	8	9	10	11		

钱 qián
money

钱币	qián bì	coin
钱包	qián bāo	wallet; purse
钱财	qián cái	wealth
捐钱	juān qián	donate money
零钱	líng qián	small change
赚钱	zhuàn qián	earn money

钱: 两把长矛"戋"把金子（金）切成一块一块的，就成了表示"金钱"的"钱"字。钱带有矛的弊端，表示权力。因此，当有钱人说话时，人们便安静地聆听并说："富人的话就是真理，穷人的话就是谎言。"

Two spears 戋 breaking gold（金）into pieces means "money": 钱. And money, taking on the vicious character of spears, means power. So, when money talks, man listens in silence and whispers: "If you are rich, you speak the truth; if you are poor, your words are but lies."

丿 广 乍 钅 钅 钅 钅 钱 钱 钱
1 2 3 4 5 6 7

针 zhēn
needle

针对	zhēn duì	directed at
针灸	zhēn jiǔ	acupuncture
针线	zhēn xiàn	needlework
针眼	zhēn yǎn	the eye of a needle
针织	zhēn zhī	knitting
打针	dǎ zhēn	an injection

针: 这个字最初写作"鍼"，是由"金"（一种金属）字和"咸"（表示咬）字合成的。简体的"针"字有一点好处，将声旁用"十"这个表示穿了线的针的字来替换，提醒我们不要贪多嚼不烂。正如谚语所言："没有两头尖的缝衣针。"

This character was originally written: 鍼, comprising 金 (metal) and 咸 (bite). The needle takes up, as it were, mouthfuls of cloth, biting its way along. The regular form 针 has a good point, with the substituted phonetic 十 resembling a threaded needle - warning us never to bite off more than we can chew, for "No needle is sharp at both ends."

丿 广 乍 钅 钅 钅 针
1 2 3 4 5 6 7

钉 dīng
nail

钉锤	dīng chuí	hammer
钉帽	dīng mào	the head of a nail
钉耙	dīng pá	(iron-toothed) rake
钉鞋	dīng xié	spiked shoes
钉子	dīng zi	nail

钉：这个字最初是一枚"丁"子状的象形文字。加了"金"字旁后，写作"钉"，后简化为"钉"。"丁"字自身表示一个强壮的成年男子或士兵。某种意义上来说，钉子就像士兵一样强壮、有用，但从不被人重视，就像俗语所说的："好铁不打钉，好男不当兵。"

Originally, this character was a pictograph of a nail: 丁. Clarified with the metal radical (金), it is now written 釘 and simplified to 钉. 丁 itself now stands for a strong male adult or soldier for, in a sense, nails are soldiers - strong, useful but never really valued. Hence the saying: "Use not good iron to make nails, nor good men soldiers."

ノ	′	╠	╞	全	钅	钉
1	2	3	4	5	6	7

户 hù
door

户口	hù kǒu	number of household; registered permanent residence
账户	zhàng hù	(bank) account
户外	hù wài	outdoor
户主	hù zhǔ	head of a family
住户	zhù hù	household;resident

户："户"字是一个单叶门状的象形文字，是构成很多与门和空间有关系的字的字根。它也表示房子或家。古代门上的合页是一条作为轴心的垂直的竖条。由于经常在开关中运动，所以被引为一句名言："户枢不蠹。"

户 is a pictograph of a one-leafed door, and constitues the radical part of numerous characters relating to doors and spaces. It is also symbolic of the house and family, the hinge of the ancient door was a vertical beam acting as a pivot; and because of its constant movement and workload, it was cited as an example in the saying: "The hinge of a door is never crowded with insects."

丶	㇇	亖	户		
1	2	3	4		

方 fāng
square

方便	fāng biàn	convenient
方法	fāng fǎ	method; way
方格	fāng gé	checks
方略	fāng luè	general plan
方向	fāng xiàng	direction
方形	fāng xíng	square
方言	fāng yán	dialect

方：这个字最初的象形文字指的是两条船绑在一起成为平底驳船的形状"囗"。这个字后被改作符号"卍"，指平面正方形中的四个区间，即地表。再后来被简化为"卐"，并最终定形为"方"。方的字意拓展为表示地区、方向，甚至于指公正或在道德方面非常拘谨。

The original version was a graphic representation of two boats lashed together to form a square barge: 囗 .This was replaced by the symbol: 卍, indicating the four regions of a square with two dimensions, i.e., the earthly surface. Modified to 卐 and finally 方, it widened its scope to mean also region, direction and even upright, or puritanical.

、	一	亠	方											
1	2	3	4											

房 fáng
room; house

房产	fáng chǎn	house property
房顶	fáng dǐng	roof
房基	fáng jī	foundations (of a building)
房间	fáng jiān	room
房客	fáng kè	tenant; lodger
房契	fáng qì	title deed

房："房"字是由"户"（表示门）字和"方"（表示四方）字组成的。它指有门（户）的方方正正（方）的东西，即房子或房间。在观察过房子或屋子后，可得出这样一句俗语式的结论："即使你拥有千间房，但晚上你躺下后也只占八尺。"

房 combines 户 (door) with 方 (square). It indicates something squarish (方) with a door (户), i.e., a house or a room. Viewing house and room squarely, one proverb draws the conclusion: "Even though your dwelling contains a thousand rooms, you can use but eight feet of space a night."

、	亠	亠	户	户	庐	房	房							
1	2	3	4	5	6	7	8							

斤 jīn
kati

斤两	jīn liǎng	weight
斤斤计较	jīn jīn jì jiào	be calculating
半斤八两	bàn jīn bā liǎng	not much to choose between the two

斤:"斤"字是一把斧头状的象形文字。最初表示斧头的意思，最后变成了一个重量单位，可能是由于古代的称量工具酷似斧首部分的缘故吧。但只有经过付出与努力才能熟练使用斧子并用斧子打制出物品。正如谚语所言："斧子敲凿子，凿子敲木头。"

斤 is a pictograph of an axe. Originally meaning "axe", it eventually became a standard measure of weight - a kati - probably because the ancient balance weight or counterpoise was shaped like an axe-head. Handling the axe with skill to produce results requires initiative and personal effort - the point of the saying: "The axe strikes the chisel; and the chisel strikes the wood."

丿	厂	斤	斤
1	2	3	4

所 suǒ
place

所得	suǒ dé	income; earnings
所谓	suǒ wèi	what is called; so-called
所以	suǒ yǐ	so; therefore; as a result
所有	suǒ yǒu	own; possess
所在	suǒ zài	place; location

所:"所"字是由"户"（门）字和"斤"（斧子）字并列而成的，指准备燃料的地方。在过去，人们总在门或房子（户）旁用斧子（斤）劈柴，所以就形成了"所"字（门外的斧头）。

所 is a juxtaposition of 户 (door) and 斤 (axe), and refers to the place where fuel is prepared. In olden times, the chopping of firewood with the axe (斤) was done near the door or house (户). Hence: 所 (axe beside house) meaning place or location.

丿	厂	ヶ	户	户	所	所	所
1	2	3	4	5	6	7	8

匠

jiàng
artisan;
craftsman

匠人	jiàng rén	artisan; craftsman
匠心	jiàng xīn	ingenuity; craftsmanship
木匠	mù jiàng	carpenter
石匠	shí jiàng	stonemason
铁匠	tiě jiàng	blacksmith

匠:"匠"字是由工匠的工具"斤"(斧头)和他的作品"匚"(一段雕空的木头,一个容器或一只箱子·)所构成。工匠技术的提高要依靠工具。这就是所说的:"工欲善其事,必先利其器。"

A n artisan: 匠 is represented by his tool: 斤 (an axe) and his work: 匚 (a hollowed-out log, essel or box). The craftsman's dependence upon his tools prompts the saying: "The workman who would do his work well should first sharpen his tools."

一	一	厂	尸	斤	匠						
1	2	3	4	5	6						

兵

bīng
soldier;
army

兵变	bīng biàn	mutiny
兵器	bīng qì	arms
兵役	bīng yì	military service
兵营	bīng yíng	barracks
步兵	bù bīng	infantry
工兵	gōng bīng	engineer (soldier)
士兵	shì bīng	soldier

兵:"兵"字是由一双挥舞战斧(斤)的手(𦥑或廾)的符号代表的。在乱世中人们对平日养兵的感慨 可归为一句话:"养兵千日,用兵一时。"

兵 is represented by two hands (𦥑 or 廾) brandishing a battle-axe (斤) - symbol of the soldier. Lamenting the necessity of maintaining an army in a belligerent world, one proverb concludes: "Feed soldiers for a thousand days, to be used for one day."

一	厂	厅	斤	丘	兵	兵					
1	2	3	4	5	6	7					

近 jìn
near

近海	jìn hǎi	coastal waters
近乎	jìn hū	close to
近况	jìn kuàng	recent development
近来	jìn lái	recently
近邻	jìn lín	neighbour
近亲	jìn qīn	close relatives

近："近"字的表意是一员武士手拿着战斧（斤）走向（辶）战场，即靠近战场。所以"近"指的是"靠近"。"远"的表意是把向前走（辶）和"袁"（走远路所必需的长袍）结合起来，而组成"遠"字。

This ideograph suggests the proper way for a warrior to advance(辶) to battle - with battle-axe 斤 in hand, i.e., near. Hence: 近, meaning "near". The ideograph for "far": 遠 combines 辶 (proceed or walk) with 袁 (a long robe, necessary for a long journey).

一	厂	斤	斤	斤	近							
1	2	3	4	5	6							

质 zhì
character; quality

质地	zhì dì	texture
质料	zhì liào	material
质问	zhì wèn	question
质疑	zhì yí	query
本质	běn zhì	innate character
品质	pǐn zhì	quality; character
人质	rén zhì	hostage

质：两把斧（斤）位于一颗贝币（指一种值钱的东西）之上，准备把它切开搞清它的价值，即"质"。"质"这对斧头保证能圆满地完成这项任务。这就是表示价值、质量、质地、品质的"质"字。

Two axes, (斤) poised above a cowrie shell (贝), representing something precious, are ready to dissect it and ascertain its worth: 質. The axes ensure a complete and thorough job. Hence: 質, denoting value, quality, nature or character.

一	厂	斤	斤	斤	质	质	质					
1	2	3	4	5	6	7	8					

新 xīn
new

新兵	xīn bīng	new recruit
新婚	xīn hūn	newly-married
新郎	xīn láng	bridegroom
新年	xīn nián	New Year
新娘	xīn niáng	bride
新奇	xīn qí	strange; new; novel
新闻	xīn wén	news

新:"亲"字代表的是可以制成棍棒的红褐色灌木。古代用此种棍棒来抽打犯人，以达到逼供的目的。由此"新"字是由代表红褐色棍棒的"亲"字与代表斧头的"斤"字组成的。

Rods, freshly chopped from the hazel bush (亲) for flexibility, were once used for flogging criminals, sometimes to extort a confession. Hence: 新, the symbol for "new", indicated by the hazel rods (亲) and the axe (斤).

1	2	3	4	5	6	7	8	9	10	11	12	13
丶	二	亠	立	立	立	辛	辛	亲	亲	新	新	新

门 mén
door; gate

门第	mén dì	family status
门户	mén hù	door
门槛	mén kǎn	threshold
门口	mén kǒu	doorway
门牌	mén pái	house number
门徒	mén tú	disciple
门诊	mén zhěn	outpatient service

门:类似"户"字表示一扇门，"門"字代表着一扇双页门。门是用来进出的，但不是所有门能随便进出。正如谚语所言："博爱之门，难开也难关。"经过演变，原先的"門"字最终被一扇敞开的"门"字所代替。

Just as 户 symbolises a one-leafed door, so 門 represents a door with two leaves. Doors provide exits and entrances, but not all are convenient, as exemplified in the proverb: "The door of charity is hard to open, and hard to shut." To simplify matters, the regular door: 門 has now been stripped down to an open doorway: 门.

1	2	3
丶	门	门

们

mén
plural sign

你们	nǐ men	you (second person plural)
人们	rén men	people; the public
他们	tā men	they; them
我们	wǒ men	we; us

们：此字的形旁为"人"字，声旁为"門"字，代表双页门。"人"和"門"合在一起就组成了"们"，指多数人们。

This character has 人 (person) as radical and 門 (door) as phonetic. 門 is a door with two leaves instead of one (as in 戸). Clarified by the radical for person (人), it is the plural sign for nouns and pronouns, applied to people: 們.

ノ 亻 亻 伫 们
1 2 3 4 5

问

wèn
ask;
enquire;
question

问答	wèn dá	questions and answers
问号	wèn hào	question mark
问候	wèn hòu	extend greetings to someone
问世	wèn shì	be published; come out
问讯	wèn xùn	inquire; ask

问：人们总爱站在门口提问。"口"字与"門"字相结合，即形成了"問"字。同时此字还具有审问或提问（虽然这可能是一种好管闲事的举动）的意思。正如谚语所言："问道于盲。"

Enquires are often made at the door, the entrance to a house. A mouth (口) at the door (門) therefore becomes a fitting ideograph for ask or enquire: 問. It can also mean question or interrogate, although to do so in an officious manner would be, according to the saying, "asking the blind man the way."

丶 冂 门 问 问 问
1 2 3 4 5 6

闻 wén

hear;
news

闻名	wén míng	famous
闻人	wén rén	celebrity
丑闻	chǒu wén	scandal
新闻	xīn wén	news
要闻	yào wén	important news

闻：此字为表意文字，当人们把耳朵贴在门上时，便产生出了"闻"字。此字引申为"新闻"之意。但靠耳朵所听到的消息并非全部值得信赖。正如谚语所言："耳闻不如目睹。"

In this ideograph, "ear" (耳) becomes "hear" (闻) when placed at the door (門). By extension 闻 also means "news", for the ear (耳) is the door (門) of knowledge or information. But not all news obtained by the ear is reliable, as the saying goes: "What the ear hears is not equal to what the eye sees."

`	丨	门	門	冂	闩	闲	闻	闻						
1	2	3	4	5	6	7	8	9						

开 kāi

open

开办	kāi bàn	set up; establish
开采	kāi cǎi	mine; extract
开除	kāi chú	expel
开动	kāi dòng	start
开端	kāi duān	beginning
开始	kāi shǐ	start
公开	gōng kāi	open

开：在"門"上加一根门闩（一）意为关"門"。两只手（廾）将门闩打开，意为"開"。但开业要比拔开门闩困难得多。正如谚语所说："创业容易，守业难。"

A bar or bolt (一) across the door (門) means to shut 門. Two hands (廾) taking away the bar (一) signifies to open: 開. But there is more to the business of opening than just unbolting the door. As the proverb says: "To open a shop is easy; the difficult thing is to keep it open."

一	二	开	开											
1	2	3	4											

富

fù
rich;
abundant

富丽	fù lì	grand; magnificent
富强	fù qiáng	prosperous and strong
富饶	fù ráo	bountiful; fertile
富庶	fù shù	rich and abundant
富翁	fù wēng	wealthy man
富裕	fù yù	wealthy

富：此字由代表屋顶的"宀"，代表高度的"高"字及代表田地的"田"字组成。它象征着一个人把从田里（田）收获的粮食高高地（"高"或"白"）堆在家里（宀），即"富"。但精神上的财富恐怕更为重要。正如谚语所说："财富多少看房屋，美德如何需看人。"

Man created this symbol for material prosperity: 富 from 宀 (roof), 高 (high) and 田 (field). Under shelter of the roof (宀), he piled up high (高 or 白) the products of his field (田) and amassed great wealth: 富. Spiritual wealth, however, is to be preferred, according to the saying: "Riches adorn the house; virtue adorns the person."

丶	冖	宀	宀	宀	宀	富	富	富	富	富	富
1	2	3	4	5	6	7	8	9	10	11	12

宝

bǎo
precious

宝贝	bǎo bèi	treasured object; baby
宝贵	bǎo guì	valuable; precious
宝剑	bǎo jiàn	a double-edged sword
宝库	bǎo kù	treasure-house
宝物	bǎo wù	treasure

宝：在古代，家中（宀）珍贵的物品恐怕要算玉（"玉"或"王"）、陶器（缶）及贝币（贝）了。由此得来"寶"字，意为珍贵。现代人只把玉看作是珍贵的物品，所以此字也就被简化为"宝"。但在商店中，"顾客才是最宝贵的而不是店中的物品。"

Among the ancients, the precious things under the roof (宀) were jade (玉 or 王), earthenware (缶) and money cowrie (貝). Hence: 寶, meaning precious. Under his roof, modern man treasures gem or jade (玉), so he simplified 寶 to 宝. But, in his shop, "customers are the precious things; goods are only grass."

丶	冖	宀	宀	宀	宀	宝	宝				
1	2	3	4	5	6	7	8				

害 hài

harm;
injure

害虫	hài chóng	harmful insect
害处	hài chù	harm
害怕	hài pà	afraid
害臊	hài sào	feel ashamed
害羞	hài xiū	bashful; shy
除害	chú hài	eliminate evil
利害	lì hai	terrible; strict

害："丰"代表一根木棍（丨）上的三条刻痕"彡"。"口"则代表由诽谤而导致的伤害，"宀"则代表在遮蔽物下所受到的伤害。由此，就产生出了"害"字。正如人们常说的那样："害人不成反害己。"

丰 represents a stick (丨) marred by notches (彡); mouth (口) suggests harm caused by slander; and roof (宀) indicates injury done under cover, i.e., secretly. From these components man created harm: 害 , fully realising that "he who harms others, harms himself"

丶	宀	宀	宀	宀	宀	宀	宀	害	害
1	2	3	4	5	6	7	8	9	10

定 dìng

fix;
decide;
certain

定单	dìng dān	order form
定购	dìng gòu	order
定婚	dìng hūn	be engaged
定价	dìng jià	fixed price
定居	dìng jū	settle down
定理	dìng lǐ	theorem
否定	fǒu dìng	deny; negative

定：此字由代表屋顶的"宀"和代表整齐有序的"正"或"疋"组成。它象征着屋檐下和平有序的生活。由此得来"定"字，意为稳定、决定。但正如谚语所说："谋事在人，成事在天。"但家中的安定比世界的安定更为重要。

This character is made up of roof (宀) and order (正 or 疋). It signifies peace and order under the roof, implanting the idea of fixed, certain or decided: 定 . Order under the roof comes before order under the heavens, although the proverb states in no uncertain terms: "It is for man to plan, but for Heaven to decide."

丶	宀	宀	宀	宀	宀	定	定
1	2	3	4	5	6	7	8

完

wán
finish;
complete

完备	wán bèi	complete
完毕	wán bì	finish; complete
完成	wán chéng	accomplish; complete
完稿	wán gǎo	complete the manuscript
完美	wán měi	perfect, flawless

完: 此字为表意文字，指代的是在头顶上（兀）加个屋顶（宀）。"兀"意为一个人（人或儿）的上半部分（"上"或"二"），即头部。在头顶上（兀）盖上屋顶（宀），一幢房子就造好了。所以"完"就是结束的意思。

This ideograph places roof （宀） over head （兀）. 兀 means that which is upon （上 or 二）a person （人 or 儿）, i.e., the head, origin or principle. So, putting on the roof（宀） over the head（兀）finishes （完） the building. Hence: 完, the end.

丶	宀	宀	宀	宀	宁	完						
1	2	3	4	5	6	7						

刀

dāo
knife

刀叉	dāo chā	knife and fork
刀架	dāo jià	tool carrier
刀具	dāo jù	cutting tool; tool
刀片	dāo piàn	razor blade
刀鞘	dāo qiào	sheath; scabbard
刀子	dāo zi	small knife; pocketknife

刀: 此字是象征刀或剑的象形字，意为挥舞刀剑来保护无辜者。但是不负责任地挥舞权力之剑，只会得到适得其反的作用。一把利刀常用来比喻一个权力极大的人。正如谚语告诫人们的那样："利刀易伤指。"

This radical is a pictograph of a knife or sword. Wielded in the cause of justice, the sword protects the innocent; but brandished irresponsibly, it is double-edged. A sharp blade is likened to a person vested with too much power, and a proverb warns: "A knife that's too sharp easily cuts the fingers."

刀	刀											
1	2											

分 fēn
divide;
separate

分别	fēn bié	differentiate
分布	fēn bù	be distributed
分界	fēn jiè	boundary
分开	fēn kāi	separate; part
分类	fēn lèi	classify
分裂	fēn liè	split; break up
分配	fēn pèi	distribute; allot

分: 此字为表意文字，由"八"字（意为区分、划分）和"刀"字（强调划分）组成，指用刀子（刀）进行划分（八）。"分"还可用来表示一部分、一些以及分钟或货币单位。

This ideograph is made up of 八 (divide), and clarified by radical 刀 (knife) to enforce the idea of dividing or separating:八. It is like dividing （八） with a knife （刀）. 分 is used also for any small division, component or part, e.g., a minute, a mark or a cent.

ノ	八	分	分												
1	2	3	4												

弓 gōng
bow;
bend;

弓箭	gōng jiàn	bow and arrow
弓弦	gōng xián	bowstring
弓形	gōng xíng	arch-shaped

弓: 此字源于中国的弓箭，即"弓"。最早被写作"㠯"，代表弯曲或颤动。如果在"弓"字上加个"丨"就变成了"引"字，意为牵引、指导或引进。虽然弓是用来进攻和防御的武器，但是，我们要牢记一句谚语："拉弓勿射。"

弓 is a radical representing a Chinese bow:弓. The ancient form shows it bent or vibrating : 㠯. Drawing the string （丨） of the bow （弓） produces the character 引, meaning to pull, guide or introduce. Though the bow is a lethal weapon for offence and defence, the proverb counsels: "Draw your bow, but don't shoot."

ㄱ	ㄱ	弓													
1	2	3													

弗

fú
not;
no

自愧弗如 zì kuì fú rú — feel ashamed of one's inferiority

弗：此字既是象形字又是表意文字，代表两根分开的棍子（)(）被一卷绳子捆起来，意为对立或否定。因此，"弗"字具有否定的意义。

This character is both pictographic and ideographic. It depicts two divergent rods ( )( ) so tied together with a coil of rope (弓) that their forces are neutralised suggesting opposition or negation; hence the meaning "not": 弗 .

㇇	㇆	弓	弗	弗								
1	2	3	4	5								

费

fèi
expenses;
squander

费力	fèi lì	strenuous
费时	fèi shí	time-consuming
费用	fèi yòng	expenses
会费	huì fèi	membership dues
浪费	làng fèi	waste; squander
免费	miǎn fèi	free of charge
学费	xué fèi	school fees

费："弗"代表了两根缚在一起的棍子向各自相反的方向弯曲，具有否定的意义。"贝"则代表了过去用来当作货币的子安贝壳。因此，把弗安置在贝字之上意味着低估了金钱的价值，实意为消耗或浪费。

The phonetic: 弗 , representing two rods bent in opposite directions being bound together, means "not". 贝 is a picture of a cowrie shell, once used as money. 弗 placed over 贝 therefore signifies under-valuing money, by inference, to waste or squander: 费 .

㇇	㇆	弓	弗	弗	弗	弗	费	费				
1	2	3	4	5	6	7	8	9				

86

剃 tì
shave

剃刀	tì dāo	razor
剃度	tì dù	tonsure
剃头	tì tóu	haircutting

剃：把"弟"字与代表刀子的"刂"相结合组成"剃"字，声旁指代的是缠绕在纺缍上的一段线，延深之意为延续中的子子孙孙。"弟"指的是不断生长的毛发就像是从纺缍上放出来的线一样。如果在它旁边再加上刀（刂），便为"剃"字，但下图中却把小弟弟（弟）和刀（刂）放在一起意为"仔细地剃"。

剃 combines 弟 (younger brother) with 刂 (knife or razor). 弟, the phonetic, depicts a thread round a spindle and means, by extension, a succession of brothers or younger brothers. The growing hair is suggested by the thread being unwound from the spindle (弟), and the addition of the razor (刂) gives us the character for shave: 剃. Our picture, however, shows how younger brother (弟) and razor (刂), put together, can mean a close shave.

丶	⺊	⼷	쓰	弓	弟	弟	弟	剃
1	2	3	4	5	6	7	8	9

矢 shǐ
arrow

矢量	shǐ liàng	vector
飞矢	fēi shǐ	flying arrow
风矢	fēng shǐ	wind vector

矢：矢的原形来源于"尖"字。就如一只箭，有尖尖的头和羽毛。后来"尖"演变成了"矢"字，以特别强调与暗中隐藏的敌人进行斗争的难度。正如谚语所说："明枪易挡，暗箭难防。"

The arrow radical, in its original form: 尖, bears a striking resemblance to an arrow with full tip and feathers. It was later modified to 尖 and finally stylised: 矢. Emphasising the difficulty of combating insidious enemies, the saying goes: "It is easy to dodge a spear in the open, but difficult to avoid an arrow shot from hiding."

丿	⺊	仁	午	矢
1	2	3	4	5

知 zhī

know

知道	zhī dào	know
知底	zhī dǐ	know the inside story
知己	zhī jǐ	bosom friend
知交	zhī jiāo	bosom friend
知觉	zhī jué	consciousness
知名	zhī míng	well-known
知识	zhī shi	knowledge

知：形旁“矢”代表敏捷，与“口”字相结合后，即为“知”字，意为在发言或阐述自己的观点时能够像快速飞出而又正中靶心的箭一样切合正题。“知”中的“口”表明“口”与“矢”一样锐利而深远。但谚语说：“知者不言，言者不知。”

The radical: 矢 (arrow) represents swiftness. Combined with 口 (mouth), it means knowledge（知）, possessed by one who can give his word or opinion with the precision and speed of an arrow（矢）. Knowledge（知）is having a mouth（口）that is as sharp and far-reaching as an arrow（矢）. Unfortunately, according to the proverb, "Those who know much talk little; those who know little talk much."

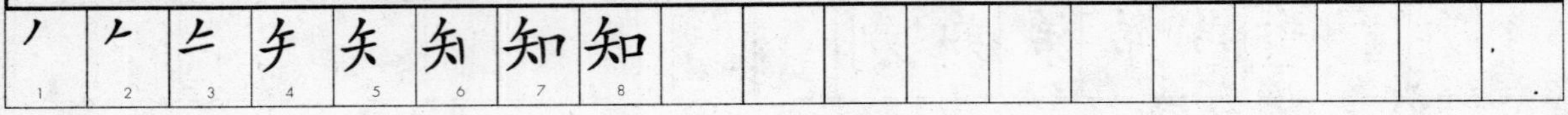

1 2 3 4 5 6 7 8

知

殹
酉

医 yī

cure; heal

医生	yī shēng	doctor
医术	yī shù	medical treatment
医药	yī yào	medicine
医院	yī yuàn	hospital
医治	yī zhì	cure; treat
军医	jūn yī	medical officer (in the army)

医：古人认为疾病是由于邪恶的影响而产生的。因此，“醫”字象征着从箭囊（医）中取箭并射杀（殳）引发疾病的恶魔。酒“酉”在治疗病痛时，是不可缺少的灵丹妙药。此字最终被简化为“医”。一句谚语说：“再聪明的医生也不会为自己疗病。”

Ancient man attribute sickness to evil influences. Healing: 醫, therefore, was symbolised by drawing arrows from the quiver（医）to shoot（殳）at the demon of disease. Wine（酉）was indispensable as an elixir. Although the modern form of healing is very much simplified: 医, the saying still goes: "A wise doctor never treats himself."

1 2 3 4 5 6 7

丑

chǒu
shameful; ugly

丑恶	chǒu è	ugly; repulsive
丑化	chǒu huà	smear; defame
丑角	chǒu jué	clown
丑陋	chǒu lòu	ugly
丑事	chǒu shì	scandal
丑态	chǒu tài	ugly performance

丑: 两种类型的魔鬼结合在一起形成了"酉", 表示丑陋的"醜"字。原先此字是把代表酒的"酉"字与来自阴间魔鬼的"鬼"字相结合, 表示隐藏着的酒鬼("酉")和魔鬼("鬼"), 实意为丑陋。现今, 它已简化成了"丑"字; 也指小丑。

Two types of spirits were integrated to form the character for shame and ugliness: spirit or liquor (酉) from a wine jar, and an evil spirit (鬼) from the invisible realm. The result is a hideous drunken (酉) devil (鬼) or 醜, representing ugliness, now hidden under the simplified form: 丑 of a clown.

丁	刀	丑	丑									
1	2	3	4									

狗

gǒu
dog

狗熊	gǒu xióng	black bear
海狗	hǎi gǒu	fur seal; ursine seal
狗腿子	gǒu tuǐ zi	hired thug; lackey; henchman

狗: 此字将形旁"犭"(或"犬")与声旁"句"相结合。"句"原意为一句话, 使人想起不停的狗叫声。"打狗还看主人面"这句谚语告诫人们对失败者进行处理时, 要三思而行。

This character for dog: 狗 fittingly combines the dog radical: 犭 (or 犬) with the phonetic: 句. 句, meaning a sentence of words, suggests barking - a distinguishing characteristic of the dog. Counselling against the thoughtless ill-treatment of the underdog, the proverb warns: "In beating a dog, first find out who the owner is."

丿	犭	犭	犭	犳	犳	狗	狗					
1	2	3	4	5	6	7	8					

猴

hóu
monkey

| 猴戏 | hóu xì | monkey show |
| 猴子 | hóu zi | monkey |

猴: 在古代, 射艺的高低对于官员的选拔起到了举足轻重的作用。单人旁（亻）代表了射手用箭（矢）射中目标（厂或コ), 由此得来了"コ"字, 指代的是贵族及太子。加上犬字旁（犭）成"猴"。把此字的意思延伸为"动物中的君主或王子", 即群猴之首。猴王是中国古典名著《西游记》中的重要角色之一。

In ancient times, skill in archery was the basis for selecting officials. In man（亻）, precision in shooting an arrow（矢）at a target（厂 or コ) represented uprightness of heart. Hence the derived meaning of nobleman or prince:侯. The addition of the animal radical:犭 extends the meaning to: "Prince among animals," a title applicable to the noble monkey:猴. Featured here is the King of Monkeys, legendary hero of the classic: "Journey to the West."

ノ	亻	犭	犭	犷	犷	犷	狨	狨	猴	猴	猴
1	2	3	4	5	6	7	8	9	10	11	12

吠

fèi
bark

| 狗吠 | gǒu fèi | bark of dogs |

吠: 此字由代表嘴字的"口"与代表狗字的"犬"相结合而成, 即"吠"。这个字表示狗为什么会叫。一则古代谚语作了极好地回答: "一犬吠影, 百犬吠声"。

Mouth（口）plus dog（犬）equals bark: 吠. This character, therefore, shows what makes a dog bark. The ancient proverb, however, explains what makes a hundred dogs bark: "One dog barks at something, and a hundred bark at the sound."

丶	口	口	口	吖	吠	吠
1	2	3	4	5	6	7

狱

yù
prison;
jail

狱吏	yù lì	prison officer; jailer
狱卒	yù zú	prison guard
地狱	dì yù	hell
监狱	jiān yù	prison
入狱	rù yù	be imprisoned
越狱	yuè yù	escape from prison

狱：把代表说的"言"放置在代表狗的"犭"和"犬"两个字根中间，就成了"狱"，即打官司之意。这表明两位诉讼者为了赢得官司，像狗一样互相争吵。"狱"同时也意为监狱，是关押失败者的地方。但对于获胜的人而言，"要想赢得官司，破财也是在所难免的。"

This ideograph places speech (言) between two different forms of dogs (犭and 犬). It represents a lawsuit: 狱, with the two suitors barking at each other like dogs. 狱 also means prison - for the loser. And, for the winner: "Win your lawsuit, and lose your money."

丿 了 犭 犭 犲 犾 犾 狱 狱

哭

kū
cry;
wail;
weep

| 哭泣 | kū qì | cry; weep |
| 哭诉 | kū sù | complain tearfully |

哭："哭"字运用了两个"口"，表示嘴部的强烈动作。两个"口"字与"犬"字相结合就是"哭"。两个嘴（口）形象地刻画出哭喊与哀嚎的情景。但正如谚语所言："再多的眼泪也不可能治愈所造成的伤害。"

This character uses two mouths(口) to express intense action of the mouth, resembling the wailing of dogs (犬); so dog (犬) with two mouths(口) means "wail": 哭. Two mouths may effectively express crying and howling, but certainly, "Two buckets of tears," according to the proverb, "will not heal a bruise."

丶 口 口 吅 吅 吅 哭 哭 哭

伏

fú
prostrate

伏安	fú ān	volt-ampere
伏兵	fú bīng	(troops in) ambush
伏法	fú fǎ	be executed
伏击	fú jī	ambush
伏贴	fú tiē	fit perfectly

伏: 把人（亻）与狗放在一起就成了"伏"字。它表明人像狗一样跪倒在另一个人面前，毫无尊严。"痛打落水狗"这句话，指的就是对恶人不要发慈悲之心。

This ideograph reduces man (亻) to the level of the lowly dog (犬). It means: "Man behaving like dog," prostrating himself or humiliating another: 伏. The saying proves true: "Flog the cur that's fallen into the water" - be merciless to bad people.

ノ	亻	亻	伊	伏	伏				
1	2	3	4	5	6				

突

tū
suddenly;
dash forward;
projecting

突变	tū biàn	sudden change
突破	tū pò	break through
突起	tū qǐ	break out; rise high
突然	tū rán	suddenly
突兀	tū wù	lofty (landscape); sudden
突袭	tū xí	surprise attack

突: "穴"是由代表分隔意义的（八）和代表屋顶的（宀）组成。"突"代表了从狗窝（穴）中冲出并攻击入侵者的狗（犬）。突字还可理解为不经警告就向对方袭击。正如谚语所说："无声狗，咬死人。"

穴 is a hole made by removing and dividing (八) rock or earth to provide a roof (宀) over the wild dog's head. 突 represents the dog (犬) rushing out of its den (穴) to attack and bite an intruder. Hence the meaning suddenly or unexpectedly - without warning, as the saying goes: "A biting dog does not show its teeth."

丶	八	宀	宀	穴	空	空	突	突	
1	2	3	4	5	6	7	8	9	

狂 kuáng
mad; wild

狂暴	kuáng bào	violent
狂吠	kuáng fèi	bark furiously
狂风	kuáng fēng	fierce wind
狂热	kuáng rè	fanaticism
狂人	kuáng rén	maniac
狂喜	kuáng xǐ	wild with joy
狂笑	kuáng xiào	laugh wildly

狂：代表声旁的"王"字是"崖"字的缩写，指代的是自由生长（坐）在泥土之中（土）的大量植物，意为自然界中的蔓生植物。"狂"还指代疯犬毫无目地的四处游荡，即"疯狂"。我们不要以疯狂来对付疯狂。我们应如谚语所劝诫人们的那样："篱笆修得牢，野狗不得进。"

王, the phonetic, is a contraction of 崖, meaning luxuriant vegetation that sprouts (坐) from the earth (土) and grows wild, indicating a rambling nature. 狂, therefore, is like a mad dog that strays or roams about aimlessly(王), suggesting the meaning: "mad or wild." Instead of advocating madness against madness, the proverb recommends prevention rather than cure: "If the fence is secure, no dog will enter."

ノ	犭	犭	犭	犭	狂	狂					
1	2	3	4	5	6	7					

犯 fàn
transgress; violate; offend

犯法	fàn fǎ	violate the law
犯规	fàn guī	break the rules
犯忌	fàn jì	violate a taboo
犯人	fàn rén	convict
犯疑	fàn yí	suspect; be suspicious
犯罪	fàn zuì	commit a crime

犯：声旁"仓"指代的是花的萌芽、开花、绽放。"狗"（犭）与"仓"相结合成了"犯"字，指代的是身处花圃中的狗，即越界犯规。由于误判许多犯罪者逃脱了法律的惩罚。此种事情屡见不鲜。正如谚语所抱怨的那样："黑狗吃肉，白狗受罚。"

The phonetic: 仓 means to blossom, sprout, expand or erupt. Dog (犭) with blossom (仓) - like dog in a flower garden - suggests heedlessness and transgression: 犯. Through miscarriage of justice, many an offender gets away with transgression; so laments the proverb: "The black dog eats the meat; the white dog is punished."

ノ	犭	犭	犯	犯							
1	2	3	4	5							

狠 hěn
fierce; vicious; cruel

狠毒	hěn dú	vicious
狠心	hěn xīn	heartless
凶狠	xiōng hěn	ferocious and ruthless

狠：声旁"艮"是古代"皀"字的缩写。"皀"字由代表眼睛的"目"与代表旋转的"匕"组成，表示转头并用一种挑衅的目光注视着对方。与"犭"旁结合后，指代的是像野兽一样具有凶猛、邪恶及残忍的特性。但有句谚语说："好狗不与鸡斗，好男不与女斗。"

艮, the phonetic, is the classical abbreviation of 皀, made up of 目 (eye) and 匕 (turn). It signifies to turn around and look a man defiantly in the face. With the addition of the dog radical(犭), indicating beastliness, it means: fierce, vicious, cruel or quarrelsome. But, concludes the proverb: "A good dog does not fight with chickens, nor a good man with his wife."

丿	犭	犭	犭	犭	犭	狠	狠	狠		
1	2	3	4	5	6	7	8	9		

狼 láng
wolf

狼狗	láng gǒu	wolfhound
狼獾	láng huān	glutton
狼藉	láng jí	scattered about in a mess
豺狼	chái láng	jackal

狼：此字由形旁"犭"与声旁"良"相结合而产生。"良"最早被写为"皀"，后演变成"皀"，指天赋从天（尸）而降。"皀"指代的是天地之间终成一体（艸），而天赋（目）最终消失（厶）了。狼意为狗的那种善良的本性已被邪恶所替代，正如谚语所说："身披羊皮，心如恶狼。"

The wolf: 狼 has dog (犭) for radical. The phonetic: 良 was originally 皀, modified to 皀 signifies a gift(目) - godly nature, coming down from above(尸). 皀, the modification, shows heaven and earth coming together (艸) with the gift (目) eventually becoming lost (厶). 狼 therefore suggests wolf - a dog that has lost its virtuous nature and acquired a vicious one. Hence the proverbial warning: "Outside he is clothed in a sheep's skin; inside he has a wolf's heart."

丿	犭	犭	犭	犭	犭	犭	狼	狼	狼	
1	2	3	4	5	6	7	8	9	10	

狮 shī
lion

狮子	shī zi	lion
狮子狗	shī zi gǒu	pug-dog
狮子舞	shī zi wǔ	lion dance
狮子座	shī zi zuò	leo (of the horoscope)

狮：此字的形旁是代表动物的"犭"。声旁"师"代表了飘扬在边关要塞（自）的第一（一）面旗（巾），即指挥官之旗，亦意为统帅或领导。而万兽之王"狮子"，就是由"犭"与代表众物之首的"师"组合而成的。

The radical is the character for dog or beast (犭). The phonetic: 师 signifies the first (一) banner (巾) over the fort (自), i.e., the banner of the commander-in-chief, and means: leader or master. Clarified by the dog radical (犭), the idea is set forth that the king or master (师) of beasts (犭) is the lion: 狮.

| ノ | 了 | 犭 | 犳 | 狗 | 狮 | 狮 | 狮 | 狮 | | | | | |
| 1 | 2 | 3 | 4 | 5 | 6 | 7 | 8 | 9 | | | | | |

猫 māo
cat

小猫	xiǎo māo	kitten
雄猫	xióng māo	tom cat
熊猫	xióng māo	panda

猫：形旁"犭"为象形文字，描绘了猫的一系列器官，即：猫头、猫须、猫爪和猫的脊背。原先的"猫"字被写为"貓"，是把代表猫的"犭"旁与代表植物萌芽部分的"苗"相结合，意为猫可以对破坏田间（田）植物幼苗（艹）的老鼠进行捕食。而猫与狗之间的不和也正像谚语所说的："狗来猫必去。"

The radical: 犭 is a pictograph depicting a feline, a cat with its head, whiskers, paws and backbone. The older form: 貓 juxtaposes cat (犭) and sprout (苗) to denote that cats eat mice - destroyers of grain sprouts (艹) in the field (田). The enmity between cats and dogs is emphasised in the proverb: "If the dog goes when the cat comes, there will be no fight." However, in the modern form: 猫, the cat (犭) goes when the dog (犭) comes."

| ノ | 了 | 犭 | 犭 | 犭 | 犮 | 猫 | 猫 | 猫 | 猫 | | | | |
| 1 | 2 | 3 | 4 | 5 | 6 | 7 | 8 | 9 | 10 | 11 | | | |

马 mǎ
horse

马鞍	mǎ ān	saddle
马鞭	mǎ biān	horsewhip
马车	mǎ chē	horse-drawn carriage
马虎	mǎ hu	careless; casual
马上	mǎ shàng	at once; immediately

马：一看到"馬"字，人们仿佛瞧见了一匹即将侧蹄扬奔的骏马形象。经过演变，马字去掉了代表眼睛与鬃毛的笔画，变为简化了的"马"字。谚语"老马识途"就是形容那些年岁已高，但经验丰富的马匹。

馬 is a picturesque representation of a brawny horse rearing. It has since undergone drastic changes, losing eyes and mane. The simplified form reduces it to three masterly strokes: 马 - a skeleton horse, advanced in age but rich in experience, inspiring the proverb: "The old horse knows the way."

フ	马	马								
1	2	3								

骡 luó
mule

骡夫	luó fū	a muleteer
骡马	luó mǎ	mules and horses
骡子	luó zi	mule

骡：声旁"累"指的是属于马类家族中的骡子。"累"最早被写成（㗊），表示三件物品（品）系在一起（糸），意为牵涉或聚积，引起麻烦的或不易管理的，身载重物或劳累的。以上这些释义充分表达了"累"子的含义。骡子以固执而闻名。骡子走路极慢，如同一句谚语所说："骑骡的人从不会觉得别人走路慢。"

The phonetic 累 gives a clue to the identity of this member of the horse（馬）family. 累 was originally（㗊）, three article（品）connected or tied（糸）together, and means involved or accumulated, troublesome or unmanageable, burdened and tired. These traits characterise the mule: 骡, a beast of burden, noted for being stubborn. Its sluggishness prompts the saying: "A person riding a mule does not realise the slowness of walking."

フ	马	马	马	马¹	马⁻	马⁻	马田	马罒	骡	骡	骡	骡	骡
1	2	3	4	5	6	7	8	9	10	11	12	13	14

骆 luò
camel

骆驼	luò tuó	camel
骆驼队	luò tuó duì	camel train; caravan
骆驼绒	luò tuó róng	camel hair cloth

骆:"马"是偏旁，指的是能够肩负重担的动物。它的声旁"各"意指不听别人劝告，毫无顾忌地独自赶路。两者结合即成"骆"字。骆驼具有突出的能自给自足的特点。骆，即一种能够在无食无水的情况下，仍具有很强的忍耐力，并可以长徒远涉的动物。

马, representing a horse or beast of burden, is the radical. 各, the phonetic, means to go one's way unconcernedly, without heeding others. This dominant characteristic of the self-sufficient camel: 骆, an animal blessed with great endurance and ability to go without food and water for weeks.

7	马	马	马	驭	驿	驿	骆	骆
1	2	3	4	5	6	7	8	9

尘 chén
dust; dirt

尘埃	chén āi	dust
尘暴	chén bào	dust storm
尘肺	chén fèi	pneumoconiosis
尘垢	chén gòu	dust and dirt
尘土	chén tǔ	dust
尘污	chén wū	soiled with dust
尘嚣	chén xiāo	hubbub; uproar

尘:此字的原形指代的是三只鹿（鹿）在土地上（土）奔跑过后留下的一阵尘土（麈）。经过演变，鹿的数量减至一只。最终，代表鹿的部分被减缩成"⺌"字。意为存在于尘土中的微粒。此字最终定型为"尘"。

The original form showed three deer（鹿）running over the earth（土）, stirring up a trail of dust（麈）. The regular form reduced the number of deer to one. The simplified form breaks it down further to tiny（⺌）particles of earth（土）, forming dust or dirt:（尘）.

丨	八	小	少	尘	尘
1	2	3	4	5	6

庆 qìng
celebrate;
congratulate

庆典	qìng diǎn	celebration
庆贺	qìng hè	celebrate
庆幸	qìng xìng	rejoice
庆祝	qìng zhù	celebrate

庆：在古代，节日期间拜访（夂）亲友并献以鹿皮（鹿）以表达衷心（心）的祝愿是一个传统的习俗。"慶"也就由此应运而生，意为庆祝、祝贺或祝福。经过演变，此字又被描述成发生在户内（广）的大事（大），即"庆"。

In ancient times it was traditional to go (夂) and offer, on a festive day, a deer's (鹿) skin with hearty (心) wishes. Hence: 慶, to celebrate, congratulate or bring a blessing. The simplified form for celebration puts it in a nutshell: something big (大) under cover or roof (广) - a big occasion indoors.

| 丶 | 亠 | 广 | 广 | 庄 | 庆 | | | | | | | | | | | |
| 1 | 2 | 3 | 4 | 5 | 6 | | | | | | | | | | | |

丽 lì
beautiful;
handsome;
elegant

| 丽人 | lì rén | a beauty |
| 美丽 | měi lì | beautiful |

丽：最初的丽字是通过一只头戴一对头饰（丽）的梅花鹿（鹿），即"麗"，来表达高贵典雅之意。经过演变，一对头饰被连在了一起，即"丽"。然而，美丽的东西并不总是值得羡慕。正如谚语所说："自古红颜多薄命，丑男之中多奇才。"

This character for beauty and elegance is a picture of the graceful deer(鹿) decorated with a pair of pendants (麗). The simplified form displays the pair of pendants linked together: 丽. Physical attractiveness is not to be envied, if we go by the saying: "Beautiful women generally suffer an evil fate; intelligent young men are seldom handsome."

| 一 | 厂 | 丆 | 兩 | 兩 | 丽 | 丽 | | | | | | | | | | |
| 1 | 2 | 3 | 4 | 5 | 6 | 7 | | | | | | | | | | |

虎 hǔ
tiger

虎伏	hǔ fú	gyro wheel
虎将	hǔ jiàng	brave general
虎劲	hǔ jìn	dauntless drive; dash
虎钳	hǔ qián	vice
虎穴	hǔ xué	tiger's den
老虎	lǎo hǔ	tiger

虎: 此字为象形字，由形旁"虎"（意为虎皮）与表示后腿的"几"相结合而成。由于老虎凶悍而残暴，所以即使一只死老虎也会让人胆颤心惊。所以就有了"骑虎难下"这一个谚语。

The character for tiger is a pictograph. It is based on the radical 虎 (tiger skin) clarified by 几 (hind legs): 虎. Characterised by its vicious ferocity, the tiger strikes fear even when dead. Hence the saying: "He who rides the tiger finds it difficult to dismount."

丨	上	上	广	卢	虎	虍	虎
1	2	3	4	5	6	7	8

号 háo or hào
shout;
mark;
number

号哭	háo kū	wail
号叫	háo jiào	howl; yell
号称	hào chēng	known as; claim to be
号令	hào lìng	order
号码	hào mǎ	number
号召	hào zhāo	call; appeal

号: 意指从口中（口）发出很响的声音（通过吹一物而发出"一"）。因此"號"字具有大叫之意。"号"字原先被写成"號"，意为人们见到老虎后，情不自禁发出的尖叫，"號"还可以被理解为是被人们大声说出或喊出的标记或号码。

号 comes from mouth (口) uttering an exclamation (the breath rising against an obstacle 一). 号 therefore means to cry out. The presence of the tiger (虎) gives the needed impetus to shout: 號. In the simplified form, the tiger is eliminated: 号. 號 also means mark or number, usually announced by the mouth, with a call or cry.

丨	口	口	므	号				
1	2	3	4	5				

象

xiàng
elephant

象鼻	xiàng bí	trunk (of an elephant)
象棋	xiàng qí	Chinese chess
象散	xiàng sàn	astigmatism
象限	xiàng xiàn	quadrant
象牙	xiàng yá	elephant's tusk; ivory
象样	xiàng yàng	presentable

象：此字为大象勾勒出一幅栩栩如生的肖像，特别是它的躯干及珍贵的象牙，即"象"。同时也指代某人在发财之后很可能就会惹祸上身，如谚语所说："猎杀大象，只求其牙。"

This character is a striking image of the elephant, emphasising its trunk and precious tusks: 象. Valuable possessions can pose a hazard to life; in the words of the proverb: "The elephant is killed because of its tusks."

ノ	⺈	⺈	乌	臼	乸	务	务	象	象	象
1	2	3	4	5	6	7	8	9	10	11

像

xiàng
portrait; image

像样	xiàng yàng	up to the mark; presentable; decent
像话	xiàng huà	reasonable; proper; right
人像	rén xiàng	portrait; image

像：此字的声旁为"象"，形旁则是代表人类的"亻"，意为肖像、画像及相似。虽然按谚语所言："画家从不崇拜上帝，因为他们对于上帝的本质可谓是了如指掌。"但人类对于世间万物的仿造复制活动却从未停止过。

In this character the phonetic 象 means elephant and also image. The radical 亻 (man) clarifies its application to man and means image, portrait or resemblance: 像. Man has been making images of everything imaginable under and above the sun. So, reasons the proverb: "No image-maker worships the gods; he knows what they are made of."

ノ	イ	亻	亻	亻	伶	伶	伊	傍	像	像	像	像
1	2	3	4	5	6	7	8	9	10	11	12	13

熊 xióng
bear

熊蜂	xióng fēng	bumble bee
熊猴	xióng hóu	Assamese macaque
熊猫	xióng māo	panda
狗熊	gǒu xióng	Asiatic black bear

熊：此字由代表熊头的"厶"、代表多毛躯干的"月"及代表熊掌的"ヒ"所组成，即"能"。熊是身强力壮及英勇无畏的象征。"能"是能力的意思 。同时，也为了把"能"与熊相区别，人们最终在"能"字下加上了代表熊掌的"灬"。这就是熊。

熊 is a representation of the bear, with its head（厶）, hairy body（月）and paws（ヒ）. The bear is a symbol of bravery, and is extremely strong and able. Hence: 能, meaning able. To differentiate bear from ability（能）four dots（灬）standing for feet are added: 熊.

厶	厶	广	台	育	育	育	能	能	能	能	能	能	熊
1	2	3	4	5	6	7	8	9	10	11	12	13	14

兔 tù
hare; rabbit

兔狲	tù sūn	steppe cat
兔脱	tù tuō	run away like a hare; escape; flee
兔子	tù zi	rabbit; hare
白兔	bái tù	white rabbit

兔：此字为象形字，意为竖起长耳蹲伏着的兔子。为了显示出兔子在逃生时的敏捷，人们还常用"狡兔三窟"及"兔子不吃窝边草"这两个谚语来形容它。

兔 is a pictograph of the squatting hare or rabbit, with its tall ears perked up. Noted for its shrewdness in the struggle for survival, the proverbial hare has three holes to its burrow - and it does not eat the grass around it.

ノ	⺈	⺈	召	召	免	兔	兔						
1	2	3	4	5	6	7	8						

冤 yuān
oppression;
injustice

冤仇	yuān chóu	enmity
冤家	yuān jiā	foe; enemy
冤屈	yuān qū	wrongful treatment
冤头	yuān tóu	enemy; foe
冤枉	yuān wang	treat unjustly

冤："一只身体弱小的兔子被囚禁在笼中（冖）即"冤"。它的引申意为不公正或错误的指控。在人类社会中，压迫的产生可以追溯到很久以前。但正如谚语所说："在压迫下所建的房子是不能得到持久的繁荣。"

An inoffensive hare (兔) confined under a cover (冖) suggests oppression: 冤. By extension, 冤 also means injustice and false accusation. Oppression has long established itself in human society but, the proverb asserts: "A house established by oppression cannot enjoy prosperity long."

丶 冖 冖 罓 罒 罒 宀 宀 冤 冤

逸 yì
escape;
leisure

逸乐	yì lè	comfort and pleasure
逸民	yì mín	hermit (in ancient times); recluse
逸闻	yì wén	anecdote
逃逸	táo yì	escape

逸：形旁"辶"指代的是奔跑后突然停下来的动作。与"兔"子结合成为"逸"，代表奔跑着的兔子。它还意为逃避或逃离现实中的世界。同时，野兔还被人们认为是难以驯服的一类动物。所以，"逸"也有闲散、挥霍、放荡之意。

The radical 辶 means to go fast and stop suddenly. Combined with 兔 (rabbit), it suggests a rabbit on the run, and means to flee, escape or retire from the world. The hare, being regarded as a profligate, 逸 also means to lead an idle and licentious life.

丿 勹 勹 兯 臽 争 兔 兔 兔 逸 逸

鼠

shǔ

rat;
mouse

鼠辈	shǔ bèi	scoundrels
鼠疫	shǔ yì	plague
老鼠	lǎo shǔ	mouse; rat

鼠: 作为象形字的"鼠"是对包括胆小的家鼠以及生性好攻击的野鼠等啮齿动物的总称。此字的每个部分都相应地代表了鼠头、鼠鬃及鼠尾。虽然老鼠能耐不小，即使是一只小老鼠也知道如何刨洞，但正如谚语所说："老鼠与猫争斗纯属自不量力。"

鼠 refers to rodents in general - from the timid mouse to the aggressive rat. It is a pictograph of the rat, showing its head, whiskers and tail: 鼠. A young rat may know how to gnaw its hole but, warns the proverb: "A rat that gnaws at a cat's tail invites destruction."

'	⺈	⺈	白	白	白	臼	臼	臼	鼠	鼠	鼠	鼠			
1	2	3	4	5	6	7	8	9	10	11	12	13			

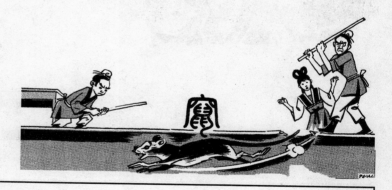

窜

cuàn

scurry; flee

窜犯	cuàn fàn	raid; make an inroad into
窜改	cuàn gǎi	tamper with; alter
窜扰	cuàn rǎo	harass
窜逃	cuàn táo	flee in disorder
鼠窜	shǔ cuàn	scurry like rats

窜: 穴是通过人们挖土掘石（八）而产生出来的洞口，老鼠居身于洞穴（穴）之中，即成了"竄"字，意为逃避或躲藏。经过演变，人们用"串"字代替了"鼠"字形成了"窜"字。作为表意文字的"串"，象征着两个物体连在一起。这就是窜字的由来。它是指通过掘（串）洞（穴）来逃生。

穴 is a hole obtained by removing or separating (八) rock or earth. A mouse (鼠) in its hole (穴) produces 竄, meaning to hide, flee or escape. The simplified form substitutes 串 for 鼠 to form 窜. 串 is an ideograph suggesting two objects (吕) strung together 串, and means to string, pierce or bore. Hence 窜, to escape by boring (串) a hole (穴).

'	⼍	⼍	宀	穴	穴	窜	窜	窜	窜	窜	窜				
1	2	3	4	5	6	7	8	9	10	11	12				

只 zhī
one; single

只身	zhī shēn	alone; by oneself
一只	yī zhī	used as a numerative or classifier

只：原先的"隻"字由代表小鸟的（隹）与代表人手的（又）相结合而成，"隻"常被用作量词来说明动物、舰船以及胳膊、眼睛、手、鞋子等领域中的数量。经过演变，最终定型为"只"。此字还具有"唯一"、"仅有"的意思。

A bird (隹) in hand (又) means "one" or "single": 隻 and is used as a numerative or classifier for birds, animals, ships and single individuals of things in pairs or sets, as arm, eye, hand, shoe, etc. It is now replaced by the simplified form: 只, which, incidentally, means "only."

丶	口	口	尸	只							
1	2	3	4	5							

集 jí
assemble; gather together

集合	jí hé	gather
集会	jí huì	assembly
集锦	jí jǐn	a collection of choice specimens
集市	jí shì	country fair; market
集体	jí tǐ	collective

集：原先的"集"字代表了三只鸟（雥）群集在树（木）顶之上。经过演化之后最终形成了"集"字，即停留在树（木）上的小鸟（隹）。"集合"一词的含义恐怕来源于群聚在一起的鸟类。但有一句谚语说："群蚊之声赛轰雷。"

The ancient character depicted three birds (雥) flocking together atop a tree (木). This was eventually contracted to 集: bird (隹) on tree (木). A gathering of birds may have created the character for "assembly" but, as the saying goes: "A gathering of mosquitoes can create a noise like thunder."

ノ	亻	亻	亽	亽	彳	隹	佳	隹	隼	隼	集
1	2	3	4	5	6	7	8	9	10	11	12

双 shuāng
a pair

双: 一只鸟（隹）在手中（又），为"隻"。两只鸟（雠）在手中（又）就成了（雙）字。 很遗憾的是，有这样一句谚语："福不成双，祸不单行。"

Just as one bird (隹) in hand (又) means single: 隻, so two birds (雠) in hand (又) stand for a pair: 雙. The simplified form shows just two hands: 双 - a clearer representation because hands, unlike birds, always come in pairs. Unfortunately, according to the saying, "Blessings never come in pairs, nor misfortunes singly."

双边	shuāng biān	bilateral
双层	shuāng céng	two layers
双重	shuāng chóng	double
双方	shuāng fāng	both sides
双亲	shuāng qīn	(both) parents
双生	shuāng shēng	twin
双喜	shuāng xǐ	double happiness

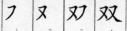

フ 又 刃 双
1 2 3 4

进 jìn
advance; enter

进: 此字由代表移动的"辶"（为"辵"字的缩写）与代表小鸟的"隹"字组合而成。因为鸟儿在飞翔的时候总是向前，从不退后，所以"進"字还具有前进之意。经过简化"廾"代替了"隹"字，最终定型为"进"。正如谚语所告诫人们的那样："不进则退。"

This character is made up of "move" (辶, contraction of 辵) and "bird"(隹). When birds "move" they always fly forward, never backward. So 進 means to "advance." In the simplified form, 廾 (order) replaces 隹 (bird), suggesting advancement and, by extension, entry: 进 - an orderly movement encouraged by the proverb: "He who does not advance loses ground."

进步	jìn bù	progress; advance
进度	jìn dù	rate of progress
进攻	jìn gōng	attack
进化	jìn huà	evolution
进食	jìn shí	have one's meal
进行	jìn xíng	be in progress
进展	jìn zhǎn	make progress

一 二 扌 井 井 讲 进
1 2 3 4 5 6 7

售

shòu
sell

售货	shòu huò	sell goods
售价	shòu jià	selling price
售卖	shòu mài	sell
出售	chū shòu	offer for sale
售票员	shòu piào yuán	ticket seller; conductor

售：此字最初是由代表两只鸟的"雠"字和代表说话的"口"字所组成。指代的是两个人在互相讨价还价。经过简化后，此字被定型为"售"。只有卖方一个人（隹）张口（口）推销他的商品。一则谚语告诫卖主："不可在森林中卖柴火，也不该在湖边卖鱼。"

The original ideograph for "sell" represented two birds (雠), the buyer and the seller, haggling with the mouth (口). The modern character shows only one bird (隹), the seller, marketing his wares with the mouth (口). The proverb explains the absence of the buyer: "Fuel is not sold in the forest, nor fish on the shore of the lake."

ノ	イ	イ´	亻宀	亻乍	亻作	亻隹	隹	隹	售	售				
1	2	3	4	5	6	7	8	9	10	11				

焦

jiāo
burnt; scorched

焦点	jiāo diǎn	focal point
焦化	jiāo huà	coking
焦黄	jiāo huáng	sallow; brown
焦急	jiāo jí	anxious
焦距	jiāo jù	focal distance; focal length
焦虑	jiāo lǜ	feel anxious

焦：此字由代表鸟字的"隹"与代表火焰的"灬"相组而成。意为燃烧或烧焦。它的延伸之意为担心或焦虑，喻意有些人总是像倍受火煎熬的鸟一样焦虑不安。正如谚语所说："杞国无事忧天倾。"

Bird (隹) over fire (灬) means "burnt or scorched": 焦, and by extension, "worried or anxious." Man has always felt like a bird over fire. In the words of the saying: "One does not live a hundred years, yet worries enough for a thousand."

ノ	イ	イ´	亻宀	亻乍	亻作	亻隹	隹	隹	焦	焦	焦			
1	2	3	4	5	6	7	8	9	10	11	12			

离

lí
part;
leave;
separate

离别	lí bié	part; bid farewell
离婚	lí hūn	divorce
离间	lí jiàn	sow discord
离境	lí jìng	leave a country or place
离奇	lí qí	odd; fantastic
距离	jù lí	distance

离: "離" 字最初用在夜莺 (一种高贵的金黄的鸟类) 身上。"禽" 意为神秘的, 而 "隹" 则指代的是鸟类。每当夜莺在春天出现时, 就预示着已到婚龄的女子就要离开她的父母远嫁他乡。因此, "禽" 又具有离开、离别之意。经过演变, "离" 字中代表小鸟部分的 "隹" 已被去掉, 最终成为了 "离" 字。

離 was formerly used for the oriole, an elegant golden bird - 禽 meaning uncanny and 隹 meaning bird. When the oriole made its rare appearance in spring, it was the signal for daughters of marriageable age to wed and leave their parental home; hence the idea of "to leave." 隹 has since separated from 禽, leaving the simplified form: 离.

、	一	亠	文	这	卤	卤	离	离	离							
1	2	3	4	5	6	7	8	9	10							

鸡

jī
chicken

鸡蛋	jī dàn	chicken's egg
鸡毛	jī máo	chicken's feather
鸡肉	jī ròu	meat of chicken
公鸡	gōng jī	cock; rooster
母鸡	mǔ jī	hen
鸡蛋糕	jī dàn gāo	sponge cake

鸡: 此字的形旁为 "鸟"。声旁为 "奚", 指代的是一位成年纺纱者 (大) 手持 (爪) 丝线 (纟或纟)。形旁与声旁构成 "鷄"。从前女犯人总是被强迫在无任何酬劳的情况下从事纺织工作, 就像笼中的母鸡一样总是要为主人无偿地下蛋。经过简化后的 "鸡" 字, 最终由 "鸟" 字与代表手的 "又" 结合而成。

The radical 鸟 stands for bird. The phonetic 奚 signifies an adult (大) with hand (爪 or) on silk thread (纟 or 纟) - a spinner. Previously women prisoners were condemned to spinning without getting any benefit, not unlike the chicken confined to the labour of laying eggs for its owner. A bird (鸟) in hand (又) produces the simplified chicken: 鸡, a really handy bird.

乛	又	又'	对	对	鸡	鸡										
1	2	3	4	5	6	7										

鸭 yā
duck

鸭蛋	yā dàn	duck's egg
鸭绒	yā róng	duck's down; eiderdown
公鸭	gōng yā	drake
母鸭	mǔ yā	duck
小鸭	xiǎo yā	duckling
鸭舌帽	yā shé mào	peaked cap

鸭：作为声旁的"甲"字意为盔甲，意指一种具有保护作用的外壳。对疾病有很强的抵抗及免疫能力的鸭子，恐怕可以算是鸟类中比较强壮的一类。因此"鸭"子指代的是一种能进行自我保护（甲）的鸟类。尽管如此，一则谚语却说："鸭子与鹅相比，鸭子就卖不出去了。"

甲 - meaning armour, protective covering or shell - is the distinguishing phonetic here. The duck is probably the hardiest of birds, with a natural immunity to disease and ability to withstand severe environmental conditions. Hence: 鸭, the well-protected （甲） bird （鸟）. Nevertheless, the proverb has the last word: "Compare a duck with a goose, and the duck will be unsaleable."

丨	冂	冋	日	甲	甲ˊ	甲丿	甲丿	鸭	鸭						
1	2	3	4	5	6	7	8	9	10						

鸽 gē
dove; pigeon

鸽子	gē zi	pigeon; dove
家鸽	jiā gē	domestic pigeon
野鸽	yě gē	wild pigeon
鸽子笼	gē zi lóng	pigeon cote

鸽："合"字意指许多（△）张嘴（口）和谐地相聚在一起。"△"代表一个整体及由三条线组合成的一个三角形。"鸽"字最终指代的是聚集成群的鸟儿们和谐地生活在一起。

合 indicates harmony of many △ mouths （口）, △ symbolising unity and agreement of three lines forming a balanced triangle. 鸽 ideographically refers to the dove or pigeon - the bird （鸟） that flocks together in peace, harmony and unity （合）.

丿	人	亽	仒	合	合	合ˊ	合丿	合丿	鸽	鸽					
1	2	3	4	5	6	7	8	9	10	11					

凤

fèng
phoenix
(male)

凤凰	fèng huáng	phoenix
凤梨	fèng lí	pineapple
凤尾鱼	fèng wěi yú	anchovy

凤："凤"字的雏形来源于代表凤凰尾部的"翄"，即"朋"。凤凰也是友谊的象征，因为它总是呼朋引伴地进行飞翔。经过演变，此字被写为"鳳"。它是鸟的象形字。在声音方面，它还结合了"风"字的特点。最终此字与代表友谊之手的"又"相结合，形成了代表友好的"凤"字。

Originally, the phoenix was represented by 翄 (朋), its tail. As it flew, it drew all birds to it in friendship. Eventually became a symbol of friendship, and a new character was adopted for the phoenix: 鳳 - a pictograph of the bird - relating it to wind (風) in sound and symbol. The simplified form substitutes a friendly hand (又) for the friendly phoenix: 凤.

丿	几	凤	凤											
1	2	3	4											

燕

yàn
swallow

燕麦	yàn mài	oats
燕鸥	yàn ōu	tern
燕隼	yàn sǔn	hobby
燕窝	yàn wō	edible bird's nest
燕鱼	yàn yú	Spanish mackerel
燕子	yàn zi	swallow
燕尾服	yàn wěi fú	tuxedo

燕：此字为对称象形字，代表一只飞翔中的燕子。燕子常常在初春时节出现在北半球的某些地区，所以也常常被人们看作是北方之鸟。"燕"子口（口）衔一根（一）嫩草（艹）正在飞过水面（灬）。

燕 is a symmetrical pictograph of the swallow flying upwards. Swallows abound in the northern hemisphere and are always a welcome sight in spring. The swallow (燕) is fondly remembered as a bird from the north (北), flying across the waters (灬) with a stalk (一) of grass (艹) in its mouth (口).

一	十	廿	廿	艹	苩	苦	苦	苗	莗	莗	燕	燕	燕	燕	燕
1	2	3	4	5	6	7	8	9	10	11	12	13	14	15	16

不 bù
not

不安	bù ān	uneasy; disturbed
不便	bù biàn	inconvenient
不断	bù duàn	continuous
不顾	bù gù	in spite of; regardless of
不客气	bù kè qi	impolite

不：此字象征着一只飞翔的小鸟逐渐消逝在人们的视野之中。代表地平线的"一"象征着阻碍鸟儿（个）飞到其终点的一道界限。"不"表示否定。对于那些还不会走却想飞翔的自负者来说，天空同样也是一道界限。

This character represents a bird flying up towards the sky and disappearing from sight, as if becoming non-existent. The horizontal stroke (一) signifies the sky as the limit, blocking the bird (个) from ever reaching its destination. Hence the idea of "net", a negative: 不 . Arrogant man, unable even to walk with his fellowman, now tries to fly; to him also, the sky is the limit.

一	丆	才	不								
1	2	3	4								

歪 wāi
crooked

歪风	wāi fēng	unhealthy trend
歪曲	wāi qū	distort; misrepresent
歪诗	wāi shī	inelegant verses; doggerel
歪斜	wāi xié	crooked

歪：此字由具有否定意义的"不"字与代表正直的"正"字组合而成的表意文字，含有弯曲之意。而"正"字又是由代表停止的"止"字与代表界限的"一"字相结合而成的，意为不要超越界限，以致迷途。正如谚语所劝诫人们的那样："身正不怕影子歪。"

歪 is an ideograph composed of two characters: 不 (not) and 正 (upright). It means: not straight, i.e., crooked. 正 itself indicates stopping(止) at a line or limit (一), without going astray, hence upright. Although imperfect, we do well to heed the proverbial counsel: "Stand upright, and don't worry if your shadow is crooked."

一	丆	才	不	歪	歪	歪	歪	歪			
1	2	3	4	5	6	7	8	9			

至 zhì
arrive; reach

至诚	zhì chéng	utmost sincerity
至多	zhì duō	at the most
至交	zhì jiāo	most intimate friend
至今	zhì jīn	up to now; so far
至上	zhì shàng	supreme; the highest

至:"至"字与"不"字具有对立的性质。"不"表示飞翔的鸟不能抵达它的终点。而原先的"⽳"为象形字,象征着鸟儿弯曲着翅膀,直朝地面飞去。演变后的"至"还有到达或接近之意。

The character 至 is the opposite of 不 which represents a bird flying straight upwards but unable to reach its destination. The original form (⽳) is a pictograph of a bird, bending its wings and darting downwards to the earth and reaching it. 至 is the modern form, meaning: arrive or reach.

一	工	云	云	卒	至							
1	2	3	4	5	6							

屋 wū
house

屋顶	wū dǐng	roof
屋脊	wū jǐ	ridge (of a roof)
屋架	wū jià	roof truss
屋檐	wū yán	eaves
屋宇	wū yǔ	house
屋子	wū zi	dwelling place

屋:代表此字声旁的"至"意为到达或接近,代表形旁的"尸"则表示一个倾斜的人物形象。"屋"就是某人到达终点(至)后,可以斜靠(尸)休息的地方。但有这样一句谚语:"先择邻,后安家。"

The phonetic 至 means to arrive or reach, and the radical 尸 is a reclining figure. 屋 is where you recline (尸) on arrival(至) - a place of rest, a house. And a house, once built, is permanently at rest; hence the saying: "Before you build a house, know your neighbourhood."

一	尸	尸	尸	屋	屋	屋	屋	屋				
1	2	3	4	5	6	7	8	9				

111

室 shì
room; chamber

室外	shì wài	outdoor
教室	jiào shì	classroom
卧室	wò shì	bedroom
会客室	huì kè shì	reception room
办公室	bàn gōng shì	office

室：表意文字"室"意为到达了（至）设在屋顶之下（宀）的终点站。因为屋子是用墙围起来的，而一堵墙是由两面组成的，所以有句谚语说："一家造墙，两家受益。"

The ideograph 室 suggests arrival（至）at a destination under a roof（宀），i.e., a room enclosed by walls. And because there are two sides to the wall, "One family builds a wall, two families enjoy it."

丶	八	宀	宀	宎	宎	宎	宎	室						
1	2	3	4	5	6	7	8	9						

龟 guī
tortoise

龟板	guī bǎn	tortoise plastron
龟背	guī bèi	curvature of the spinal column
龟甲	guī jiǎ	tortoise-shell
龟缩	guī suō	withdraw into passive defence
乌龟	wū guī	tortoise

龟：此字是长寿的象征，因为乌龟的年龄可以超过150岁。乌龟是无理性、冷血、而无害的动物。它还被形容是一种"肉里壳外"的动物。但是，"龟"字的演变过程很漫长，如同乌龟本身的演变一样。

The tortoise is a symbol of longevity, having a life span of over 150 years. Unreasoning and coldblooded but harmless, it is described as an animal with its "flesh inside and bones outside." The character for tortoise is a pictograph, with an evolutionary history as slow and steady as the creature itself.

丿	勹	夕	乌	刍	白	龟								
1	2	3	4	5	6	7								

万 wàn
myriad;
10,000

万般	wàn bān	all the different kinds
万端	wàn duān	multifarious
万分	wàn fēn	very much; extremely
万古	wàn gǔ	eternally; forever
万能	wàn néng	omnipotent

万：此字是根据蝎子而演变过来的象形字。它可用于对数字10,000的简称。经过演变后它变为印度梵文中的"卐"，最终定型成"万"字。"万岁"这个词则是皇帝的代名词。但有句谚语则说："皇帝虽富有，但想要靠钱达到长生不老是不可能的。"

A pictograph of the scorpion: 萬 was used for 10,000 or myriad by sound loan. When it came to simplification, the Indian swastika: 卐 (meaning also 10,000) was borrowed and stylised to 万. The term 万岁 (10,000 years) became the title of the emperor, despite the saying: "The emperor has money but he cannot buy myriads of years to live."

一	丁	万									
1	2	3									

易 yì
change;
easy

易经	Yì Jīng	The Book of Changes
轻易	qīng yì	easily
容易	róng yì	easy
易燃物	yì rán wù	combustibles; inflammables

易：此字的构成与能够随背景不断变色的晰蜴极其相似。晰蜴变色"易如反掌"。它的延伸之意为变化或容易。

易 bears the likeness of a chameleon, a lizard that changes its colour easily to blend with its background. This change of colour is "as easy as turning over one's palm". Hence the extended meaning: change or easy.

丨	冂	日	日	月	彐	易	易				
1	2	3	4	5	6	7	8				

龙

lóng

dragon

龙船	lóng chuán	dragon boat
龙卷	lóng juǎn	spout
龙虾	lóng xiā	lobster
龙眼	lóng yǎn	longan
龙钟	lóng zhōng	senile
龙卷风	lóng juǎn fēng	tornado

龙：此字最早为象形字"龖"。象征具有贵族血统的"龙"由代表翅膀的"乞"与代表身躯的"月"和"童"字声旁的"立"相组合而成。"龙"字同时也具有皇室和荣耀之意。正如谚语所说："有钱即是龙，无钱便是虫。"

The primitive form was a pictograph of the dragon: 龖. The regular form: 龙, although resembling the royal creature, is made up of 乞 (contraction of 飞, wings), 月 (body), and 立 (contraction of the phonetic 童, slave boy). 龙 also means imperial or glorious; hence the saying: "With money you are a dragon, without it you are a worm."

一	ナ	九	龙	龙									
1	2	3	4	5									

角

jiǎo

horn; corner; 10-cent piece

角尺	jiǎo chǐ	angle square
角度	jiǎo dù	angle
角落	jiǎo luò	corner; nook
角膜	jiǎo mó	cornea
角质	jiǎo zhì	cutin
号角	hào jiǎo	bugle
鹿角	lù jiǎo	antler

角："角"由表示强壮的"力"和表示肉体的"月"组成。形旁"月"似一个带有条纹的号角。由于号角末尾的部分比较细，所以"角"字还具有边角之意。同时"角"还是一种计算货币的单位。一角等于10分。

The radical 角 resembles a horn with its streaks. It is probably a combination of 力 (strong) and 月 (flesh). Because the horn terminates in an angle and tapers to a point, 角 can mean angle or corner. 角 is also a 10-cent piece, a mere tenth or "corner" of a dollar.

⺈	⺈	⺈	舟	角	角	角						
1	2	3	4	5	6	7						

解 jiě

divide;
untie;
explain

解除	jiě chú	remove
解答	jiě dá	answer; explain
解雇	jiě gù	discharge; dismiss
解决	jiě jué	solve; dispose of
解开	jiě kāi	untie
解闷	jiě mèn	divert oneself from boredom
解剖	jiě pōu	dissect

解：此字将形旁"角"字与"刀"和"牛"字相结合，意为用刀劈开牛角，即"解"。同时，牛角经过磨制变细后，还可作解结之用。因此，此字又含有拆开、解开之意。《说文解字》这本书专门解释中文字的来源。

This character combines the radical for horn（角）with knife（刀）and ox（牛）. To cleave the horn of an ox requires the use of a knife; hence 解: to divide. The horn of an ox is also shaped into bodkins（刀）for untying knots. So 解 also means to untie, undo, unravel and, by extension, explain. The ancient lexicon 说文解字 explains the origin of Chinese characters.

丿 ク 广 月 角 角 角 角 觪 觪 觪 解 解

毛 máo

hair; fur;
10-cent
piece

毛笔	máo bǐ	writing brush
毛纺	máo fǎng	wool spinning
毛巾	máo jīn	towel
毛孔	máo kǒng	pore
毛毯	máo tǎn	wollen blanket
毛线	máo xiàn	knitting wool
毛衣	máo yī	wollen sweater

毛：此字是用来形容人类或动物毛发的象形文字。与身体其它部分相比，头发恐怕算是无足轻重了。"毛"字还具有微小、粗糙之意。同时，它还可作为货币的计量单位。一毛等于10分。虽然，我们的头发不能以数量来计算，但正如谚语所说："动及分毫，触及全身。"

毛 is a pictograph of the hair of man or beast. Compared with other parts of the body, the hair is insignificant and valueless. 毛 also means little, unpolished, or the common 10- cent piece. Our hairs may not be numbered but, says the proverb: "Pull a hair and the whole body may be affected."

丿 二 三 毛

尾

wěi
tail; end

尾巴	wěi ba	tail
尾灯	wěi dēng	tail light; tail lamp
尾欠	wěi qiàn	balance due
尾声	wěi shēng	epilogue; end
尾随	wěi suí	tag along; follow at somebody's heel
尾追	wěi zhuī	in hot pursuit

尾: "尾"字由代表身体倾斜状态的"尸"作为形旁, 与代表头发的"毛"字作为声旁而组成。在篆刻文字中, "毛"字被颠倒过来, 表明毛发向下长就是尾巴。尾巴常用来摇动。但当某人很强大, 而统治者虚弱时, 那就"尾大不掉"了。

尾 has 尸 (a recumbent body) as radical and 毛 (hair) as phonetic. In the seal form 毛 is inverted, indicating hair growing downwards from the body (尸), suggesting a tail. The tail is meant to be wagged by the body but when the people are strong and the ruler weak, "The tail is too large to wag" (尾大不掉).

ㄱ	ㄱ	尸	尸	尼	屋	尾					
1	2	3	4	5	6	7					

老

lǎo
old;
aged

老板	lǎo bǎn	boss; employer
老成	lǎo chéng	experienced; steady
老将	lǎo jiàng	veteran; old-timer
老练	lǎo liàn	seasoned; experienced
老年	lǎo nián	old age
老实	lǎo shi	honest; frank

老: 在篆刻体中, 此字由代表毛发的"屮"与代表人字的"儿"和与代表变换不定的"匕"字组合而成。当人上了年纪后, 原先的黑发就会逐渐由黑变灰或变白。"老"字是从原形为"耂"而演化为"老"。为了鼓励年轻人尊重老人, 有一句谚语强调说: "年轻时耻笑老人, 年老后就被别人耻笑。"

The seal character for "old" grew out of 毛 (hair), 儿 (person) and 匕 (change). When the hair of man turns gray or white, its colour has changed, indicating old age: 耂, now arbitrarily shrunk to 老. To encourage respect for white hair, the old saying warns: "Laugh at the old, and age will laugh at you."

一	十	土	耂	耂	老						
1	2	3	4	5	6						

116

票 piào
bill; ticket; ballot

票额	piào é	the sum stated on a cheque or bill; denomination
票房	piào fáng	booking office
票根	piào gēn	counterfoil; stub
票价	piào jià	the price of a ticket

票：在篆刻文字中，此字被写作"燓"，表明用四只手（𦥑）点燃火（火），使之冒烟（彡）来发出信号。此字还有一种篆体形式，即"燓"，代表的是顽皮的鬼火精灵。经过演变，最终定型为"票"字。它由"西"字与"示"字组合而成。

The early seal form: 燓 represents an ancient method of signalling fire (火) with rising smoke (彡) manipulated by four hands (𦥑). This suggests ticket or ballot form of sign. Another seal form: 燓 depicts the mischievous fairy of the phantom-fire, a dreaded natural phenomenon. It stands for bill or warrant - things also dreaded. The modern arbitrary form: 票 may be remembered as a bank bill, a western (西) token (示).

一	一	一	一	一	一	一	一	一	票	票
1	2	3	4	5	6	7	8	9	10	11

爬 pá
crawl; creep; climb

爬虫	pá chóng	reptile; insect
爬竿	pá gān	climbing pole; pole-climbing
爬犁	pá lí	sledge
爬山	pá shān	mountain-climbing
爬行	pá xíng	crawl; creep

爬：此字是由"爪"和"巴"组合而成的象形字。"爪"指代的是右手掌向下，用手指支撑而休息。"巴"指的是翅起尾巴的蛇。因此，"爬"还具有爬行之意。但爬行也不是一帆风顺的，正如谚语所说："发扬美德就像爬山一样艰难，而邪恶的产生犹如顺水推舟一样简单。"

爬 combines two pictographs: 爪 and 巴. 爪 (claw) is the right hand, palm down, resting on the finger-tips; 巴 (boa) is a snake raised on its tail. Hence 爬: to crawl, creep or climb, like a snake. Climbing is not plain sailing according to the saying: "Following virtue is like climbing a hill; following vice is like sailing downstream."

	厂	爪	爪	爪	爪	爪	爬			
1	2	3	4	5	6	7	8			

为

wèi or wéi

because;
to be;
to do

为何	wèi hé	why
为难	wéi nán	feel awkward; make things difficult
为期	wéi qī	by a definite date; duration
为人	wéi rén	behave; conduct oneself

为: 此字的象形字"禹"原来指代的是一只具有人类躯体(夒)特点的母猴。后来夒简化成了代表爪子的"爭"字，是因为母猴爱使用爪子。所以，此字在演变过程中就形成了另一种形式"㯢"，代表用手梳理丝织物，以去除其中的无用部分。但最终此字还是被定型为"为"。

A pictograph based on reason, 禹 originally was a female monkey with a human body: 夒 because of the resemblance. It was changed to a form of two claws: 爭 because the female monkey was most prone to claw. To include the meaning "to do, to be" it took on a more human form: 㯢, a hand carding textile fibres to remove unessentials, leading to the simplified form: 为.

`	丿	为	为									
1	2	3	4									

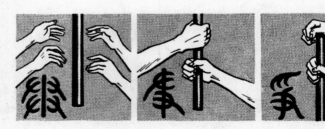

争

zhēng

contend;
fight;
quarrel

争辩	zhēng biàn	argue
争吵	zhēng chǎo	quarrel
争持	zhēng chí	refuse to give in
争斗	zhēng dòu	fight; struggle; strife
争夺	zhēng duó	fight
争论	zhēng lùn	controversy;

争: 此字为表意文字，意为两只手在拖拉某一物体。原先的字形也勾勒出了双手在争夺中的形态。虽然最终还是左手胜了右手，但这其中并无任何优势可言。也正如谚语所说："陶器不能碰瓷器，鸡蛋不能碰石头。"

This ideograph features two hands tugging at an object. The older forms graphically portray the quarrel or fight between two pairs of hands. Though the left hand conquers the right, no advantage is gained. Hence: "Pottery and fine porcelain must not fight" and "Eggs must not quarrel with stones."

丿	勹	刍	刍	刍	争							
1	2	3	4	5	6							

受

shòu
receive;
accept

受苦	shòu kǔ	suffer
受难	shòu nàn	suffer calamities
受罚	shòu fá	be punished
受害	shòu hài	victimised
受气	shòu qì	be bullied
受伤	shòu shāng	be wounded
受益	shòu yì	benefit from

受：此字指代的是货物的装载。一只手（⺥）在岸上递货，另一只手（又）在船上（舟）接货。在篆体文字中，船被写作"⺼"，最终被缩写为"⺆"和"冖"。作为表意文字"受"字还具有收到、接受和忍受之意。

This character represents the loading of goods. A hand (⺥), on the bank, delivers the goods while another hand (又), in the boat, (舟) receives and stows them away in the hold. In the seal forms the boat can be seen in symbol: ⺼, eventually contracted to ⺆ and 冖. The ideograph 受, by extension, means "receive, accept, endure."

一	⺈	⺈	⼞	⼞	严	受	受				
1	2	3	4	5	6	7	8				

骨

gǔ
bone

骨骼	gǔ gé	skeleton
骨灰	gǔ huī	ashes of the dead
骨架	gǔ jià	framework
骨节	gǔ jié	joint
骨牌	gǔ pái	dominoes
骨气	gǔ qì	moral integrity
骨肉	gǔ ròu	flesh and blood

骨：人类身体的基本框架是由骨头与肉合成的。正因为如此，"骨"字由代表骨头的"冎"字与肉字组合而成，并不是"骨头上都长肉的。正如谚语所说："皮包骨头怎能胖？"

The bones form the framework of the body and they are closely associated with the flesh. The character for bone: 骨 therefore combines pictographs of the bone (冎) and flesh (肉). However, courtesy demands that you ask for a bone if you want flesh, despite the saying: "You can't get fat from a dry bone."

丶	冂	冎	冎	冎	严	骨	骨	骨			
1	2	3	4	5	6	7	8	9			

皮

pí
skin; leather

皮袄	pí ǎo	fur-lined jacket
皮包	pí bāo	leather handbag
皮带	pí dài	leather belt
皮蛋	pí dàn	preserved egg
皮肤	pí fū	skin
皮箱	pí xiāng	leather suitcase
皮鞋	pí xié	leather shoes

皮：此字由代表手部动作的"又"，代表动物皮毛的"丿"及代表小刀的"刀"字组合而成。好名声就像一张上好的毛皮一样可以流芳百世。正如谚语所说："人死留名，虎死留皮。"

Three components make up the character for skin: 又, the hand that flays; 丿, the animal skin; and 刀, the knife. The animal skin, being durable, may be compared to the reputation of a man, as in the saying: "Man dies and leaves a name; the tiger dies and leaves a skin."

一	厂	广	皮	皮							
1	2	3	4	5							

风

fēng
wind

风采	fēng cǎi	elegant demeanour
风干	fēng gān	air-dry
风格	fēng gé	style
风光	fēng guāng	scene; view
风浪	fēng làng	stormy waves; storm
风靡	fēng mǐ	fashionable

风：此字的篆体为"飌"，有人认为昆虫（它）是在风与水汽（尺）的影响下产生的。此字原形是由"日"、"丿"与"凡"三部分组成，即"飌"。因为人们认为风的产生与阳光有直接关系。经过简化后，此字代表阳光与昆虫的部分被去掉了，最终定型为"风"字，正如人们常说的那样："人言似舵，随风转。"

The seal form: 飌 is based on man's belief that insects(它) are born under the influence of the wind or vapour (尺). An older form: 飌 - from 日 (sun), 丿 (motion) and 凡 (extension) - suggests that wind is produced by the action of the sun. The simplified form, however, cuts out the sun and insects, leaving the motion and extension; 风, which goes to prove that "Man's words are like grass - they sway with the wind."

丿	几	凡	风								
1	2	3	4								

公 gōng
public; impartial

公道	gōng dào	reasonable
公共	gōng gòng	public
公分	gōng fēn	centimetre (cm)
公民	gōng mín	citizen
公式	gōng shì	formula
公司	gōng sī	company; corporation
公用	gōng yòng	for public use

公：此字由"八"（代表划分和相对）与"厶"（代表私有和自私）两部分组合而成的象形字。"公"指代的是一只缩在茧子里的蚕，意为为了公共的利益对私有财产（厶）进行分配（公）。因此，"公"字还具有公共和公正的意义，同时也反对（八）自私自利（厶）。

公 is made up of a 八 (division, opposition) and 厶 (private, selfish), a pictograph of a silkworm coiled in its cocoon. It implies the division (八) of private (厶) property for the benefit of the public. Hence 公: meaning public or impartial, i.e., opposed (八) to private or selfish (厶).

ノ	八	公	公							
1	2	3	4							

私 sī
personal; private; selfish

私奔	sī bēn	elopement
私立	sī lì	privately run
私人	sī rén	private
私事	sī shì	private (or personal) affairs
私语	sī yǔ	whisper
无私	wú sī	selfless

私："禾"，即谷物，是人类的主要食物，一种具有很高价值的财产。声旁"厶"指代的是身藏茧中的蚕，意为私人或自私。在古代，收获的粮食（禾），一部分用来交税，剩下的就变为了私有财产（厶），这也正是"私"字的由来。即：归于自己的那部分粮食。引申意思为个人、私有和自私。

The radical 禾 stands for grain, man's staple food, a highly valued possession. The phonetic 厶, representing a silkworm hidden in its cocoon, symbolises private or selfish. Grain (禾) in ancient days was used to pay taxes and the residue was personal (厶) property. Hence 私: my share of grain, i.e., personal, private or selfish.

一	二	千	禾	禾	私	私				
1	2	3	4	5	6	7				

丝
sī
silk

丝绸	sī chóu	silk cloth
丝带	sī dài	silk ribbon; silk braid; silk sash
丝毫	sī háo	a bit
丝绒	sī róng	velvet
丝状	sī zhuàng	filiform
肉丝	ròu sī	meat floss

丝："纟"的篆体为"⊗"，这也是丝字的声旁。"⊗"所代的是两只茧，在它下面的"∧"指代的是经过搓捻后形成的一股线。此字还曾被写作"纟"，说明由许多丝线才能织成绸。经过演变，完全相似的两部分被合在了一起，变为现在的"丝"字。

⊗ is the seal form of 纟, the radical for silk. The upper ⊗ represents two cocoons; the lower part ∧, the twisting of several strands into a thread. 纟 is duplicated to stand for silk, indicating that many threads are required to form silk: 絲. In the modern version the two identical components are woven together and simplified to 丝.

ㄥ	纟	纟	丝	丝									
1	2	3	4	5									

线
xiàn
thread

线虫	xiàn chóng	nematode
线段	xiàn duàn	line segment
线描	xiàn miáo	line drawing
线绳	xiàn shéng	cotton rope
线索	xiàn suǒ	clue
光线	guāng xiàn	traditional thread binding (of Chinese books)

线：此字由代表形旁的"纟"与声旁的"戋"组合而成，即"缕"（由很多股丝汇集而成）。另一种说法是"缕"采用"泉"的音，意为像泉水一样丝丝不断。正所谓："线无针不能用，舟无水不能行。"

The radical is 纟 (silk). The phonetic 戋 means small, fine or split into bits - the common work of many spears （戈）. Hence 缕: thread, made up of minute （戋）strands of silk （纟）. Another version is 缐, with 泉 (spring) as phonetic. Here the thread is likened to a continuous flow of water from a spring. Whichever the version: "The thread cannot pass without a needle;" or "The boat cannot cross without water."

ㄥ	纟	纟	纟	纟	纩	线	线					
1	2	3	4	5	6	7	8					

红 hóng
red

红豆	hóng dòu	red beans; red seeds
红海	Hóng Hǎi	Red Sea
红利	hóng lì	bonus
红润	hóng rùn	rosy
红晕	hóng yùn	blush; flush
红运	hóng yùn	good luck

红：红色是一种欢乐吉祥的颜色，也是最能取悦于中国人的颜色。因为红色不是丝（纟）的本色，只有经过加工漂染（工）之后，才能得到"红"色。但红色也并不总代表幸运，正如谚语所说："自古红颜多薄命。"

Red is a happy, auspicious colour, most pleasing to the Chinese. Because it is not the natural colour of slik (纟), extra work (工) has to be put in to dye it red: 红. Red, however, is not always propitious, as in the saying: "Beautiful women are often unfortunate."

| 乡 | 纟 | 纟 | 纟 | 红 | 红 | | | | | | | | | |
| 1 | 2 | 3 | 4 | 5 | 6 | | | | | | | | | |

给 gěi
give; provide; supply

| 给以 | gěi yǐ | give; grant |

给：朋友与亲戚之间互赠礼品，尤其是丝绸（纟），可以增进双方之间团结与和谐（合），这就是此字的由来。"给"意为给以或提供。事实上给以本身就是幸福，因为给以所感受到的快乐要比接受所感受到的快乐大得多。

Gifts foster unity and harmony (合) between friends and relatives; and what better present than silk (纟), a material appreciated by all. Hence 给, meaning to give and, by extension, to provide or supply. The practice of giving brings blessings, for there is more happiness in giving than there is in receiving.

| 乡 | 纟 | 纟 | 纟 | 纠 | 纠 | 纱 | 给 | 给 | | | | | | |
| 1 | 2 | 3 | 4 | 5 | 6 | 7 | 8 | 9 | | | | | | |

123

结

jié

knot;
produce;
settle

结拜	jié bài	become sworn brothers or sisters
结冰	jié bīng	freeze
结彩	jié cǎi	adorn or decorate
结果	jié guǒ	result; outcome
结合	jié hé	combine
结婚	jié hūn	get married
结论	jié lùn	conclusion

结: 声旁"吉"意为幸运、吉利，是值得人们宣布的事情。而形旁"纟"（丝）则指代的是一些注定能获得成功的事情，例如：协议的签定所获得的丰收、联结等。图中所示是一件值得宣布的事，即喜结良缘。

The phonetic 吉 means fortunate - from 事 (affair) and 口 (mouth) - an affair worth announcing. In this character, the radical 纟 (silk) enforces the idea of tying or making secure something fortunate, e.g., concluding a contract, producing fruitage or tying a knot 结. Illustrated is the successful conclusion of an affair worth announcing - the tying of the matrimonial knot.

乚	纟	纟	纟	纠	结	结	结	结					
1	2	3	4	5	6	7	8	9					

纸

zhǐ

paper

纸板	zhǐ bǎn	paperboard; cardboard
纸币	zhǐ bì	paper money; currency note
纸盒	zhǐ hé	box; carton
纸花	zhǐ huā	paper flower
纸牌	zhǐ pái	playing cards

纸: 声旁"氏"原先指代的是扎根于水底后飘浮（€€）在水面的植物（屮）。形旁"纟"指代的是用只有铺开才能用于写字的材料。虽然丝（纟）一般的纸张就像水中的植物（氏）一样无毒无害，但需要注意的是："纸笔杀人不见血。"

The phonetic 氐 (clan) was originally a floating plant (屮)spread out flat (€€) over the water surface, rooting itself to the bottom. Silk (纟) - the radical - is also spread out when used as a writing material. Hence 纸: paper - the writing material like silk (纟) that lies flat and apparently harmless as the water-plant(氐). But beware: "Paper and brush may kill a man; you don't need a knife."

乚	纟	纟	纟	红	纸	纸							
1	2	3	4	5	6	7							

网 wǎng
net

网罗	wǎng luó	trap
网球	wǎng qiú	tennis
电网	diàn wǎng	electrified barbed wire
发网	fà wǎng	hair net
鱼网	yú wǎng	fish net
蜘蛛网	zhī zhū wǎng	cobweb

网：此字是一个象形字。原先的"綱"字是由代表丝绸的"纟"字与代表陷阱及圈套的"罔"所组成。此字最终定型为"网"。但正如谚语所说："人们总是一天打鱼，一天晒网。"

This character started as a pictograph of a net: 网. It was cast aside and replaced by the regular form 綱, comprising 纟 (silk) and 罔 (trap) - without much success. So the primitive pictograph of the net was taken up again for the modern simplified form 网, demonstrating that "There is a day to cast your nets, and a day to dry your nets."

丨	冂	冂	冈	网	网							
1	2	3	4	5	6							

细 xì
fine;
tender;
careful

细胞	xì bāo	cell
细长	xì cháng	tall and slender
细工	xì gōng	fine workmanship
细节	xì jié	minute detail
细菌	xì jūn	germ
细密	xì mì	fine and closely woven
细腻	xì nì	exquisite

细：代表声旁的"田"字最早被写成"囟"，指代的是由高处俯视儿童嫩嫩的脑门。"细"字表示像丝织（纟）一般的纤细、脆弱、柔软。"细水长流"是一句谚语，告诫人们要勤俭持家。

In this character, the phonetic 田 was originally written: 囟, a top view of the child's skull showing the tender fontanelles. Hence 细: meaning tender, fine, soft, like the silken (纟) hair around the fontanelles (囟). Small beginnings are not to be despised for, just as resources last a long time if used sparingly, "A small stream flows without interruption."

乙	纟	纟	纟	纠	细	细	细					
1	2	3	4	5	6	7	8					

经 jīng

classic; already; pass through

经常	jīng cháng	frequently
经典	jīng diǎn	classics
经度	jīng dù	longitude
经费	jīng fèi	funds
经管	jīng guǎn	be in charge of
经过	jīng guò	pass through; pass by

经: 声旁"坙"最早被写成"巠", 指代的是被风水先生所观测(壬)到的, 不同寻常, 深藏于地下(一)的水流(巛)。同时, 原先的声旁"坙"象征织布机上的线。用丝线(系)织出的珍贵的丝织物, 就像集智慧为一体的古典文学(經)一样。经典作品是被历代人传颂的文化遗产。

The phonetic 坙 was originally 巠- an allusion to water currents (巛) under the ground (一) that the geomancer examines (壬) something deep, not superficial in the regular form, the phonetic resembles warp threads on a loom: 坙. Just as silk threads (系) are woven into precious fabrics, so wisdom is woven into enduring classics: 經, a literary heritage that has already passed through many hands.

乙	纟	纟	纠	经	经	经	经
1	2	3	4	5	6	7	8

终 zhōng

end; final

终点	zhōng diǎn	destination; finishing line
终古	zhōng gǔ	forever
终归	zhōng guī	eventually; after all
终究	zhōng jiū	eventually; in the end
终身	zhōng shēn	lifelong

终: 此字的声旁为"冬", 它的篆体为"夂", 意为绑在一股丝绸末端的带子(夂)。加上表示冰的"冫", 指代的是一年之终, 即冬天。形旁"纟"表示丝线的末端。最后"纟"与"冬"结合就成了"终"。

This character has 冬 (winter) for its phonetic. Its seal form was a bundle of silk tied at the end by a band to suggest "end": 夂. Ice (冫) was added to signify winter, the end of the year. The presence of the silk radical (纟) extends the idea to "the winter of the silk thread" i.e., the final part of it, the end: 终.

乙	纟	纟	纟	纱	终	终	终
1	2	3	4	5	6	7	8

药

yào
medicine

草药	cǎo yào	medicinal herbs
药方	yào fāng	prescription
药房	yào fáng	dispensary
药水	yào shuǐ	lotion; liquid medicine
药丸	yào wán	pill
服药	fú yào	take medicine
火药	huǒ yào	gunpowder

药：草药（艹）就像音乐一样可以抚慰人们的心灵，也可以使人们保持健康（乐）。经过简化后的"药"字把"艹"与"约"（很约束，阻止）字相结合，意指草药可以阻止疾病的产生。尽管草药可以治愈多种疾病，但"粗俗之人是无药可治的。"

Medicinal herbs（艹）, like music that soothes the mind, restore harmony（乐）to the body; hence 藥 the symbol for medicine. The simplified form 药 combines 艹 (herbs) with 约 (agree, restrain), implying that herbs restrain sickness. Though there are herbal remedies for all sorts of ailments: "No medicine can cure a man of vulgarity."

一 十 艹 艹 艻 苭 药 药 药
1 2 3 4 5 6 7 8 9

学

xué
learn;
study

学费	xué fèi	tuition fee
学府	xué fǔ	an institution of learning
学科	xué kē	branch of learning; subject
学生	xué shēng	student; pupil
学识	xué shí	knowledge

学：表意文字的"学"具有教导、启迪之意，指代的是教师交叉（爻）着双手（臼）用于驱散笼罩在（冖）学生（子）脑海中的疑团。这就是指学习。学习对孩子的成长很关键，正如人们常说的："养儿不教如养驴，养女不教如养猪。"

This ideograph signifies enlightenment - the master's laying on of hands（臼）crosswise 爻 upon the darkness which covers（冖）the mind of his disciple（子）. It implies to learn or study. Learning is essential to the upbringing of a child, hence: "To raise a son without learning is raising an ass; to raise a daughter without learning is raising a pig."

丶 丷 丷 ⺍ 兴 学 学 学
1 2 3 4 5 6 7 8

写 xiě
write

写实	xiě shí	write or paint realistically
写稿	xiě gǎo	write for (a magazine, etc.)
写生	xiě shēng	draw, paint or sketch from nature
写作	xiě zuò	writing

写："寫"意为在屋檐下（宀）的一只喜鹊（舄）。喜鹊作为一种象征吉祥的鸟，喜爱干净并喜欢衔叼及藏匿发光的物体。因此"寫"被解释为在屋檐下进行整理。其延伸之意为整理思绪并把所想好的写出来。经过演变，此字最终被简化为"写"。

寫 originally was a picture of a magpie 舄 under a roof （宀）. Regarded as a bird of good omen, the magpie is a tidy bird with the habit of picking up bright objects and hiding them. 寫 therefore suggests order under the roof; by extension, to set one's ideas in order; to write, now simplified to 写.

'	'	'	写	写									
1	2	3	4	5									

印 yìn
print;
stamp;
seal

印发	yìn fā	print and distribute
印盒	yìn hé	seal box
印花	yìn huā	revenue stamp
印刷	yìn shuā	printing
印象	yìn xiàng	impression
印章	yìn zhāng	seal
盖印	gài yìn	affix one's seal

印：用右手（爪）按住一个印章（卩），即"印"。原先的意思是在粘土上印盖图案。经过演变成了在纸上印盖图案。随着活字印刷的产生，此字的意思又进了一步，意为盖印或印刷。

The right hand（爪）pressing a seal（卩）formed the character for seals used for stamping impressions on clay: 印. These, in time, gave way to inked impressions on paper. With the invention of block printing and movable type, the character enlarged its meaning to include stamping and printing.

'	匚	爪	印	印									
1	2	3	4	5									

shū
book; writings

书包	shū bāo	schoolbag
书报	shū bào	books and newspapers
书本	shū běn	book
书店	shū diàn	bookshop
书法	shū fǎ	calligraphy
书房	shū fáng	study room

书: "書" 是用笔 (聿) 进行语言或文字表述的产物。它表示手 (⺕) 握住一枝笔 (|) 在牌匾上画出的一条横线 (一)。形旁 "日" 指代的是口中 (口) 的言语 (一)。但书中所说的并非全部正确。所以人们还是不要照本宣科盲目相信书本上所说的为好。

書 is the product of a pen (聿) that speaks (日) books and writings. It indicates a stylus (|) in hand (⺕) scratching a line (一) on a tablet (一). 日, the radical, is the mouth (口) with a word (一) in it. Because not everything the pen speaks is truth, "It is better to have no books than to rely blindly on them."

㇇	㇖	书	书								
1	2	3	4								

書畫畫畫画

huà
painting; drawing

画报	huà bào	pictorial
画家	huà jiā	painter; artist
画架	huà jià	easel
画廊	huà láng	gallery
画室	huà shì	studio
画像	huà xiàng	portrait
画展	huà zhǎn	art exhibition

画: "畫" 是由象征着书画家画笔的 "聿", 和作品的 "田" 及画框底部的 "凵" 组合而成。简化后的 "画" 字是由代表作品的 "田" 字与代表框架的 "凵" 组合。画蛇添足的行为纯粹多余。人们的需要也一定要切合实际, 不要 "画饼充饥"。

畫, a painting or drawing, is symbolised by the artist's brush (聿) and his picture (田); of the frame there now remains only the bottom part (凵). However, the simplified form: 画 restores the picture (田) with its frame (凵). "Painting a snake and adding legs" (画蛇添足) would be superfluous. Hence the need to be practical: "You cannot satisfy your hunger by merely drawing a loaf."

一	厂	帀	币	雨	酉	画	画				
1	2	3	4	5	6	7	8				

wáng
king; ruler

国王	guó wáng	king
王朝	wáng cháo	imperial court; dynasty
王储	wáng chǔ	crown prince
王法	wáng fǎ	the law
王宫	wáng gōng	(imperial) palace
王牌	wáng pái	trump card
王室	wáng shì	royal family

王：三条横线（三）分别代表上天、人类与土地。由垂直的"丨"相连后便形成了代表在天地之间具有绝对权威的君王，即"王"。而早先作为象形字的"王"代表一串只有君王才能佩戴的翡翠念珠。

Three horizontal planes (三) representing heaven, man and earth, connected by a vertical structure (丨), form the character for king: 王 - the one vested with power, between heaven and earth, to rule uprightly over man. Originally 王 was a pictograph of a string of jade beads (王) which only the royalty could afford. It eventually became the symbol for king.

一	二	干	王										
1	2	3	4										

yù
jade; gem

玉雕	yù diāo	jade carving; jade sculpture
玉器	yù qì	jade article
玉色	yù sè	jade green; light bluish green
玉蜀黍	yù shǔ shǔ	maize; corn
玉簪	yù zān	jade hairpin

玉："三"象征着三块吊在一起代表君主身份的翡翠。为了与"王"字加以区别，就加上了"、"。"玉"便成了上等与纯洁的象征。因为真正的玉往往身藏于粗石之中，很难发现。人们常说："玉不琢，不成器。"

三 represents 3 pieces of jade strung together as a symbol for king: 王 The dot (、) was added to form 玉 (jade), distinguishing it from 王 (king). Highly valued as a symbol of excellence and purity, jade may be found in its crude form, hidden in rough stone. Hence the saying: "Jade which is not chiselled and polished is not an article of beauty."

一	二	干	王	玉									
1	2	3	4	5									

国 guó
country; nation

国宾	guó bīn	state guest
国策	guó cè	national policy
国产	guó chǎn	made in our country
国都	guó dū	national capital
国法	guó fǎ	the law of the land
国防	guó fáng	national defence

国: "国"字是由象征土地与边界的"口"与嘴（口），及矛（戈）组成。因此"国"代表一定范围内的土地、人民及武器。简化后，只有"玉"放在表示国界的"口"中，成为"国"。而君主对于臣民的需要就像人民对于食品的需要一样热切，正如人们所说："人是国家源，粮为人必需。"

国 is composed of 口 (boundary), (land), 口 (mouth) and 戈 (spear). 国 therefore means land, people and weapons within a boundary - a country. The simplified form puts only 玉 (jade, representing king) within the boundary (口) to produce nation: 国. But a king needs subjects as much as subjects need food: "People are the nation's source; food is the primary need of the people."

1	2	3	4	5	6	7	8
丨	冂	冂	冋	囝	国	国	国

现 xiàn
appear; reveal; now

现场	xiàn chǎng	scene (of an incident)
现成	xiàn chéng	ready-made
现代	xiàn dài	modern times; the contemporary age
现款	xiàn kuǎn	ready money; cash

现: 代表形旁的"王"意为翡翠，代表声旁的"见"则代表人"儿"的双眼"目"，意为观看。"现"字同时还描述出宝石发光时的景象。同时，它也告诫人们外表具有很强的欺骗性，是靠不住的。正如谚语所说："具有美德的人往往没有华丽的外表，并且不擅于花言巧语。"

The radical is 玉 (jade, gem) contracted to 王. The phonetic 见, representing eyes (目) of man (儿) means to see. So 现 means the sight of a sparkling gem, its appearance at that very moment. Appearances may be revealing or deceptive. According to the saying: "Fine words and appearance are seldom associated with virtue."

1	2	3	4	5	6	7	8
一	二	干	王	玒	玑	现	现

理

lǐ
texture;
reason;
manage

理性	lǐ xìng	reason
理由	lǐ yóu	reason; ground argument
理发	lǐ fà	haircut; hairdressing
理想	lǐ xiǎng	ideal
理智	lǐ zhì	reason; intellect

理: 此字由代表形旁的 "王" 字与代表声旁的 "田" 字与 "土" 字组合而成。人们把切割翡翠与分割田地相提并论，因为切割翡翠与分割田地都应遵循一定的规则与原则。因此，"理" 字的引申之意为 "原因、原则"。有句谚语说："一个没有原则的天才不如一个有原则的笨蛋。"

王 (gem) is the radical, and the phonetic 里 is made up of 田 (field) and 土 (land). 理 compares the cutting of a gem to the dividing of field and land, both done according to fixed rules and principles; hence the extended meaning: reason, principle. The old saying highlights the importance of a moral standard: "A man of talent without principle is inferior to a simpleton with principle."

一	二	千	王	玨	玑	珥	珥	理	理	理
1	2	3	4	5	6	7	8	9	10	11

主

zhǔ
owner;
master

主办	zhǔ bàn	direct; sponsor
主持	zhǔ chí	chair (a discussion); host (a banquet)
主动	zhǔ dòng	initiative
主队	zhǔ duì	home team; host team
主妇	zhǔ fù	housewife; hostess

主: 作为象形字的 "主" 为一盏冒着火焰的油灯。它意为君主或主人手托闪烁着亮光的油灯来传播光明。如果你想要在事业上成功的话，下面的建议或许可以带来一些启迪："用人不疑，疑人不用。"

主 is a pictograph of a lampstand with the flame rising above it. It symbolises a man who spreads light - a lord or master. To shed light, the master himself needs the enlightening counsel: "If you suspect a man, don't employ him; if you employ a man, don't suspect him."

、	二	二	辛	主
1	2	3	4	5

住 zhù

live;
reside;
stay

住户	zhù hù	household; resident
住口	zhù kǒu	shut up; stop talking
住手	zhù shǒu	stay one's hand; stop
住宿	zhù sù	stay; put up; get accommodation

住："人"字与"主"字组合，即为"住"。在古代，男人（人）往往是一家之主（主）。于是"住"字就含有了居住、逗留之意。在现代社会中，有些丈夫仍旧是一家之主。

人 (man) is combined with 主 (master) to form 住 meaning to dwell. In ancient days, the man (人) was always master (主) of his dwelling; so the combination 住 suggests to dwell, to stay. In modern times, however, some husbands still boss the house; others house the boss.

ノ	イ	イ	伫	伫	住	住						
1	2	3	4	5	6	7						

全 quán

complete;
perfect

全部	quán bù	whole; complete; total; all
全才	quán cái	a versatile person; all arounder
全场	quán chǎng	the whole audience; all those present

全：此字最早被写为"全"或"全"，表示合起来的（亼）工作（工），意为完成。例如：原件装配好了，工作完成了。经过演变，此字变成了由代表玉的"王"或"玉"字与代表镶嵌的"入"组合而成的"全"，表示完美。虽然追求完美不是至关重要的事，但正如谚语所说："宁取烂玉，不要精瓦。"

This character was first written 全 or 全 combining 亼 (joined) with 工 (work). It means completed, i.e., the components are assembled and the work finished. However, the modern character, classified under 入 (in), could be interpreted as a jade (王 or 玉) skilfully inlaid (入), and so flawless and perfect: 全. But perfection is not always the crucial thing: "Better an imperfect jade than a perfect tile."

ノ	人	亼	今	全	全						
1	2	3	4	5	6						

133

米 mǐ
rice
(uncooked)

米波	mǐ bō	metric wave
米粉	mǐ fěn	rice-flour noodles; vermicelli
米酒	mǐ jiǔ	rice wine
米粒	mǐ lì	gain of rice
米色	mǐ sè	cream-coloured
米制	mǐ zhì	the metric system

米：象形字"米"代表水稻的根茎。最早是由九粒谷子"❊"所组成。经过演变后，最终形成了"米"字。象征着脱粒后的谷物（米）被分播在四个方块（十）之中。虽然吃饭用的碗代表着廉洁的生存之道，但俗语说："用通过不正当手段获取的米煮饭，煮不出香喷喷的米饭。"

米 is a pictograph of a rice stalk. Its original form depicted nine grains of rice ❊. This was modified to 米 and finally 米, symbolising grains (米) separated in the four quarters (十) by threshing. Although the rice-bowl may represent an honest means of living, "Rice obtained by crookedness will not boil up into good food."

、	゛	⺊	半	米	米					
1	2	3	4	5	6					

气 qì
breath;
vapour;
air

气喘	qì chuǎn	asthma
气氛	qì fēn	atmosphere
气愤	qì fèn	indignant; furious
气候	qì hòu	climate
气力	qì lì	effort; energy
气球	qì qiú	balloon
气温	qì wēn	air temperature

气：此字指代的是由上升的蒸气而形成的朵朵白云。最早"气"是由代表太阳（☉）与代表火焰的（火）组合而成，即可以产生蒸汽的"氣"。经过演变后，"氣"意为冒着热气（气）的米饭（米），最后简化为"气"。此字含有空气、蒸气、气息及生气之意。

气 represents curling vapours rising and forming clouds. Ancient forms show the sun (☉) and fire (火) which cause the vapours: 氣. The regular form 氣, however, depicts the vapour (气) ascending from boiling rice (米) now simplified to 气, meaning air, vapour, breath, energy or anger.

ノ	广	气	气							
1	2	3	4	5						

饱

bǎo
eat to the full

饱含	bǎo hán	filled with
饱和	bǎo hé	saturation
饱满	bǎo mǎn	full; plump
饱学	bǎo xué	learned

饱：最早"饱"字由代表声旁的"包"字与代表食物的"食"字组合而成。篆体中的"包"字被写作"甩"，指代的是母体中的胚胎，意指包起来。"饱"指代的是所有被胃包起来的食物，即吃得很饱。但有句俗语说："宁要饥与纯，不要肥与堕。"

包 the phonetic combines with 食, the radical for food, to form 饱 (satiated). The seal form of 包 is 甩, depicting a foetus enclosed in the body; hence the meaning wrapped up. 饱 therefore means food all wrapped up in the stomach, i.e., fully satisfied. However, as the saying goes: "Better be hungry and pure than well-filled and corrupt."

ノ	㇏	饣	饣	饣	饣	饣	饱				
1	2	3	4	5	6	7	8				

饿

è
hungry

挨饿	āi è	go hungry
饥饿	jī è	hunger; starvation

饿："饿"字由作为形旁的"食"与代表我字的"我"结合而成，意为喂我。同时，另一个代表饥饿的字为"饑"。它可以解释为：一点儿（幾）食物（食），简化字为"饥"，指代的是放在小桌（几）上的食物（饣）。虽然人们都会有饥饿的时候，但廉者是不会承受嗟来之食的。

This character is based on the radical for food: 食. It literally means feed (食) me (我) - a fitting sign for hunger. Another character for hunger is 饑, literally: little (幾) food (食) simplified to 饥, i.e., food (饣) on small table (几). Although hunger is no respecter of persons, "Even a hungry person will refuse food offered in contempt."

ノ	㇏	饣	饣	饣	饣	饣	饿	饿	饿		
1	2	3	4	5	6	7	8	9	10		

馆 guǎn
hotel;
restaurant

旅馆	lǚ guǎn	hotel
美术馆	měi shù guǎn	art gallery
体育馆	tǐ yù guǎn	gymnasium; stadium
图书馆	tú shū guǎn	library

馆: 早先的"馆"字由"食"与"官"组合而成。象征声旁的"官"字指代的是城中(自)的官邸(宀)。"食"与"官"合在一起指代的是卖食品的场所(例如: 酒店、餐馆或饭庄等)。所以有人说: "酒店老板从不会为你的胃口之大而担心。"

The food radical 食 combines with 官 to produce 馆, a public building. The phonetic 官 (official) originally meant the residence of an official - the hall (宀) of the city (自). 食 (food) together with this suggests a public building doing food business - inn, hotel or restaurant. Hence: "An innkeeper never worries if your appetite is big."

丿	𠂉	饣	饣	饣	馆	馆	馆	馆	馆	馆
1	2	3	4	5	6	7	8	9	10	11

饮 yǐn
drink

饮茶	yǐn chá	drink tea
饮弹	yǐn dàn	be hit by a bullet
饮恨	yǐn hèn	nurse a grievance
饮料	yǐn liào	drink; beverage
饮泣	yǐn qì	weep in silence
饮食	yǐn shí	food and drink; diet

饮: 此字由代表形旁的"食"字与代表声旁的"欠"字组合而成。原先作为象形文字的"欠"意为张嘴呼吸, 就如饮酒一样"𣢇"。而"𣢇"经过演变后成了"㒫", 指代的是从人体(儿)上散发出的气味(彡)。这个字的原形极像一只酒瓶"酉"。这也是一个表示食物的部首。

Based on the food radical 食, this character has a significant phonetic 欠, suggesting breath. 欠 originally was a pictograph of a man opening his mouth to catch his breath, as in drinking: 𣢇. This was modified to 㒫, representing air waves (彡) emanating from the man (儿). The primitive form of the character for drink shows clearly a drinking flask (酉) as part of the food radical.

丿	𠂉	饣	饣	饮	饮	饮							
1	2	3	4	5	6	7							

车 chē

cart;
carriage;
chariot

汽车	qì chē	motor vehicle; automobile
车床	chē chuáng	lathe
车费	chē fèi	fare
车祸	chē huò	road accident
车间	chē jiān	workshop
车辆	chē liàng	vehicle; car

车：此字指代的是用鸟瞰的方式来观察一辆车。而"車"字是由代表车体的"田"，代表双轮的"二"及代表轮轴的"丨"组合成的。原先的"車"并不像马车、战车或大车那样多变。但不管如何变化，车过总会留辙。如人们办事一样，应该做到"前事不忘，后事之师"才对。

車 represents a bird's eye view of a cart, showing its body (田)the two wheels (二)and the axle (丨). The primitive forms of 車 are as varied as carts, carriages and chariots. But, whatever the form, where there is a cart in front there is a track behind; so "Take warning from the wrecked cart ahead of you."

一	左	놀	车						
1	2	3	4						

轰 hōng

bang;
boom (noise; uproar)

轰动	hōng dòng	cause a sensation; make a stir
轰击	hōng jī	shell; bombard
轰隆	hōng lōng	rumble; roll
轰鸣	hōng míng	thunder; roar
轰炸	hōng zhà	bomb

轰：此字原先是由三个车字组合而成，即"轟"，代表许多马车在行进过程中所发出的声响。经过演变，位于底部的两个"車"字被"双"字所代替，成为"轰"。"又"本身指代右手。在吃饭时右手不停地往嘴里送食物，表示"再次"。

轟 is the triple form of the noisy cart (車). It serves as a fitting symbol for any loud or explosive sound like the rumbling of many carts. In the simplified form, 又 (again; ditto) replaces each of the two lower carts to produce 轰. 又 itself is a simplified picture of the right hand; and the right hand, returning repeatedly to the mouth in eating, suggests "again".

一	左	놀	车	轰	轰	轰	轰		
1	2	3	4	5	6	7	8		

轮 lún
wheel

轮班	lún bān	in shifts; in relays
轮齿	lún chǐ	teeth of a cogwheel
轮船	lún chuán	steamer
轮渡	lún dù	ferry
轮换	lún huàn	rotate; take turns
轮机	lún jī	turbine
轮胎	lún tāi	tyre

轮: 此字的形旁为"车", 声旁为"侖", 意为马车。因为只有靠轮子, 车辆才能前进。马车的轮子排列有序, 协调一致, 运行稳健。同时也象征那些用竹片写好有序地捆绑在一起(亼)进行保存的古代文件(冊)。

輪 the wheel that moves the cart, has 車 (cart) for radical. 侖, its phonetic, is suggestive, not only of the orderly arrangement of 侖, the spokes of a wheel, but also their unity and stability. It signifies a collection (亼) of ancient documents preserved on bamboo slips tied together in an orderly manner (冊).

一 𠂉 车 车 轩 轮 轮 轮
1 2 3 4 5 6 7 8

库 kù
storehouse

军械库	jūn xiè kù	armoury
仓库	cāng kù	storehouse; warehouse
库藏	kù cáng	have in storage
库存	kù cún	stock; reserve
库房	kù fáng	storehouse

库: 代表屋顶的"宀"象征着一间小棚屋, 而"广"则代表了半间敞着前脸的篷子。"库"的原意为搁放马车的篷子。但不久它便被用来贮藏粮食及其它物品。最后此字便具有了货栈、谷仓及仓库的意思。

Just as 宀 is a picture of a roof, representing hut, so 广 is half a hut - a shed or shop with an open front. 库 originally was a shed (广) for carts (车). But, before long, it came to be used for storing grain and all sorts of goods. Hence (库) a storehouse, warehouse, granary or depot.

丶 宀 广 广 庄 庄 库
1 2 3 4 5 6 7

军

jūn
army; soldiers

军备	jūn bèi	armament; arms
军部	jūn bù	army headquarters
军操	jūn cāo	military drill
军车	jūn chē	military vehicle
军队	jūn duì	armed forces
军法	jūn fǎ	military criminal code
军港	jūn gǎng	naval port

军：篆体的"車"字指代的是由一群士兵（冖）护送下的战车（军）。正所谓"养兵千日，用兵一时。"而在那关键的时候，"胜者为王，败者为寇"。

The seal form of this character shows a war chariot (車) escorted by a surrounding force of soldiers (冖) - an army: 軍 . Armies are maintained for years, to be used on a single day. And on that crucial day: "The conquerors are crowned kings; the defeated are branded bandits."

丶	冖	冖	写	军	军									
1	2	3	4	5	6									

斩

zhǎn
chop off

斩断	zhǎn duàn	chop off
斩首	zhǎn shǒu	behead; decapitate

斩："斩"字由代表战车的"車"字与代表士兵手中利斧的"斤"字组合而成，具有手舞利斧砍杀敌人之意。它也可以理解为用手舞动（車）战斧（斤）。但斩杀一名敌人并不能解决一切麻烦。正如俗话所说："斩草还需除根。"

斩 probably has reference to a war chariot (車) with warriors wielding axes (斤) to cut off the enemy. It may also mean to whirl or brandish (車) a battle axe (斤). But cutting off an enemy does not eradicate the source of trouble; hence the saying: "When cutting the weeds, get rid of the root."

一	士	车	车	车	斩	斩	斩							
1	2	3	4	5	6	7	8							

轿 jiào
sedan-chair

轿车	jiào chē	car
轿子	jiào zi	sedan chair
花轿	huā jiào	bridal sedan chair

轿: 此字由代表运输工具的"車"字与代表轿子的"乔"字组合而成。声旁"乔"由描述人弯身前倾的"夭"与表示高度的"高"字组合产生。虽然身居高位和有权势的人往往会选择轿为交通工具, 但正如俗话所说: "坐轿抬轿都是人。"

轿 is composed of 車 (vehicle) and 乔, something high and stately - the sedan chair. The phonetic 乔 combines 夭 (man leaning forward) with a contracted form of 高 (high). Although the high and mighty travel in sedans, "He who rides in the chair is a man; he who carries the chair is also a man."

一	土	车	车	车	车	轩	轩	轿	轿				
1	2	3	4	5	6	7	8	9	10				

软 ruǎn
soft; weak; pliable; yielding

软钢	ruǎn gāng	mild steel; soft steel
软骨头	ruǎn gú tou	a weak kneed person; a spineless person; a coward
软骨	ruǎn gǔ	cartilage
软化	ruǎn huà	soften; win over by soft tactics

软: 此字由代表具有良好机动性的"車"字与"欠"字组合而成, 意为柔软的、虚弱的、易弯的、灵活的。"欠"象征着一个人(儿)张口喘气(彡)。此字还被写作"輭"。而代表声旁的"耎"字则象征着男子(大)柔软的胡须(而)。

The mobility of the carriage (車) is used to good effect in this character. Combined with 欠, it produces 软, meaning soft and weak or pliable and flexible, 欠 signifying a man (儿) gasping for breath (彡), i.e., exhausted, deficient. 软 may also be written 輭, the phonetic 耎 representing the soft beard (而) of a man (大).

一	土	车	车	车	软	软	软											
1	2	3	4	5	6	7	8	9	10	11	12	13	14	15	16	17	18	19

连 **lián**

link;
join;
connect

连忙	lián máng	promptly; at once
连日	lián rì	for days on end; day after day
连同	lián tóng	together with; along with
连续	lián xù	continous; successive

连：早先此字由"車"字与"辶"组合而成，表示通过车辆把各地方连接起来。"連"字还象征着一队正在行进中（辶）的马车。代表链子的•"鏈"字则表示连在一起的（連）一串金属（金）。

Carts (車) on the move (辶) form a connecting link (連) between places, leaving a continuous track, not broken like the track of man. (連) also represents a string of carriages (車) moving along (辶) as if connected. By the same token 鏈 , the character for chain, is made up of rings of metal 金 linked (連) together.

一	乞	车	车	车	诓	连			
1	2	3	4	5	6	7			

莲 **lián**

lotus

莲花	lián huā	lotus flower
莲蓬	lián péng	seedpod of the lotus
莲子	lián zi	lotus seed

莲：莲花是一种飘浮在水面上的植物（艹），像连起来的一串花（連）。因为它出淤泥而不染，所以它也是纯洁的象征。而加上"氵"的"漣"字，则象征着一连串的水波，即水中涟漪。

蓮 the lotus, is a prolific water plant (艹) that spreads continuously (連) like a flowery chain. It epitomises purity because it grows out of mud but remains undefiled. From 連 (connect) also comes the character 漣 (ripples) based on the water radical 氵 - ripples being a continuous succession (連) of waves.

一	十	艹	艹	艿	莒	莲	荳	莲	莲
1	2	3	4	5	6	7	8	9	10

父 fù
father

父母	fù mǔ	father and mother; parents
父亲	fù qin	father
父权制	fù quán zhì	patriarchy
父兄	fù xiōng	father and elder brothers; head of a family

父：父亲总是通过表扬儿子来抬高自己。"父"字的篆体为""，象征着一位右()手持权力之棍(丨)的严父。经演变，代表权力的棍子(丨)消失了，成了""，最终变为"父"。很显然，"治国易，而治家难。"

The Chinese proverb defines father as "a man who, in praising his son, extols himself". Accordingly the seal form depicts father as a disciplinarian - the right hand wielding the rod of authority (丨). Eventually the rod is contracted: and then broken: 父. Apparently: "It is easy to govern a kingdom but difficult to rule one's family."

丿 八 夕 父

巾 jīn
napkin; towel handkerchief

巾帼	jīn guó	woman
餐巾	cān jīn	napkin
手巾	shǒu jīn	hand towel
头巾	tóu jīn	headdress
围巾	wéi jīn	scarf

巾：此字为象形字，象征着一块系在腰间的用于清洁的抹布。古时候用于擦灰尘的手巾是挂在腰间的。"冂"代表一块布的两头，而"丨"则代表垂吊在腰带上。同时，"巾"也是偏旁能组成许多与布有关的字。

巾 is a pictograph of a small piece of cloth used for cleaning, dusting or wiping. In ancient times it was worn, suspended from the girdle. 冂 represents the two extremities of the cloth hanging (丨) from the girdle. 巾 forms the radical of a series of characters relating to cloth in general.

丨 冂 巾

布 bù
cloth

布道	bù dào	preach
布丁	bù dīng	pudding
布防	bù fáng	place troops on garrison duty
布告	bù gào	notice; bulletin; proclamation
布谷鸟	bù gǔ niǎo	cuckoo

布：此字由代表布的形旁"巾"与声旁"父"结合而成。"父"字的篆体为"📜"。"父"是一幅手持权力之棍（丨）的右手（ㄋ）的画面，意为纪律、命令。正如人们所说："织布太快只能织次布，急于结婚的女孩只能搭个蠢丈夫。"

This character is based on the radical for cloth: 巾. The phonetic 父 (father) is discernible as ㄋ in the seal form 📜. ㄋ is a picture of the right hand (ㄋ) with the rod of authority (丨), and implies discipline, control and order - as essential in weaving as in marrying. So the saying goes: "Hasty weaving produces shoddy cloth; a girl who marries in haste has a fool for a husband."

一	ナ	オ	右	布							
1	2	3	4	5							

帚 zhǒu
broom; duster

扫帚	sào zhǒu	broom
扫帚星	sào zhou xīng	comet

帚：此字的篆体为"📜"，后演变为"帚"。它由象征着手的"ㄋ"字，双层布料的"巾"字及手柄（丨）结合而成"帚"（帚）。由于是手（扌）拿扫帚（帚），所以就成了"扫"。有句俗话说："个人自扫门前雪，哪管别人瓦上霜。"

In the seal form 📜, broom is suggested by a hand (ㄋ)with an improvised broom (帚) - double cloth (巾) attached to a handle (丨) Although a helping hand (扌) can easily turn 帚 (broom) into 扫 (sweep), "No one will sweep a public hall used by everyone."

ㄱ	ㄱ	ㅋ	ㄹ	尹	帚	帚	帚				
1	2	3	4	5	6	7	8				

妇

fù

wife;
married
woman

少妇	shào fù	young married woman
夫妇	fū fù	husband and wife
妇产科	fù chǎn kē	(department of) gynaecology and obstetrics
妇女	fù nǚ	woman

妇：原先此字是由"女"字和"帚"字所组成，即"婦"，指代的是已婚妇女。经过演化，由"女"字和代表帮手的"ヨ"组合成"妇"。同时"妻"字也可做为对已婚妇女的称呼。此字象征着手持（ヨ）扫帚（十）的妇女（女）。但不管"妻"字如何写，"一女不能嫁二夫。"

Woman (女) with broom (帚) is the symbol for wife or married woman: 婦, simplified to 妇 - woman (女) with helping hand (ヨ). Another character for wife is 妻 - woman (女) with broom (十) in hand (ヨ). Whatever the character, "She who is the wife of one man cannot eat the rice of two."

| ㇀ | 女 | 女 | 圠 | 妇 | 妇 | | | | | | |
| 1 | 2 | 3 | 4 | 5 | 6 | | | | | | |

帝

dì

emperor

皇帝	huáng dì	emperor
上帝	shàng dì	God
帝国	dì guó	empire
帝王	dì wáng	emperor; monarch
帝制	dì zhì	autocratic monarchy; monarchy

帝：找出能够适合于皇帝的象征物可不容易。此字的原型为"帝"和"帝"，意为身穿龙袍的真命天子。经过演变，此字又添加上了代表双臂的两笔，即"帝"。后来下半部分则演变为"米"形成了"帝"，最后定型为"帝"。俗话说："伴君如伴虎。"

Creating a symbol to suit the emperor can be a thorny problem. The ancient forms 帝 and 帝 represented him with long robes and designated by 一 (上, superior). Two arms were later added: 帝. Then the bottom was changed to 米 (朿, thorns) to produce 帝 and finally 帝. Hence the saying: "To attend on the emperor is like sleeping with a tiger."

| 丶 | 亠 | 宀 | 六 | 产 | 产 | 产 | 帝 | 帝 | | | |
| 1 | 2 | 3 | 4 | 5 | 6 | 7 | 8 | 9 | | | |

dài

girdle;
bring

录音带	lù yīn dài	recording tape
热带	rè dài	the tropics
带累	dài lěi	implicate; involve
带领	dài lǐng	lead; guide
带路	dài lù	show the way act as a guide

带: 此字为象形字, 指代的是古人使用的带有吊饰的腰带, 即 "業"。而处在底部的 "帀" 象征着叠在一起的两条 "巾"。此字还可以指常挂在腰间上的物品。所以 "带" 字还具有携带、穿戴之意。

带 is a pictograph of the ancient girdle, embellished with trinkets hanging from it: 業. At the bottom of the character are the robes, represented by 帀 - two 巾, one over the other. 带 also means to bring or take along, as articles are often carried, tucked in or worn at the girdle.

一	十	卄	卅	艹	带	带	带	带
1	2	3	4	5	6	7	8	9

 mào

hat;
cap

帽徽	mào huī	insignia on a cap
帽子	mào zi	headgear; hat; cap; label; tag; brand

帽: 声旁 "冒" 字意为冒失, 是由代表眼睛的 "目" 字与代表盖着的 "冃" 组合而成。"冃" 指盖着 "口" 某物 "一" 或 "头"。而 "冒" 字与代表声旁的 "巾" 字组合之后, 便成为了 "帽" 字。帽子不可能总是戴起来很合适, 所以我们不能 "以帽取人。"

The phonetic 冒 means rash, acting with eyes (目) covered (冃). 冃 indicates a cover (冂) for something (一), viz. the head (一). 冒 combines with the radical 巾 (cloth) to produce 帽 (hat, cap). A cap does not always fit the head of the wearer because "Many a good man can be found under a shabby hat."

丨	冂	巾	巾	帄	帄	帽	帽	帽	帽	帽	帽
1	2	3	4	5	6	7	8	9	10	11	12

常 cháng
always; constantly

常会	cháng huì	regular meeting
常见	cháng jiàn	common
常年	cháng nián	through the year; perennial
常人	cháng rén	man in the street
常用	cháng yòng	in common use
常驻	cháng zhù	resident; permanent

常: 此字由代表布料的偏旁（巾）与声旁 "尚" 组合而成。"尚" 指代的是房屋的上半部分，有屋顶（宀），烟囱（丨）和能够遮挡（口）风雨的屋脊（八）。"尚" 还可以代表一直飘扬在指挥所上方的旗帜。

常 is made up of the radical 巾 (cloth) and phonetic 尚 (elevated). 尚 is a picture of the upper part of a house with a roof (宀), a smoke hole (口), and a ridge (丨) which divides (八) wind and rain. 尚 represents the banner raised as a signal in front of the general's headquarters and which flies constantly: 常.

丨	丬	业	业	尚	尚	尚	常	常	常	常
1	2	3	4	5	6	7	8	9	10	11

帮 bāng
help; assist

帮忙	bāng máng	help; give a hand; do a favour
帮手	bāng shou	helper; assistant
帮凶	bāng xiōng	accomplice; accessary
帮助	bāng zhù	help; assist

帮: 在封建社会，帝王都是依靠贵族的支持来一统天下的。此字的篆体为 "𡉉" 和 "帛"。"𡉉" 意为在贵族统治下的（彐）土地（土）与庄稼（业）。"帛" 则指代的是捐献的丝绸或财物。在现在的 "帮" 字中，声旁 "邦" 是由代表木材的 "丰" 及代表城市的 "阝" 组合而成。"帮" 也可作为州或国家之意。

In feudal times the emperor relied on the support of his nobles. The seal form of the character for such aid combines 𡉉 with 帛. 𡉉 denotes the crops (业) and land (土) under the noble's rule (彐). 帛 signifies the silk or wealth donated.
In the modern form the phonetic 邦 means state or country represented by woods (丰) and city (阝).

一	二	三	丰	邦	邦	帮	帮	帮
1	2	3	4	5	6	7	8	9

衣 yī
clothes

衣橱	yī chú	wardrobe
衣服	yī fu	clothing; clothes
衣架	yī jià	coat hanger; clothes-rack
衣鱼	yī yú	silverfish; fish mouth; bookworm

衣：此字象征着衣物的外部轮廓。上半部分指代的是带有袖子的外衣，下半部分则指代的是飘动着的长裤。作为象形字的"衣"也同时为许多与衣物有关的词语充当形旁。但正如人们所说的，我们不可以帽取人。"你可以换衣服，但你不能改变一个人。"

衣 delineates the outlines of clothing: on the top, the outer garments with sleeves; at the bottom, the flowing trousers. This pictograph serves as a radical for characters relating to clothing. Apparently, clothes do not make the man, according to the saying: "You can change the clothes; you cannot change the man."

`丶`	`亠`	`宀`	`衤`	`衣`	`衣`					
1	2	3	4	5	6					

裤 kù
trousers

短裤	duǎn kù	shorts
裤子	kù zi	trousers; pants

裤：此字是由形旁的"衣"与声旁字"库"组合而成。"库"指代的是中式宽松而肥大的裤子。此字还可被写作"袴"，它的声旁"夸"（意为大话或大声喊叫），形旁则为"衣"（代表衣物）。而"衫"字则是由代表衣物的"衣"同代表为人体保暖的羽毛的"彡"组合而成。

裤 meaning trousers, is based on the radical 衣 (clothing). The ample storage space of loose Chinese trousers is suggested by the phonetic 库 (store). 裤 may also be written: 袴, the phonetic 夸 meaning big (大) talk or exclamation (亏). 衫 or robe, the other basic article of clothing (衣) is likened to feathers (彡) that warm the body.

`丶`	`丆`	`丬`	`衤`	`衤`	`衤`	`衤`	`衤`	`衤`	`裤`	`裤`	`裤`
1	2	3	4	5	6	7	8	9	10	11	12

被 bèi

bedclothes;
blankets

被捕	bèi bǔ	be arrested
被单	bèi dān	(bed) sheet
被动	bèi dòng	passive
被俘	bèi fú	be captured; be taken prisoner
被告	bèi gào	defendant; the accused

被: 此字指代的是床布或毯子。声旁 "皮" 或 "叕" 指代的是用手中的 (⺕) 尖刀 (⼑) 剥下动物的皮毛 (⽑)。此字同时还具有忍受和被动的意义。而由 "衣" 字与 "包" 字组合成的 "袍" 字指代的是可以裹在身体外边进行保暖的长袍或长外套。

被 bedclothes or blankets, are regarded as cloth (衣) skin (皮). The phonetic 皮 or 叕, represents the skin (⽑) flayed by hand (⺕) with knife (⼑). 被 may also mean to suffer, a sign of the passive. However, 袍 (literally, cloth 衣 wrap 包) refers to the long robe or outer garment wrapped round the body to keep it warm and active.

`	⼀	⼂	⼓	⼔	⼕	⼖	⼗	被	被
1	2	3	4	5	6	7	8	9	10

表 biǎo

express;
show;
manifest

表层	biǎo céng	surface layer
表达	biǎo dá	express; convey; voice
表决	biǎo jué	decide by vote; vote
表露	biǎo lù	show; reveal
表面	biǎo miàn	surface; face

表: 此字是由 "衣" 字与 "毛" 字组合而成，意为表露或表达。原先的衣物表面都被一层皮毛所覆盖。转意之后的 "表" 在文学上指代的是衣物或外表，但外表往往会引起误导。但正如人们所说："人不可貌相，水不可斗量。"

表 combining 衣 with 毛, means to show or make known. Clothes (衣) were originally skins with hair (毛) on the outside. 表 literally means the outside of clothes - the manifestation or outer appearance which may be a false front. It is said that when a boy is small you can see the man, but "A man cannot be known by his looks, nor can the sea be measured with a bushel basket."

一	二	卡	圭	丰	表	表	表
1	2	3	4	5	6	7	8

片 piàn
slice;
piece

片段	piàn duàn	part; passage; extract; fragment
片刻	piàn kè	a short while; an instant; a moment
片时	piàn shí	a short while; a moment

片: 在生活中，人们等不到看到树长大成材被劈成两半（即"爿"和片）的时候。"爿"指代的是可以做床用的木板，而"片"则指代的是一块或一片木头。把"爿"与"片"相结合后，就成了"鼎"。"鼎"字的形旁部分分别由代表木材的"木"（爿）和作为偏旁的"片"组合而成。正如俗话所说："要想早上种树，晚上成材是不可能的。"

Man cannot wait to saw a tree (木) vertically into two halves: 爿 and 片. 爿 serves as a strong plank for his bed and 片 as a symbol for a slice or piece. With 爿 and 片 he forms a tripod for an urn: 鼎. He uses 木 and its components 爿 and 片 as radicals. And so the saying goes: "He plants a tree in the morning and wants to saw planks from it in the evening."

ノ	ゲ	广	片
1	2	3	4

床 chuáng
bed

单人床	dān rén chuáng	single bed
双人床	shuāng rén chuáng	double bed
床单	chuáng dān	bedsheet
床垫	chuáng diàn	mattress
床位	chuáng wèi	berth; bunk; bed
床罩	chuáng zhào	bedspread

床: 代表木材的"爿"意为用于打造木床所需要的厚木板。将"爿"与"木"木材相结合后，便成为"牀"字（意为木床）。此字的另一种写法为"床"，是由代表屋顶的"广"字与代表木材的"木"字结合而成。人们造床是为了睡觉而用。但"如果睡不着的话，请不要埋怨床。"

爿, the left half of a tree (木), represents a thick, strong plank used for a bed. By adding 爿 to 木 you can make 牀 (bed) - literally, strong plank (爿) of wood (木). Another way is by placing 木 (wood) under 广 (roof): 床. As you make your bed, you must lie on it, so "if you can't sleep, don't complain about your bed."

丶	亠	广	广	庄	庄	床
1	2	3	4	5	6	7

墙

qiáng
wall

墙壁	qiáng bì	wall
墙角	qiáng jiǎo	a corner formed by two walls
墙脚	qiáng jiǎo	the foot of a wall; foundation

墙：此字篆刻体的声旁为“啬”，意为谷物（来）被存入（入）在具有双层墙壁的谷仓内（回）。声旁“爿”是为了强调墙壁的坚硬，同时也是一种力量的象征。由于墙壁是由粘土与泥土（土）混合制成的，所以此字最终被写为“墙”。城墙虽然可以起到防御作用，但城市的创造还要归功于人类的贡献，而不是墙。

The seal form of the phonetic 啬 signifies grain 来 stored within (入) a double-walled granary (回) The idea of wall is reinforced by the radical 爿, a symbol of strength. Since walls are made of clay or earth (土), the character may also be written: 墙. Walls may fortify a city, but "Men, not walls, make a city."

1	2	3	4	5	6	7	8	9	10	11	12	13	14
一	十	土	𡈽	坩	坩	坴	埣	埣	墙	墙	墙	墙	墙

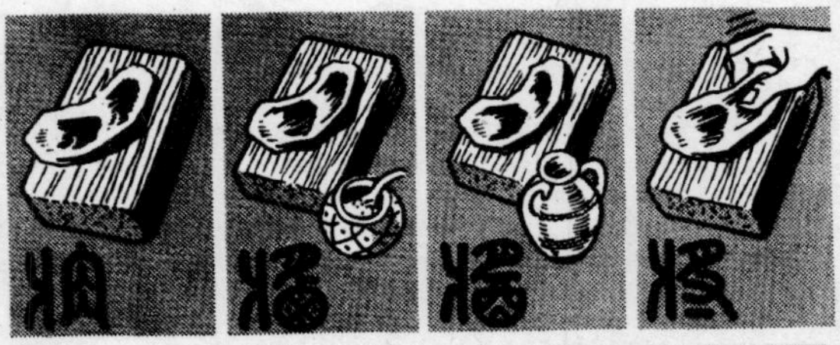

将

jiāng
take; hold;
handle;
shall; will

将近	jiāng jìn	close to; nearly; almost
将军	jiāng jūn	general
将来	jiāng lái	future

将：此字具有很多种篆体形式，分别具有不同的含义：
“𤖅”意为放在肉板（爿）上的肉（肉）。
“𤖅”意为放在肉板（爿）上的肉（月）及食盐（卤）。
“𤖅”意为放在肉板上（爿）的肉（月）及盐水（酉）。
“将”意为手（寸）把一块肉（月）放在肉板上。
此字的延伸之意为奉献、滋养、帮助、处理，还有将来的意义。此字还可以用于称呼领导者和军队的将官。

将 has many seal forms and varied meanings:
𤖅 is a meat block (爿) with meat (肉).
𤖅 shows the meatblock (爿) with meat (月) and salt (卤).
𤖅 represents the meatblock (爿) with meat (月) and brine (酉).
将 signifies the hand (寸) placing meat (月) upon the block.
Hence the extended meanings: offer, present; nourish, help; take, hold; handle, manage. 将 is a character with a future, often used for shall or will; it is even used to mean leader or general.

1	2	3	4	5	6	7	8	9
丶	冫	丬	丬	丬	丬	将	将	将

壮 zhuàng

strong;
eminent;
impressive

壮胆	zhuàng dǎn	embolden; boost somebody's courage
壮丽	zhuàng lì	majestic; magnificent
壮烈	zhuàng liè	heroic; brave
壮士	zhuàng shì	hero; warrior
壮实	zhuàng shi	sturdy; robust

壮: 此字在文学上的意义为能够给人们留下深刻印象（爿）的人（士），或自命不凡的人。延伸之意为强壮、壮实。 与"壮"字相像的"妆"字意为通过化妆整理能给人留下深刻印象的女人。

壮 literally means a strong and impressive (爿) personage (士) or one who professes to be so; by extension, strong and able-bodied. An analogous character is 妆 (adorn, disguise) - an impressive (爿) woman (女), i.e., one who adorns herself with make-up.

`	冫	ヰ	丬	壯	壮						
1	2	3	4	5	6						

装 zhuāng

pack;
fill;
pretend

装扮	zhuāng bàn	dress up; disguise
装备	zhuāng bèi	equip; equipment; outfit
装胡涂	zhuāng hú tu	pretend not to know
装货	zhuāng huò	loading (cargo)
装甲车	zhuāng jiǎ chē	armoured car

装: 此字的声旁为"壮"，意为强壮、壮实。最早此字用来形容人的外表。作为形旁的"衣"字，意为身着不属于自己身份地位的服装，含有欺诈、蒙骗之意。它的延伸之意还包括：包装、装假或装填。

壮 the phonetic, means strong or robust. It was originally, concerned with appearance. The addition of the radical 衣 (clothing) suggests putting oneself in another's clothing and filling it - to deceive; by extension, to pack, fill, pretend: 装 .

`	冫	ヰ	丬	壯	壮	壯	壯	壯	袈	裝	装
1	2	3	4	5	6	7	8	9	10	11	12

夕

xī
evening

夕烟	xī yān	evening mist
夕阳	xī yáng	the setting sun
夕照	xī zhào	the glow of the setting sun; evening glow

夕：夕字描绘出了一幅在薄暮之时跃升至地平线上的一轮下半部被青山遮挡住的弦月的景象。此字的延伸之意为薄暮、黄昏。对人类来说，月亮的升起意为机遇的到来。但正如谚语所说："机遇不可能从天而降。"

夕 is a picture of the crescent moon emerging on the horizon at dusk, its lower part obstructed by a mountain. Hence the extended meaning: dusk, evening. To man the rising moon presents opportunities but the proverb laments: "How seldom in life is the moon directly overhead!"

ノ 夕 夕
1 2 3

多

duō
many; much

多半	duō bàn	the greater part; most
多方面	duō fāng miàn	many-sided; in many ways
多民族	duō mín zú	multinational
多余	duō yú	unnecessary; superfluous

多：经过昼夜在田野中的辛勤劳作，人们终于在渡过一个又一个夜晚（夕）之后，收获了劳动的果实。代表许多夜晚的"多"字意为许多、很多。经过辛勤劳作后所收获的丰厚（多）的果实（果）产生出了一个新字，即"夥"。正如谚语所说："一分耕耘，一分收获。"

From morning to evening man toiled in the field, and evening (夕) after evening (夕) he noted the fruitage of his labour. "Many evenings" (多) soon came to mean "many". His hard work bore much (多) fruit (果), producing a new word: 夥 (fruitful) and demonstrating the principle: "Sow much, reap much; sow little, reap little."

ノ 夕 夕 夕 多 多
1 2 3 4 5 6

够 gòu
enough

够本	gòu běn	break even
够朋友	gòu péng you	be a friend indeed
够受的	gòu shòu de	quite an ordeal
够意思	gòu yì si	really something; terrific; generous; really kind

够："句"是由代表勾子的"勹"和"口"字（具有诱惑之意）组合而成。"多"意为很多、许多。所以，"够"字含有足够、充分之意。但并非事事如此，正如谚语所说："百年创业，毁于一旦。"

句 is to hook (勹) with the mouth (口) to entice; 多 means much many. 够 therefore signifies to entice many, i.e., enough. But enough is not always enough, according to the proverb: "To complete a thing a hundred years is not sufficient, to destroy it, a day is more than enough."

ノ	勹	勺	句	句	句	句	够	够	够	够		
1	2	3	4	5	6	7	8	9	10	11		

外 wài
outside

外币	wài bì	foreign currency
外边	wài bian	outside; out
外表	wài biǎo	outward appearance; exterior
外宾	wài bīn	foreign guest
外公	wài gōng	(maternal) grandfather

外：此字是由代表夜晚的"夕"和含有占卜之意的"卜"相组合而成。而占卜（卜）只有在天黑之前破解加热后的乌龟身上的纵横条纹才能奏效。由此，"外"还指代外边、外围之意。借助外界的帮助，许多人花起钱来十分慷慨。因为他们相信这句谚语："有钱能使鬼推磨。"

外 is composed of 夕 (evening) and 卜 (divine). Divination (卜) by interpreting the vertical (|) and horizontal (-) cracks of a heated tortoise-shell, was deemed effective only before (or outside of) evening. Hence 外: meaning outside or foreign. And for such outside or foreign help many will pay handsomely - those who place trust in the saying: "Much money moves the gods."

ノ	夕	夕	列	外				
1	2	3	4	5				

梦

mèng
dream

梦话	mèng huà	words uttered in one's sleep; somniloquy
梦幻	mèng huàn	illusion; dream; reverie
梦境	mèng jìng	dreamland; dreamworld; dream

梦：此字篆刻体的构成足以引起人们的恶梦。此字原先意为双眼（目）紧闭（冖）之后所梦见的可怕景象（首），即"莧"。因为人们常在夜间熟睡时做梦，所以"夕"字最终取代了"目"字，变为"莧"，最终定型为"梦"（意为夜间之树）。不幸的是："美好的梦想总是破灭得很快。"

The seal forms of dream are horrifying enough to evoke a nightmare. No wonder the original character 莧: means bad sight (首) with covered (冖) eyes (目). Dreams being evening visions, 夕 replaces 目 in the new form: 莧, now simplified to 梦 (evening trees) - a pleasant dream. Unfortunately, "A beautiful dream is soon ended."

一	十	才	木	朩	杧	材	林	栐	梦	梦						
1	2	3	4	5	6	7	8	9	10	11						

夜

yè
night

开夜车	kāi yè chē	work deep into the night; burn the midnight oil
夜班	yè bān	night shift
夜半	yè bàn	midnight
夜工	yè gōng	night job
夜盲	yè máng	night blindness

夜：此字的篆体为"夜"，意为人们（大）在夜间（夕）侧身而睡（丿）。经过演化，"夜"表示某人（亻）夜间（夕）在屋内（宀）侧身而睡（乀）。假如睡觉只指晚上的话，那么白天也可视为晚上，因为有人白天也睡觉。正如我们图中所示。

The seal character 夜 depicts man (大) sleeping on his side (丿) in the evening (夕). The modern form 夜 shows man (亻) under cover (宀) lying on his other side (乀) also in the evening (夕). If night can be suggested by sleep, as in both these forms, then day can be transformed into night, as demonstrated by our sleepy characters shown here.

丶	亠	广	疒	疒	夜	夜	夜									
1	2	3	4	5	6	7	8									

从 cóng
follow; from

从容	cóng róng	calm; unhurried; leisurely
从此	cóng cǐ	from this time on; henceforth
从简	cóng jiǎn	conform to the principle of simplicity

从："從"字代表两个人（从）的行走（彳）与止步（止）。在篆体中"彳"与"止"结合成为"辵"。而经过演变后的简体"从"则指代跟在某人之后的另一个人。跟着别人走十分简单。正如谚语所说："论事容易，做事难。"

從 represents two men (从) walking (彳) and stopping (止). In the seal form, 彳 and 止 are united into 辵 (going). The simplified form is 从 - a man following another man - a simple task, in view of the saying: "To know the truth is easy; but, ah, how difficult it is to follow it!"

| ノ | 人 | 丩 | 从 | | | | | | | | | | |
| 1 | 2 | 3 | 4 | | | | | | | | | | |

得 dé
get; obtain

得到	dé dào	get; obtain; gain; receive
得分	dé fēn	score
得奖	dé jiǎng	win or be awarded a prize
得胜	dé shèng	win a victory; triumph
得益	dé yì	benefit; profit

得：此字的形旁"彳"指代的是步伐，声旁是"寻"，意为伸手（寸）去抓已经映入眼帘（见或㫃）的物品，含有索取之意。但获得财物并非一件容易之事，正如谚语所说："赚钱如同土中挑针，而花钱则如清水冲沙。"

彳, the radical, means step. The phonetic 寻 to lay hands (寸) on what one has in view (见 or 㫃) - signifies to obtain. However, laying hands on money not easy: "Money comes like earth picked up with a pin, but goes like sand washed away by water."

| ノ | ク | 彳 | 彳 | 彳 | 得 | 得 | 得 | 得 | 得 | 得 | | | |
| 1 | 2 | 3 | 4 | 5 | 6 | 7 | 8 | 9 | 10 | 11 | | | |

德 dé

virtue; goodness

德国	Dé Guó	Germany
德行	dé xíng	moral integrity; moral conduct
德育	dé yù	moral education
品德	pǐn dé	moral character

德："直"意为经过十只（十）眼睛（目）检测过的垂直物体（一）。而"心"则指心脏。所以，声旁"悳"中含有心直口快之意，形旁"彳"象征着通向美德的大门。因此，一个人的道德如何还要依据他的实际行动来判定。正如谚语所说："说得好不如做得好。"

直 means straight (一) as tested by ten (十) eyes (目). 心 is the heart. So the phonetic 悳 denotes a straight heart. Clarified by the radical for step (彳) to mean the way to virtue or goodness, 德 is defined by the saying: "To talk good is not being good; to do good, that is being good."

| ノ | ク | 彳 | 彳 | 彳 | 彳 | 徍 | 徝 | 徲 | 德 | 德 | 德 | 德 | 德 |
| 1 | 2 | 3 | 4 | 5 | 6 | 7 | 8 | 9 | 10 | 11 | 12 | 13 | 14 | 15 |

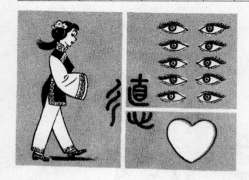

律 lǜ

law; rule; discipline

| 律吕 | lǜ lǚ | bamboo pitch-pitch-pipes used in ancient china; temperament |
| 律师 | lǜ shī | lawyer; barrister; solicitor |

律：声旁"聿"指代的是书写的规则，象征着手握（彐）一支笔（丨）在牌匾上进行书写（一）。形旁"彳"意为使用某些法律程序来保护市民。但"为了某些事而诉诸于法律是得不偿失的。"

The phonetic 聿 signifies written regulations - hand (彐) with pen (丨) writing lines (一) on tablet (一). The radical 彳 (step) suggests steps taken to enforce them as law to protect the citizens. However, "Going to the law is losing a cow for the sake of a cat."

| ノ | ク | 彳 | 彳 | 彳 | 彳 | 律 | 律 | 律 |
| 1 | 2 | 3 | 4 | 5 | 6 | 7 | 8 | 9 |

待 dài

treat; deal with

待命	dài mìng	await orders
待续	dài xù	to be continued
待遇	dài yù	treatment; remuneration

待: 此字的右半部分"寺"指代的是法律法规（寸），可以像生长的植物（彳）一样不断生效的地方。形旁"彳"意指对他人要以诚相待。但如果要做到："人人为我，我为人人"，还需要一定耐心并加之自身的不断努力。

寺 is a court where the law or rule (寸) is applied continually, like the growth of a plant (彳). The radical 彳 indicates the step or way to treat others with propriety, requiring patience and application of the golden rule: "Do to others as you would have them do to you."

ノ	ク	彳	彳	衤	往	往	待	待
1	2	3	4	5	6	7	8	9

功 gōng

merit; achievement

功德	gōng dé	merits and virtues
功课	gōng kè	schoolwork; homework
功劳	gōng láo	contribution; meritorious service; credit
功能	gōng néng	function

功: 此字是由代表肌肉的"力"字与代表工匠所使用的丁字尺的"工"结合而成。在工作中尽之全力，而获得成就，即为"功"。另一方面在工作中出力少，即为"劣"，意为糟糕的或低级的。

Strength (力) is here symbolised by muscles, and work (工) by a carpenter's square. Strength exerted in work produces 功 - merit or achievement. On the other hand, little (少) strength (力) results in 劣, meaning bad or inferior.

一	T	工	巧	功				
1	2	3	4	5				

加

jiā
add;
increase

加班	jiā bān	work overtime
加倍	jiā bèi	double; redouble
加法	jiā fǎ	addition
加害	jiā hài	injure; do harm to
加紧	jiā jǐn	step up; speed up; intensify
加宽	jiā kuān	broaden; widen

加：此字为表意文字，意为增加或增长。将“力”与“口”相结合，意为在劝说过程中动用武力，但在劝说过程中动用武力永远也不会被人们所赞同。虽然强权永远也不可能成为公理，但公理却总是强有力的。

This ideograph means to add to or increase. It adds strength (力) to mouth (口) by applying force to words. Adding violence to persuasion cannot always be justified. Although might is never right, right is always might.

㇇	力	力	加	加
1	2	3	4	5

协

xié
together
co-operate

协定	xié dìng	agreement; accord
协会	xié huì	association; society
协力	xié lì	unite efforts; join in a common effort
协商	xié shāng	consult; talk things over

协：三股力量合在一起（劦）象征在一个团体中十个人（十）的力量，意为共同合作，即“協”。在工作中，如果缺少了协作，就会出现失误。正如谚语所说：“缺少协作，两人喂马马必瘦，两个补船船必漏。”

Triple-strength (劦) signifying the multiple efforts of ten (十) persons in unity, indicates wholehearted cooperation: 協. Without cooperation, shared responsibility leads to neglect. "If two men feed a horse, it will be thin, if two men mend a boat, it will leak."

一	十	协	协	协	协
1	2	3	4	5	6

劳 láo
work; labour

劳动	láo dòng	work; labour
劳工	láo gōng	labourer; worker
劳累	láo lèi	tired; run down
劳力	láo lì	labour force
劳碌	láo lù	work hard; toil

劳：此字象征着借助灯光（炏）在屋内（冖）辛勤地工作（力），即"劳"。但过分地耗费精力是徒劳无益的，就像水中捞月或磨砖为镜一样。

劳 is to toil (力) indoors (冖) by the light of many fires (炏). Burning the midnight oil or the candle at both ends is a waste of effort. "It is labour lost, trying to catch the moon in the water or polishing brick to make a mirror."

一	十	艹	艹	芦	劳	劳						
1	2	3	4	5	6	7						

光 guāng
light; glory

光彩	guāng cǎi	lustre; splendour; radiance; honourable; glorious
光辐射	guāng fú shè	ray radiation
光顾	guāng gù	patronize
光辉	guāng huī	radiance; brilliance

光：原先的"炗"字是由代表二十的"廿"与代表火焰的"火"字组合而成，意为二十团火焰。经过演变成为"灶"，意为手持火炬（火）的一个人（儿）。不论此字的形式如何，"光"意味着光明和荣耀。但这种光明和荣耀是不能持续很久的，正如谚语所说："明亮的黎明并不总能代表晴朗的一天。"

The ancient form 炗 means twenty (廿) fires (火). The modern form 灶 portrays a man (儿) bearing a torch (火). Whatever the form, 光 means brightness and glory which, unfortunately, never lasts. Hence: "A bright dawn does not always make a fine day."

丨	丷	业	业	屶	光							
1	2	3	4	5	6							

159

先

xiān
first;
before

先辈	xiān bèi	elder generation; ancestors
先导	xiān dǎo	guide; forerunner
先后	xiān hòu	early or late; priority one after another
先进	xiān jìn	advanced
先生	xiān sheng	teacher; mister

先：此字的上半部分"屮"意为从地面上（一）生长出来的植物（屮），意为生长。下半部分则代表行进中的双腿。从字面上来解释，"先"意为依靠人的双脚（儿）前进（屮），争夺第一。而与人打交道时切记要做到"先礼后兵"。

The top part 屮 is a small plant (屮) issuing from the ground (一); thus indicating progress. The lower part is a picture of marching legs. Accordingly, 先 means to advance 屮 on one's feet (儿) - to be first. And to progress with people, remember: "Courtesy first, force later" (先礼后兵).

| 丿 | 一 | 屮 | 生 | 步 | 先 | | | | | | | | |
| 1 | 2 | 3 | 4 | 5 | 6 | | | | | | | | |

洗

xǐ
wash;
bathe

洗尘	xǐ chén	give a dinner of welcome (to a visitor from afar)
洗涤	xǐ dí	wash; cleanse
洗发剂	xǐ fà jì	shampoo
洗劫	xǐ jié	loot; sack
洗澡	xǐ zǎo	have a bath; bathe

洗：此字将代表形旁的"氵"与代表声旁的"先"字组合而成，意为要想清洁或梳洗必须第一（先）需要水（氵）。那么什么东西最先应该被清洗呢？正如谚语所说："净化的心灵，如同日常清洗碗碟一样重要。"

The radical is 氵 (water) and the phonetic 先 (first). This suggests that you must have water (氵) first (先) to wash or clean: 洗. And what needs to be cleansed first? According to the proverbial exhortation: "Cleanse your heart as you would cleanse a dish."

| 丶 | 冫 | 氵 | 氵 | 汇 | 汁 | 沣 | 浐 | 洗 | | | | | |
| 1 | 2 | 3 | 4 | 5 | 6 | 7 | 8 | 9 | | | | | |

海

hǎi
sea;
ocean

海岸	hǎi àn	coast; seashore
海豹	hǎi bào	seal
海滨	hǎi bīn	seaside
海产	hǎi chǎn	marine products
海盗	hǎi dào	pirate; sea rover
海港	hǎi gǎng	seaport; harbour
海军	hǎi jūn	navy

海："每"字指代的是一位正在哺乳孩子的妇女。"每"字是由代表母亲的"母"字与代表发芽的"⺊"组合而成，意为经常不断地重生。"海"指代的是大海，意为总是（每）拥有大量水资源的地方（氵）。

母 is a picture of a woman with breasts for suckling a child, signifying mother (母).
每 compares a mother (母) with a sprout (⺊) always reproducing; hence meaning every, always.
海 represents the sea, where there is always (每) plenty of water (氵).

丶	冫	氵	氵	汇	汇	海	海	海	海				
1	2	3	4	5	6	7	8	9	10				

林

lín
forest

艺林	yì lín	art circles
竹林	zhú lín	bamboo grove
林产品	lín chǎn pǐn	forest products
林带	lín dài	forest belt
林立	lín lì	stand in great numbers (like trees in a forest)
林木	lín mù	forest; woods

林：按照谚语所说："无丝不成线，无树不成林"。代表树的"木"字为象形字。两个"木"字意为树丛或树林。三个"木"字组合在一起，即为"森"，指代的是茂密生长的树林。

"A single fibre does not make a thread; a single tree does not make a forest," so goes the saying. The character for tree is a pictograph: 木. Two trees form a company - a grove or forest: 林. Three trees make a crowd, signifying dense or overgrown: 森.

一	十	才	木	朩	朳	材	林						
1	2	3	4	5	6	7	8						

枝
zhī
branch

枝杈	zhī chà	branch; twig
枝接	zhī jiē	scion grafting
枝叶	zhī yè	branches and leaves; non-essentials
枝子	zhī zi	branch; twig

枝: 此字是由代表树木的 "木" 字与代表树叉的 "支" 字组合而成。"支" 指代的是右手 (又) 握着的一个树枝 (十), 意为分枝。又因为树叉是构成树木的一部分, 所以正可谓是 "一枝晃动, 百枝齐摇"。"枯" 字意为枯萎, 指代的是一棵经历过十代人 (口) 的古树。

枝 is a branch (支) of a tree (木). 支 itself is a picture of the right hand (又) holding a twig (十) and means branch. Because branches form an integral part of a tree, "One branch moves, a hundred branches shake." 枯 means withered, like an old (古) tree (木) - one that has passed through ten (十) generations or mouths (口).

一	十	才	木	𣎴	朾	朾	枝								
1	2	3	4	5	6	7	8								

病
bìng
painting; drawing

流行病	liú xíng bìng	epidemic disease
心脏病	xīn zàng bìng	heart trouble; heart disease
病倒	bìng dǎo	be down with an illness; be laid up
病假	bìng jià	sick leave
病态	bìng tài	morbid state

病: 此字的形旁为 "疒" (疒), 指代的是躺在床上 (爿) 的一个病人 (一)。声旁 "丙" (疒) 指代房中 (宀) 的火 (火), 即发高烧。"病" 字还含有缺点与错误之意。正如谚语所说: "再聪明的医生也不会为自己治病。"

The radical for disease 疒 (疒) is made up of a horizontal line (一) - the position of a sick person - and the bed (爿). The idea of sickness is reinforced by the phonetic 丙 (疒) - fire (火) in the house (宀), referring to high fever. 病 also means defect or fault, and it is said: "A wise doctor never treats himself."

丶	亠	广	疒	疒	疒	疒	病	病	病						
1	2	3	4	5	6	7	8	9	10						

疼

téng
pain;
ache

疼爱	téng ài	be very fond of
疼痛	téng tòng	pain; ache; soreness

疼:"冬"字与代表疾病的形旁"疒"结合后,含有疼痛之意。当然,老年人与年轻人对"疼"的看法不一样。年轻人认为:缺少了欢乐就是痛苦。而老年人则认为:没有痛苦就是幸福。

Just as fire or fever suggests sickness, winter (冬) or intense cold is here combined with the radical for sickness (疒) to signify pain: 疼. However, young and old do not feel pain alike. In youth, the absence of pleasure is pain; in old age, the absence of pain is pleasure.

1 丶	2 宀	3 广	4 疒	5 疒	6 疒	7 疗	8 疚	9 疼	10 疼							

疾

jí
disease;
ailment

眼疾	yǎn jí	eye trouble
疾病	jí bìng	disease; illness
疾风	jí fēng	strong wind; gale
疾苦	jí kǔ	sufferings; hardship

疾:疾病的降临尤如突然射出的利箭一样,出乎人们的意料。因此"疾"含有疾病的意思。此字是由代表疾病的形旁"疒"和代表箭字的"矢"组合而成。正如谚语所说:"病从口入,祸从口出。"

Disease strikes suddenly and unexpectedly like an arrow. Hence 疾, meaning disease, made up of the radical for sickness (疒) and arrow (矢). According to the proverb: "Diseases enter by the mouth; misfortunes issue from it."

1 丶	2 宀	3 广	4 疒	5 疒	6 疒	7 疒	8 疟	9 疾	10 疾						

163

道 dào
way; path

道德	dào dé	morals; morality; ethics
道贺	dào hè	congratulate
道教	Dào Jiào	Taoism
道具	dào jù	stage property; prop

道："首"是一个象形文字，代表了人类长有头发（首）的脑袋，意为头脑或首领。将"首"与"辶"相结合后，产生出了"道"，意为通向美德之路。将代表头脑的"首"字与代表足部的"辶"相结合，意为在同一条路上行进。同时，道教也是源于中国本身的一种宗教。有一句谚语说："信道容易，得道难。"

首 is a pictograph of a hairy (首) head (辶) and means head or chief. Combined with 辶 or 辵 (go), it produces 道 - the way of virtue. Head (首) and feet (辶) advancing on the same path symbolises the Tao (道) of which it is said: "To believe in the Tao is easy; to keep the Tao is difficult."

丶	丷	丷	丷	产	首	首	首	首	道	道	道
1	2	3	4	5	6	7	8	9	10	11	12

面 miàn
face

面对	miàn duì	face; confront
面对面	miàn duì miàn	facing each other; face-to-face
面粉	miàn fěn	wheat flour; flour
面积	miàn jī	area
面颊	miàn jiá	cheek

面：形旁"口"指代的是人脸的轮廓，而"百"说明眼睛是人类身体中最突出的部分。在与人打交道时，我们往往会注重人的外表而不是心灵。但无论何时，"我们都不应该当面一套，背后一套。"

This radical incorporates 口, an outline of the face, with 百 (head) featuring the eyes (目) as its most prominent part. Because a person is identified by his face, we know a man's face, not his mind. Nevertheless, "Be able to say in his face what you say behind his back."

一	一	丆	丂	而	而	而	面	面		
1	2	3	4	5	6	7	8	9		

瞎 xiā
blind

瞎扯	xiā chě	talk irresponsibly; talk rubbish
瞎话	xiā huà	untruth; lie
瞎闹	xiā nào	act senselessly; mess about; fool around; be mischievous

瞎: 此字意为受伤的（害）眼睛（目）。声旁"害"代表在遮盖物下（宀）由刻有痕迹（三）的木棍或言语（口）所造成的伤害。另一个表示"瞎"的表意文字为"盲"，意为失去（亡）的双眼（目）。尽管聋哑人与盲人身有残疾，但"盲人的听觉十分灵敏，而聋人的眼睛非常敏锐。"

瞎 stands for injured (害) eyes (目). The phonetic 害 (harm) represents injury from a stick (|) with notches (三) or injury by mouth (口) under cover (宀). Another ideograph for blind is 盲 or lost (亡) eyes (目). Despite their handicap, "The blind are quick at hearing; the deaf are quick at sight."

丨	冂	冂	月	目	目`	目̀	盰	盰	盰	睅	瞎	瞎	瞎	瞎
1	2	3	4	5	6	7	8	9	10	11	12	13	14	15

睡 shuì
sleep

睡觉	shuì jiào	sleep
睡莲	shuì lián	water lily
睡梦	shuì mèng	sleep; slumber
睡眠	shuì mián	sleep
睡醒	shuì xǐng	wake up
睡衣	shuì yī	night clothes; pyjamas

睡: 此字指代的是垂下（垂）的眼皮（目），意为睡觉。声旁"垂"或"坴"意指长满树叶的树枝垂向地面（土）。但有时紧闭双眼睡觉也并非安全，正如谚语所说："伴君如伴虎。"

睡 is to have the eyes or eyelids (目) hanging down (垂) - to sleep. The phonetic 垂 or 坴 depicts a bough loaded with leaves (㣺) hanging down towards the earth (土). Sleep, even if your eyes are closed, is not always a peaceful affair. According to the saying, "Attending to the Emperor is like sleeping with a tiger."

丨	冂	冂	月	目	目́	目̃	盰	睡	睡	睡	睡	睡
1	2	3	4	5	6	7	8	9	10	11	12	13

胃

wèi
stomach

胃病	wèi bìng	stomach trouble; gastric disease
胃口	wèi kǒu	appetite; liking
胃溃疡	wèi kuì yáng	gastric ulcer
胃酸	wèi suān	hydrochloric acid in gastric juice
胃痛	wèi tòng	gastralgia
胃液	wèi yè	gastric juice

胃：此表意文字是由两个象形文字所组成。上半部分的"⊗"代表装满大米的小包，下半部分"⅁"则代表一块肉。由此得来了"胃"字，意为装有大米的肉口袋。虽然吃饱之后便可高枕无忧，但正如谚语所说："宁可饥肠辘，不要饱与贪。"

This ideograph combines two pictographs. The upper one is pouch filled with rice: ⊗ ; the lower, a piece of flesh: ⅁. Hence, stomach - a fleshy pouch filled with rice. Although a full stomach begets a contented mind "Better be hungry and pure than well-filled and corrupt."

丨 冂 冃 冊 田 甲 胃 胃 胃

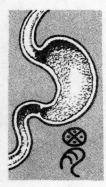

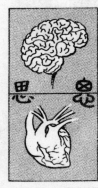

思

sī
think

| 思潮 | sī cháo | trend of thought; ideological trend; thoughts |
| 思考 | sī kǎo | think deeply; ponder over; reflect on |

思：象形文字的"⊗"是由代表脑壳的"⊗"与代表心脏的"心"组合而成。推理与感知的能力结合在一起，代表一种平衡的心态。有句俗话说："闻其言，明其思。"

This ideograph combines the skull (⊗) with the heart (心) to produce thought: ⊗. The faculties of reasoning and feeling are here exercised to create a balanced mind. And, according to the saying, "If you wish to know the mind of a man, listen to his words."

丨 冂 日 用 田 田 思 思 思

情 qíng
feeling; affection

情报	qíng bào	intelligence; information
情操	qíng cāo	sentiment
情敌	qíng dí	rival in love
情调	qíng diào	sentiment; emotional appeal
情感	qíng gǎn	emotion; feeling

情："青"字代表绿色。"丹"表示自然的颜色，"生"表示生长的植物，与代表心脏的形旁"忄"相结合后，意指对人产生出的一种纯真自然的情感，即"情"。人们有时会为没有深厚的感情而感到痛苦。有句话说："人情薄如纸。"

青 is green - the colour (丹) of nature and growing plants (生). With the addition of the radical for heart (忄) the character stands for those feelings which are pure or natural to the heart of man: 情. Lamenting the lack of depth and substance in such feelings, the saying goes: "Human feelings are as thin as sheets of paper."

`	八	忄	忄一	忄二	忄主	忄青	情	情	情	情
1	2	3	4	5	6	7	8	9	10	11

放 fàng
release

放出	fàng chū	give out; let out; emit
放大	fàng dà	enlarge; magnify; amplify
放胆	fàng dǎn	act boldly and with confidence
放荡	fàng dàng	dissolute; dissipated

放：此字意为释放、解放，是把"攵"赶进牧场或一块开阔的空间。形旁"攵"（攵）代表手握小棍的手，声旁"方"指代的是方形场地或一块开阔的空间。马匹或牛群总是在吃草时被放出去，吃完后就赶回来。然而："君子一言，驷马难追。"

放 means to release - to drive out 攵 into an open space or pasture (方). The radical 攵 (攵) is a hand with stick; the phonetic 方 is a square or open space. Horses or cattle released for grazing can always be rounded up, but "Words once released cannot be recaptured by the swiftest steeds."

`	二	方	方	方	放	放	放		
1	2	3	4	5	6	7	8		

政

zhèng
government

政变　zhèng biàn　coup d'etat
政策　zhèng cè　policy
政党　zhèng dǎng　political party
政敌　zhèng dí　political opponent
政法　zhèng fǎ　politics and law
政府　zhèng fǔ　government
政客　zhèng kè　politician

政：形旁"攵"代表右手紧握象征权利的木棍，声旁"正"指代的是一只脚（止）走在笔直的路上（一）。由此可以看出，"政"强调一种正规的行政机构，即政府。

The radical 攵 represents the right hand wielding the rod of authority. The phonetic 正 signifies a foot (止) walking the straight way (一). Hence 政 which means government, an upright (正) administration (攵) - an enforcement for good.

| 一 | 丁 | 下 | 疋 | 正 | 正 | 正 | 政 | 政 | | | | | | | |
|1|2|3|4|5|6|7|8|9|

叫

jiào
call

叫喊　jiào hǎn　shout; yell; howl
叫好　jiào hǎo　applaud
叫唤　jiào huàn　cry out; call out
叫苦　jiào kǔ　complain of hardship or suffering; moan and groan

叫：此字的原形"吶"是由代表大声呼喊的"口"字与代表计量工具的"斗"字组成。古时候，此字由一个勺子（勹）和十（十）字组成，即"斗"。小贩们对自己的货品赞不绝口，真可谓是"老王卖瓜，自卖自夸。"

叫 is to call out (口) the measure (斗). The ancient form of 斗 depicts a measuring ladle (勹) with ten (十): 斗 .Although vendors shout out their wares, a melon seller never cries "Bitter melons!" nor a wine seller "Thin wine!"

| 丨 | 𠮛 | 口 | 叫 | 叫 | | | | | | | | | | | |
|1|2|3|4|5|

听 tīng
hear; listen

听从	tīng cóng	obey; heed; comply with
听话	tīng huà	be obedient
听觉	tīng jué	sense of hearing
听说	tīng shuō	be told; hear of
听写	tīng xiě	dictation
听众	tīng zhòng	audience; listeners

听:"直"代表纠正（鱼或壬）一位听者心中（心）所想，或者是某人耳朵（耳）的信徒（壬），意为遵从或听从。经过简化后的"听"字是由"口"字与"斤"字相结合而成的，意为用耳朵听懂别人所说的话。但现实中的许多人都对别人的劝诫充耳不闻。

直 is the rectification (鱼 or 壬) of the heart (心) of a listener or disciple (壬) by his ear (耳), hence to listen or obey. The simplified form 听 combines 口 (mouth) with 斤 (discerning), i.e., to discern what comes from the mouth by listening. It may even suggest that most people today listen with their mouths!

丨	口	口	吁	听	听	听						
1	2	3	4	5	6	7						

聋 lóng
deaf

聋哑	lóng yǎ	deaf and dumb; deaf-mute
聋子	lóng zi	a deaf person

聋：因为龙是兽之王（其它的依次为：独角兽、凤凰、乌龟），所以它可以对任何事情都采取充耳不闻的态度，由此得来"聋"字。听觉不好的不必太失望，因为有一句俗话说："在聋人的世界里，有一只耳朵的人就是国王了。"

Because the dragon is king of the supernatural creatures (the others being the unicorn, the phoenix and the tortoise), it can afford to turn a deaf ear to anything. Hence dragon's 龙 ear (耳) meaning deaf: 聋. But let not those who cannot hear well lose heart: "In the kingdom of the deaf, the one-eared man is king!"

一	广	尤	龙	龙	龙	龚	斉	斉	聋	聋		
1	2	3	4	5	6	7	8	9	10	11		

喜

xǐ

happiness;
pleasure

喜爱	xǐ ài	like; love; be fond of; be keen on
喜欢	xǐ huān	like; love; happy; elated; filled with joy
喜酒	xǐ jiǔ	wedding feast
喜剧	xǐ jù	comedy

喜: 此字是由代表歌唱的"口"字与代表音乐的"壴"结合而成。"壴"在古代指代的是放在架子上 (豆) 鼓面展开 (一) 的鼓, 一人用右手 (屮) 在敲鼓。"口"则代表一张正在歌唱中的嘴。要记住, 无私的奉献就是幸福。当你使两个人快活时, 其中一个可能就是你自己。

喜 or happiness is expressed by 壴 (music) and 口 (singing). 壴 depicts the ancient drum on its stand (豆) with its stretched skin (一) and a straightened right hand (屮) striking it. 口 represents the mouth singing. True happiness, however, comes from unselfish giving; and when you make two people happy, one of them is probably you.

一	十	士	吉	吉	吉	壴	壴	壴	喜	喜	喜				
1	2	3	4	5	6	7	8	9	10	11	12				

春

chūn

spring

春光	chūn guāng	sights and sounds of spring
春季	chūn jì	spring; springtime
春卷	chūn juǎn	spring roll
春天	chūn tiān	spring; springtime

春: 此字的篆体为 "𣊫", 指代的是在阳光照耀下 (日) 植物的萌芽 (屮) 与生长。而春天是一个气候多变的季节, 就同它每年到来的时间也是不固定的一样。这一点正像谚语所说: "春天就像继母的脸一样多变。"

𣊫 the seal character for spring (春) signifies the growth and outburst (屮) of vegetation (屮) under the influence of the sun (日). As unpredictable and changeable as the weather, spring comes either early or late each year. Hence the proverb: "Spring has a stepmother's face."

一	二	三	声	夫	表	春	春	春						
1	2	3	4	5	6	7	8	9						

唱

chàng
sing

唱词	chàng cí	libretto; words of a ballad
唱歌	chàng gē	sing (a song)
唱工	chàng gōng	art of singing; singing
唱片	chàng piàn	gramophone record

唱："昌"是由代表太阳的"日"与代表言语的"口"字组合而成，延伸之意为喘息。同时，"昌"字还具有繁荣昌盛之意，就如太阳发光，嘴巴吐字一样。"唱"意为从嘴中唱出的优美的声音，它比日常的说话要动听。

昌 is composed of 日 (sun) and 曰 (speak). 曰 is the mouth (口) that exhales a breath; by extension, exhalation and emanation. So 昌 means prosperous or splendid, just as the sun sends forth rays and the mouth puts forth words.

唱 therefore refers to singing which produces a more refined quality of the voice than an ordinary conversation.

㇑	ㅁ	口	叮	叩	吅	唱	唱	唱	唱	唱
1	2	3	4	5	6	7	8	9	10	11

歌

gē
song

歌本	gē běn	song book
歌词	gē cí	words of a song
歌喉	gē hóu	(singer's) voice
歌剧	gē jù	opera
歌谱	gē pǔ	music of a song

歌："可"字指代的是从嘴里（口）发出赞许（丁）的欢呼声，意为可能或可以。"哥"字是由两个"可"字组成，原来指代歌唱，现在用来称呼兄长。"歌"是将代表气息的"欠"字与代表歌唱的"哥"字组合而成。

可 is an exclamation of approval (丁) from the mouth (口) and means can or may.

哥 is 可 doubled, suggesting singing, now used for addressing elder brother by sound loan.

歌 adds breath (欠) to singing (哥) to produce a song.

一	㇕	一	可	可	可	哥	哥	哥	哥	歌	歌	歌	歌
1	2	3	4	5	6	7	8	9	10	11	12	13	14

如

rú
like;
as

如常	rú cháng	as usual
如此	rú cǐ	so; such; in this way
如果	rú guǒ	if; in case; in the event of
如何	rú hé	how; what
如今	rú jīn	nowadays; now

如：此字为表意文字，由"女"与"口"组成，表示像女人般地说话。女人常常用语言影响和左右男人，正如俗话所说："男人所创下的事业，往往毁在女人的手中。"

Ideographically, 如 is to speak (口) like or as a woman (女) that is, appropriately to the circumstances and the disposition of the man she desires to influence. Testifying to such persuasive, womanly skill is the saying: "The walls of a city are raised by men's wisdom but overthrown by women's wiles."

1	2	3	4	5	6
ㄑ	夕	女	如	如	如

客

kè
guest;
visitor

客船	kè chuán	passenger ship
客串	kè chuàn	be a guest performer
客队	kè duì	(sports) visiting team
客房	kè fáng	guest room
客观	kè guān	objective

客："夊"代表正在走路的行人。"各"代表不听劝诫（口）而继续赶路（夊），延伸之意指代个体。"客"意为客人，是在别人屋内（宀）进行休息的人。毫无疑问，当客人离开的时候，最高兴的恐怕还是主人。

夊 represents a man following his own way. 各 signifies his going his way (夊) without heeding advice (口); by extension, each or every.
客 is a guest - one who has his way under another's roof (宀). No wonder the saying goes: "The host is happy when the guest is gone."

1	2	3	4	5	6	7	8	9
丶	宀	宀	宀	歺	安	客	客	客

比 bǐ
compare

比方	bǐ fang	analogy; instance
比分	bǐ fēn	score
比价	bǐ jià	price relations; parity; rate of exchange
比率	bǐ lǜ	ratio; rate
比赛	bǐ sài	match; competition

比：此字的篆刻体显示出此字是"从"字的颠倒体。它指代的是站在一起，互比身高的两个人。正如谚语所说："比上不足，比下有余。"

The seal form of 比 reveals this character as an inverted form of 从 (follow). It represents two men standing as if to compare heights. "When compared with those above," so goes the saying, "there is something lacking; but compared with those below, there is something to spare."

一	上	上	比									
1	2	3	4									

从比

北

背 背

背 bèi
back; oppose
carry on the back

背痛	bèi tòng	backache
背地里	bèi dì li	behind somebody's back; privately; on the sly
背后	bèi hòu	behind; at the back; in the car
背脊	bèi jǐ	the back of the human body

背：一个人面朝南，与另一个人背靠背而坐就是"北"字。"背"字指代某人转身背向另一个人，意指相反。所以"背"字由"北"与"月"组成。此字还具有反抗、反对及身肩背扛之意。

A person sitting facing the south (as is the custom) and back to back with another suggests north: 北. Turning one's back on another signifies opposition. Hence 背, referring to the back (北) of the body (月), may mean to oppose or to carry on the back.

ィ	┤	┤	北	北	北	背	背	背				
1	2	3	4	5	6	7	8	9				

凶

xiōng
unfortunate;
ominous

凶残	xiōng cán	fierce and cruel; savage and cruel
凶恶	xiōng è	fierce, ferocious; fiendish
凶猛	xiōng měng	violent; ferocious
凶杀	xiōng shā	homicide; murder

凶：此字意为倒霉、晦气，指代的是不幸落入（乂）坑中（凵）的人。然而，灾难并不是伴随着某些事故而到来的。正如谚语所说："祸从口出。"

凶 means unfortunate, symbolised by a man falling upside down (乂) into a pit (凵). Calamities do not always come by accident. According to the proverb, "Calamity comes by means of the mouth."

ノ	乂	凶	凶								
1	2	3	4								

答

dá
reply;
answer

答案	dá àn	answer; solution; key
答辩	dá biàn	reply (to a charge, query or an argument)
答复	dá fù	answer; reply

答：美丽的竹子（竹）含有合谐（合）之意，在此表示答案或答复之意。然而，所给出的答案总是不相同的，如同竹子的长度是长短不一的一样。也正像很多人总爱用啰嗦的语言来回答很简明的问题一样。

Because of its beauty, design and harmony (合) the bamboo (竹) is used here as a perfect example of an answer or reply: 答 . However, like bamboos, answers come in various lengths. Many a short question is evaded by a long answer.

ノ	𠂉	𠂇	𠂊	竹	竹	竺	笂	答	答	答	答
1	2	3	4	5	6	7	8	9	10	11	12

篮 lán
basket

投篮	tóu lán	(basketball) shoot a basket
篮球	lán qiú	basketball
篮圈	lán quān	(basketball) ring; hoop
篮子	lán zi	basket

篮："血"指代的是在一个装满物品的瓶子（血）前弯下身来（卧），看看里边有些什么。延伸之意为监督被囚禁在狱中的犯人。加上形旁"竹"字后，意为可以携带物品的竹制容器，即"篮"。

卧 is to bend over (卧) a full vase (血) to examine its contents; by extension, to oversee those who are confined in a prison. When the bamboo radical 竹 is added, we have a bamboo container to confine goods for safe transportation - a basket: 籃 now simplified to 篮.

ノ	⺮	⺮	⺮	竺	竺	竿	笁	笁	笁	篮	篮	篮	篮	篮	篮
1	2	3	4	5	6	7	8	9	10	11	12	13	14	15	16

井 jǐng
well

矿井	kuàng jǐng	pit; mine
油井	yóu jǐng	oil well; neat; orderly
井场	jǐng cháng	well site
井架	jǐng jià	derrick

井：此字的篆体"井"意为由八户人家共享的土地，中间有一口公用水井。"井"字同时也揭示出人们爱挑剔的毛病。例如：如人们打水时常常埋怨井的深度，而不是绳子的长度。

Originally the seal form 井 represented fields divided among eight families, with the well in the middle plot to serve the public. The well also serves to expose man's inclination to faultfinding: "One does not blame the shortness of the rope, but the deepness of the well."

一	二	亍	井						
1	2	3	4						

石 shí
stone

石斑鱼	shí bān yú	grouper
石壁	shí bì	cliff; precipice
石雕	shí diāo	stone carving; carved stone
石膏	shí gāo	gypsum; plaster stone

石：此字指代的是悬崖（厂）上掉落下来的一块岩石（口）。"岩"字指代的是像小山（山）一样险峻的岩石（石）或悬崖。由于岩石十分坚硬，所以也指代完整及完善。有一句谚语说："人正不怕影斜，水落才能石出。"

石 is a picture of a piece of stone or rock (口) falling from a cliff (厂).
岩 is a steep rock (石) or cliff that looks like a hill (山). The rock, being strong, symbolises integrity. Hence: "Slander cannot destroy an honest man; when the flood recedes the rock appears."

一	丆	不	石	石								
1	2	3	4	5								

仙 xiān
fairy; recluse

仙丹	xiān dān	elixir of life
仙姑	xiān gū	female immortal; sorceress
仙鹤	xiān hè	red-crowned crane
仙境	xiān jìng	fairyland; wonderland; paradise
仙人掌	xiān rén zhǎng	cactus

仙：此字的原形为"僊"，指代的是一个人（人）开动脑筋（囟）运用四肢（舁）向上爬升。代表官印的"卪"意指晋升。经过演变后的"仙"字由代表人类的"亻"与"山"字结合而成，意为隐士或仙人。

The ancient form 僊 signifies a human (人) who rises by climbing with his head (囟) and four hands (舁) probably after the manner of a monkey. An official seal (卪) is added to denote promotion. The modern form 仙 associates person (亻) with mountain (山), suggesting recluse and fairy.

丿	亻	仈	仙	仙								
1	2	3	4	5								

高 gāo
high; tall

高傲	gāo ào	supercilious; arrogant
高潮	gāo cháo	high tide; upsurge; climax
高大	gāo dà	tall and big; tall
高度	gāo dù	altitude; height
高贵	gāo guì	noble; high; elitist

高: 此字为象形字，一座高塔（冂）座落在高出地面的地基上（冂），并有一个大厅（口）。此字具有高耸之意。当涉及到地位问题时，人人都想向高处爬升。但人们应牢记："爬得越高，摔得越狠。"

高 is a pictograph of a high tower or pavilion 冂 on a lofty sub-structure(冂) equipped with a hall (口). It stands for high. When it comes to position, no person stoops so low as the one most eager to rise high in the world. But beware: "He who climbs too high will have a heavy fall."

丶	亠	亠	亠	古	户	高	高	高	高					
1	2	3	4	5	6	7	8	9	10					

京 jīng
capital city

京城	jīng chéng	the capital of a country
京剧	jīng jù	Beijing opera

京: 此字是由"高"字演变而来的，代表支点的"亅"字取代了"高"字的下半部分。"亅"表示一个小支点，用来传达中央的指示。所以，"京"有一国之都的意思。正如谚语所说："能言之人谈国事，寡言之人谈家事。"

京 is derived from 高 (high). It is a contraction of 高 with the lower part replaced by 亅, a pivot, conveying the idea of loftiness and centrality. So lofty is the capital city that it is said: "One who can speak, speaks of the city; one who cannot, talks merely of household affairs."

丶	亠	亠	亠	古	宁	京	京							
1	2	3	4	5	6	7	8							

空 kōng

empty
spare time

空洞	kōng dòng	cavity; empty
空防	kōng fáng	air defence
空话	kōng huà	empty talk; idle talk
空欢喜	kōng huān xǐ	rejoice too soon
空间	kōng jiān	space
空军	kōng jūn	air force

空：此字的部首为"穴"。而洞穴是靠挖掘（八）岩石或泥土而得来的一个空间（宀）。当一个"穴"通过劳动（工）挖成后，就"空"了。同时，空还具有空闲与休息之意。

The radical is 穴 (cave) - a space (宀) obtained by the removal or separation (八) of rock or earth. When a cave (穴) is excavated by labour (工) we have the character for empty: 空. 空 also means at leisure or free from work.

`	八	宀	宀	穴	空	空	空
1	2	3	4	5	6	7	8

船 chuán

boat;
ship

船埠	chuán bù	wharf; quay
船壳	chuán ké	hull
船尾	chuán wěi	stern
船坞	chuán wù	dock; shipyard
船员	chuán yuán	(ship's) crew
船长	chuán zhǎng	captain; skipper
船只	chuán zhī	shipping; vessels

船：此字指代的是载有八个（八）或八张嘴（口）的一叶孤舟（舟），暗指诺雅方舟。"舟"为象形字，声旁"㕣"意为海岸。所以，"船"字还有沿海（沿）之舟（舟）的意思。船与水之间的关系就像针不能离开线一样。没有了水，船就寸步难行。

As a memory aid, 船 could refer to a boat (舟) with eight (八) survivors or mouths (口) - an allusion to Noah's Ark. The radical 舟 is a picture of a boat. The phonetic 㕣 probably means a coast; so 船 is a coastal (沿) vessel (舟). No matter how useful such a vessel is, "Like a thread without a needle, a boat is useless without water."

`	丿	刀	刀	舟	舟	舟	舟	舟	船	船
1	2	3	4	5	6	7	8	9	10	11

贫

pín
poor

贫乏	pín fá	poor; short; lacking
贫寒	pín hán	poor; poverty-stricken
贫困	pín kùn	poor; impoverished; in straitened circumstances
贫民	pín mín	poor people; pauper

贫：形旁"贝"指代的是原来用作货币的子安贝，是财富的象征。"分"则代表驱逐或分离。所以，"贫"可意为使某人失去（分）财富（贝），变穷。穷人应该牢记这句话："穷人与富人交往只会更穷。"

The radical 贝, a picture of a cowrie shell once used as money, represents wealth. 分 is to divide or scatter. So 贫 is to squander (分) one's wealth (贝) - to be poor. Even the poor cannot afford to ignore the warning: "If the poor associates with the rich, he will soon have no trousers to wear."

ノ	八	分	分	分	谷	贫	贫					
1	2	3	4	5	6	7	8					

圆

yuán
round;
dollar

圆规	yuán guī	compasses
圆滑	yuán huá	smooth and evasive; slick and sly
圆满	yuán mǎn	satisfactory
圆圈	yuán quān	circle; ring
圆舞曲	yuán wǔ qǔ	waltz
圆型	yuán xíng	circular; round

圆：意作圆圈或被用作货币单位的"圆"字经历了许多演变。最早被写作"○"。象形字"○"意为像子安贝（贝）一样的圆形（○）。此字后来写作"員"。最终，此字定型为"圆"。尽管此字最终加了一个"口"，但货币所具有的价值依然是起浮不定的，正如谚语所说："用钱买物要比用物换钱容易得多。"

This character for round or dollar has undergone many changes since its original form: ○. The ideograph 員 meaning round (○) like a cowrie (贝), soon replaced it. Then it was altered to 圆, being reclarified and surrounded by 口. Although hollowed out to 圆 the dollar is still changeable; it's easier to change dollars into goods than goods into dollars!

丨	冂	冂	冈	冈	圎	圆	圆	圆			
1	2	3	4	5	6	7	8	9	10		

儿

ér
infant; child

儿歌	ér gē	children's song; nursery rhymes
儿科	ér kē	(department of) paediatrics
儿女	ér nǚ	sons and daughters; children

儿：此字为象形字，指代的是脑门（O）沿尚未长合的爬行中的婴儿到能够摇摇摆摆走路的儿童（兒），意为成长中的儿童。经过演变，最终定成为"儿"。但养育孩子的艰辛是不能言表的，正如谚语所说："不养儿，不知父母辛。"

儿 is a pictograph of the growing child, from the crawling infant with open fontanels (O) to the little toddler (兒) with wobbly legs, now simplified to its present form: 儿 . The loving care shown in the delineation of this character calls to mind the saying: "To understand your parents' love, raise your own children."

丿 儿

士

shì
scholar; gentleman

士兵	shì bīng	rank-and-file soldiers; privates
士女	shì nǚ	young men and women
士气	shì qì	morale
士绅	shì shēn	gentry
士卒	shì zú	soldiers; privates

士：此字为表意文字，指代的是在人群中只占有很少一部分的学者或智者（士），即只有十分（十）之一（人）。"士"指代的是经过长时间培养出来的通达世界万物的人。正如谚语所说："十年树木，百年树人。"

According to this ideograph, a scholar or learned man (士) is a rarity: one (一) out of ten (十). He is also acquainted from one to ten, i.e., with all things. Scholars are a country's treasure, and with good reason: "It takes a tree ten years to grow up; it takes a century to educate man."

一 十 士

做 zuò
make; produce

做东	zuò dōng	play the host
做法	zuò fǎ	way of doing or making a thing
做工	zuò gōng	do manual work; work
做鬼	zuò guǐ	play tricks; play an underhand game
做客	zuò kè	be a guest

做：此字是将"亻"旁与"故"字结合而成，意为生产、劳作。同时还具有某人（亻）为了一件毫无意义的事情而辛勤劳作（攵），直至年老（古）。正如谚语所说："千年之作，毁于一旦。"

The word combines man (亻) with a cause (故) to produce an effect. Hence meaning: to make or produce. It also suggests man (亻) toiling 攵 until he gets old (古) sometimes for a fruitless cause. In the words of the proverb: "The hard work of a hundred years may be destroyed in an hour."

ノ	亻	亻	什	什	估	估	做	做	做	做
1	2	3	4	5	6	7	8	9	10	11

众 zhòng
crowd; many

众多	zhòng duō	multitudinous; numerous
众人	zhòng rén	everybody
众望	zhòng wàng	people's expectations

众：篆体的"𥃤"指代的是在他人目光（⑪）注视下的三个或三个以上的人（𠈌）。经过演变成为"眾"。此字最终定型为"众"，代表叠在一起的三个人，具有"一群"之意。你跟着一群人比较容易，要让一群人跟着你就很难。正如谚语所说："千人之军易找，千人之首难寻。"

The seal form 𥃤 shows three or many persons 𠈌 as viewed by the eye ⑪ .Modified to 眾, it was again altered to 众 - three persons, representing a crowd. It's easier to follow the crowd than to get the crowd to follow you. In the words of the proverb: "An army of a 1000 is easy to find; but, ah, how difficult to find a general!"

ノ	人	个	众	分	众		
1	2	3	4	5	6		

价 jià
price; value

估价	gū jià	estimate the value of; evaluate
讲价	jiǎng jià	bargain
价格	jià gé	price
价目	jià mù	marked price
价值	jià zhí	value worth

价: 此字为表意文字，把一个买者（亻）与卖者（贾）相结合，即"價"。卖者总会对自己的物品（西）按照子安贝（贝）的价值进行标价，即"价"。但有些价格昂贵的物品并非物有所值。

The ideograph for price (价) is derived by putting man (亻), the buyer against the seller (贾). 贾 , the seller, marks up the price to cover (西) his goods with value in cowries (贝). Paradoxically, the highest price you can pay for anything is to get it for nothing.

丿 亻 亻 价 价 价
1 2 3 4 5 6

话 huà
speech; words

话别	huà bié	say a few parting words; say good-bye
话柄	huà bǐng	subject for ridicule
话旧	huà jiù	talk over old times; reminisce
话剧	huà jù	modern drama; stage play

话: "话"意为言语，是由指代言语的"言"字与代表舌头的"舌"字组合而成。"讲"表示用有序（冓）的言（言）语进行表达或表述。"冓"指代的是建筑物的框架。"讲"最终简化为"讲"。同时，一个人的心智可以通过言语表达出来。正如谚语所说："智者谦逊，笨者狂。"

话 , meaning words or speech, is signified by words (言) of the tongue (舌).
讲 , meaning to speak or explain, is suggested by words (言) set in order (冓), 冓 being a graphic representation of the framework of a building. 讲 is simplified to 讲 . Sense is often linked with speech: "The full teapot makes no sound; the half empty teapot makes much noise."

丶 讠 讠 讠 讠 讠 话 话
1 2 3 4 5 6 7 8

语
yǔ
language

语词	yǔ cí	words and phrases
语调	yǔ diào	intonation
语法	yǔ fǎ	grammar
语汇	yǔ huì	vocabulary
语句	yǔ jù	sentence
语气	yǔ qì	tone; manner of speaking

语："吾"字指代的是五（五）张嘴（口）。古代可以用作表达"我们或我"。人称代词"吾"字与"言"字相结合后，就形成了"语"字。而言语既可以表达思想，也可以被某些人用来隐瞒自己真实的思想。

吾, or five (五) mouths (口), stands for we, I, our or my. So our or my (吾) words (言) become language (语). Language is used in many ways. Some people use it to express thought, some to conceal thought, but most use it to replace thought.

`	讠	讠	订	语	语	语	语	语				
1	2	3	4	5	6	7	8	9				

去
qù
go; leave

去处	qù chù	place to go; whereabouts
去垢剂	qù gòu jì	detergent
去路	qù lù	the way along which one is going; outlet
去年	qù nián	last year

去：此字为象形字，指代的是带有盖子"土"的空容器"厶"。"去"字含有离去之意，指代的是移走容器的盖子和容器中的物品。"来"字意为到来，象征着正在茁壮成长的小麦或大麦。同时，也象征着人们对于上天所赐福的收获所怀有的一种感激之情。

去 is a pictograph of an empty vessel (厶) and its cover (土). The meaning "go" comes from the removal of the cover and contents of the vessel.
来, meaning "come", is a pictograph of growing wheat or barley, gratefully acknowledged as having come from the heavens above.

一	十	土	去	去			
1	2	3	4	5			

回 huí
return

回避	huí bì	evade; dodge
回驳	huí bó	refute
回程	huí chéng	return trip
回答	huí dá	answer; reply; response
回顾	huí gù	look back; review
回击	huí jī	return fire; counterattack

回: 此字指代的是卷曲的云彩、水中的漩涡或以轴为中心而转动或卷曲的某一物体。因此,"回"字还具有卷入或返回之意。

回 represents an eddy, like the curling clouds of smoke or whirlpools in water; or probably an object that rolls or turns on an axis; hence the idea of revolving or returning.

1	2	3	4	5	6
丨	冂	冂	冋	回	回

凸 tū
convex; protruding

凸窗	tū chuāng	bay window
凸轮	tū lún	cam
凸面镜	tū miàn jìng	convex mirror
凸透镜	tū tòu jìng	convex lens
凹面镜	āo miàn jìng	concave mirror
凹透镜	āo tòu jìng	concave lens
凹陷	āo xiàn	hollow; depressed

凸: 此字的构造决定了它所包含的意义,即凸出。"凹"字也是一个象形字,意为凹部、凹痕。

凸 to protrude, is graphically represented by the shape of this character.
凹 a hollow or dent, is another primitive character clearly indicated by its shape.

1	2	3	4	5
丨	凵	冫	凸	凸

1	2	3	4	5
丨	凵	凵	凹	凹

巢

cháo
nest

巢穴	cháo xué	den; lair
匪巢	feǐ cháo	bandits' lair
鸟巢	niǎo cháo	bird's nest

巢: 篆体 "巢" 指代的是在树顶窝中的三只幼鸟。经过演变，此字成为了 "巢"。但果实的出现，往往代替了鸟窝的存在。虽然这种情况不会持续很久，但正如俗语所说："打破鸟巢，便一无所有。"

The seal form: 巢 depicts three fledglings in a nest on top of a tree. In the regular form: 巢 the birds remain, but the nest is missing, displaced by fruit (果), though not for long, according to the saying: "If you upset a nest, you cannot expect to find any whole eggs underneath.

‹	‹‹	‹‹‹	‹‹‹	峇	峇	峇	峃	單	巢	巢								
1	2	3	4	5	6	7	8	9	10	11	12	13	14	15	16	17	18	19

附　录
Appendix

汉语拼音与国际音标
Chinese Phonetic Alphabet (Hanyu Pinyin) and International Phonetic Alphabet

韵母　FINALS				声母　INITIALS	
汉语拼音 (Chinese Phonetic Alphabet)	国际音标 International Phonetic Alphabet	汉语拼音 (Chinese Phonetic Alphabet)	国际音标 International Phonetic Alphabet	汉语拼音 (Chinese Phonetic Alphabet)	国际音标 International Phonetic Alphabet
i	i	ian	iæn	b	p
u	ʊ	uan	uan	p	p′
ü	y	üan	yan	m	m
er	ər	en	ən	f	f
a	a	in	in	d	t
ia	ia	uen	uən	t	t′
ua	ua	un	yn	n	n
e	ɣ	ang	aŋ	l	l
o	o	iang	iaŋ	g	k
uo	uo	uang	uaŋ	k	k′
ie	iɛ	eng	əŋ	h	x
üe	yɛ	ing	iŋ	j	tɕ
ai	ai	ong	uŋ	q	tɕ′
uai	uai	iong	yŋ	x	ɕ
ei	ei			zh	tʂ
uei	uei			ch	tʂ′
ao	au			sh	ʂ
iao	iau			r	ʐ
ou	ou			z	ts
iou	iou			c	ts′
an	an			s	s
				y （字母）	i
				w （字母）	w

汉语的数字表达法
Numbers

1–100 的数字表达方式：
The Chinese count using the decimal system. Counting from 1 to 100 is as follows:

1	2	3	4	5	6	7	8	9	10
一 yī	二 èr	三 sān	四 sì	五 wǔ	六 liù	七 qī	八 bā	九 jiǔ	十 shí
十一 shí yī	→	→	→	→	→	→	→	→	二十 èr shí
二十一 èr shí yī	→	→	→	→	→	→	→	→	三十 sān shí
三十一 sān shí yī	→	→	→	→	→	→	→	→	四十 sì shí
四十一 sì shí yī	→	→	→	→	→	→	→	→	五十 wǔ shí
五十一 wú shí yī	→	→	→	→	→	→	→	→	六十 liù shí
六十一 liù shí yī	→	→	→	→	→	→	→	→	七十 qī shí
七十一 qī shí yī	→	→	→	→	→	→	→	→	八十 bā shí
八十一 bā shí yī	→	→	→	→	→	→	→	→	九十 jiǔ shí
九十一 jiǔ shí yī	→	→	→	→	→	→	→	→	一百 yī bǎi

汉语的月、星期表达法
Days and Months

1）月的表达方式:
   The months of the year in Chinese are:

一月	yī yuè	January	七月	qī yuè	July
二月	èr yuè	February	八月	bā yuè	August
三月	sān yuè	March	九月	jiǔ yuè	September
四月	sì yuè	April	十月	shí yuè	October
五月	wǔ yuè	May	十一月	shí yi yuè	November
六月	liù yuè	June	十二月	shí èr yuè	December

2）星期的表达方式:
   The names of Monday to Saturday in Chinese are:

星期一	xīngqī yī	Monday	星期四	xīngqī sì	Thursday
星期二	xīngqī èr	Tuesday	星期五	xīngqī wǔ	Friday
星期三	xīngqī sān	Wednesday	星期六	xīngqī liù	Saturday

* 英文中 Sunday 的汉语表达方式为星期日。

索 引
Index

A

爱	ài	65
安	ān	2

B

八	bā	29
白	bái	14
半	bàn	61
伴	bàn	61
帮	bāng	146
宝	bǎo	82
饱	bǎo	135
贝	bèi	38
被	bèi	148
背	bèi	173
笔	bǐ	56
比	bǐ	173
表	biǎo	148
冰	bīng	41
兵	bīng	77
病	bìng	162
表	biǎo	148
不	bù	110
布	bù	143

C

常	cháng	146
唱	chàng	171
巢	cháo	185
车	chē	137
尘	chén	97
齿	chǐ	33

愁	chóu	58
丑	chǒu	89
出	chū	37
川	chuān	44
船	chuán	178
床	chuáng	149
春	chūn	170
聪	cōng	67
从	cóng	155
窜	cuàn	103

D

答	dá	174
大	dà	7
带	dài	145
待	dài	157
刀	dāo	84
岛	dǎo	46
道	dào	164
旦	dàn	15
得	dé	155
德	dé	156
帝	dì	144
电	diàn	43
钉	dīng	74
定	dìng	83
东	dōng	17
兑	duì	29
多	duō	152

E

恶	ě, è	68

饿	è	135		龟	guī	112
恩	ēn	69		贵	guì	39
儿	ér	180		国	guó	131
耳	ěr	27		果	guǒ	63

F

H

犯	fàn	93		海	hǎi	161
方	fāng	75		害	hài	83
房	fáng	75		号	háo, hào	99
放	fàng	167		好	hǎo	2
飞	fēi	46		禾	hé	57
费	fèi	86		合	hé	69
吠	fèi	90		黑	hēi	54
分	fēn	85		狠	hěn	94
风	fēng	120		轰	hōng	137
凤	fèng	109		红	hóng	123
夫	fū	8		猴	hóu	90
弗	fú	86		虎	hǔ	99
伏	fú	92		户	hù	74
富	fù	82		话	huà	27
父	fù	142		画	huà	129
妇	fù	144		话	huà	182
				回	huí	184
				慧	huì	68
				火	huǒ	52

G

甘	gān	59				
高	gāo	177				
鸽	gē	108				

J

歌	gē	171		鸡	jī	107
给	gěi	123		集	jí	104
工	gōng	25		疾	jí	163
弓	gōng	85		家	jiā	4
公	gōng	121		加	jiā	158
功	gōng	157		甲	jiǎ	15
狗	gǒu	89		嫁	jià	4
够	gòu	153		价	jià	182
古	gǔ	30		尖	jiān	11
骨	gǔ	119		见	jiàn	23
馆	guǎn	136		贱	jiān	39
光	guāng	159		将	jiāng	150

匠	jiàng	77
焦	jiāo	106
角	jiǎo	114
轿	jiào	140
叫	jiào	168
结	jié	124
解	jiě	115
姐	jiě	65
今	jīn	70
金	jīn	72
巾	jīn	142
近	jìn	78
进	jìn	105
经	jīng	126
京	jīng	177
井	jǐng	175
军	jūn	139

K

开	kāi	81
课	kè	63
客	kè	172
空	kōng	178
口	kǒu	24
哭	kū	91
库	kù	138
裤	kù	147
狂	kuáng	93

L

来	lái	62
篮	lán	175
狼	láng	94
牢	láo	60
劳	láo	159
老	lǎo	116
雷	léi	43
离	lí	107

理	lǐ	132
李	lǐ	6
立	lì	9
力	lì	12
丽	lì	98
连	lián	141
莲	lián	141
林	lín	161
龙	lóng	114
聋	lóng	169
鲁	lǔ	49
轮	lún	138
骡	luó	96
骆	luò	97
律	lǜ	156

M

马	mǎ	96
猫	māo	95
毛	máo	115
帽	mào	145
美	měi	51
妹	mèi	64
门	mén	79
们	mén	80
梦	mèng	154
米	mǐ	134
面	miàn	164
明	míng	14
墨	mò	54
木	mù	5
目	mù	23

N

男	nán	12
你	nǐ	21
念	niàn	71

鸟	niǎo	45
牛	niú	60
奴	nú	19
怒	nù	31
女	nǚ	1

P

爬	pá	117
怕	pà	32
皮	pí	120
片	piàn	149
票	piào	117
贫	pín	179

Q

妻	qī	5
栖	qī	6
气	qì	134
金	qiān	70
钱	qián	73
墙	qiáng	150
情	qíng	167
庆	qìng	98
秋	qiū	57
取	qǔ	28
去	qù	183
全	quán	133

R

人	rén	7
日	rì	13
如	rú	172
软	ruǎn	140

S

伞	sǎn	44
山	shān	45
扇	shàn	48
上	shàng	18
少	shǎo, shào	10
舌	shé	26
身	shēn	32
生	shēng	37
狮	shī	95
十	shí	30
石	shí	176
豕	shǐ	3
矢	shǐ	87
是	shì	35
室	shì	112
士	shì	180
手	shǒu	20
售	shòu	106
受	shòu	119
书	shū	129
鼠	shǔ	103
双	shuāng	105
水	shuǐ	40
税	shuì	58
睡	shuì	165
思	sī	166
私	sī	121
丝	sī	122
所	suǒ	76

T

他	tā	22
太	tài	9
贪	tān	71
疼	téng	163
剃	tì	87

天	tiān	8	先	xiān	160
田	tián	11	仙	xiān	176
听	tīng	169	现	xiàn	131
凸	tū	184	线	xiàn	122
秃	tū	59	想	xiǎng	66
突	tū	92	象	xiàng	100
土	tǔ	36	像	xiàng	100
兔	tù	101	小	xiǎo	10
			笑	xiào	56
			协	xié	158
W			写	xiě	128
			新	xīn	79
歪	wāi	110	心	xīn	31
外	wài	153	姓	xìng	38
完	wán	84	凶	xiōng	174
万	wàn	113	兄	xiōng	28
王	wáng	130	熊	xióng	101
网	wǎng	125	休	xiū	16
忘	wàng	67	学	xué	127
尾	wěi	116	雪	xuě	42
为	wéi, wěi	118			
胃	wèi	166			
未	wèi	64	**Y**		
闻	wén	81			
问	wèn	80	鸭	yā	108
我	wǒ	21	言	yán	24
屋	wū	111	炎	yán	53
恶	wù	68	燕	yàn	109
			羊	yáng	50
			洋	yáng	52
X			药	yào	127
			也	yě	22
西	xī	17	夜	yè	154
夕	xī	152	衣	yī	147
习	xí	47	医	yī	88
洗	xǐ	160	义	yì	51
喜	xǐ	170	忆	yì	66
细	xì	125	逸	yì	102
瞎	xiā	165	易	yì	113
下	xià	18	银	yín	72
鲜	xiān	50	饮	yǐn	136
			印	yìn	128

英	yīng	55	壮	zhuàng	151
永	yǒng	40	子	zǐ	1
有	yǒu	62	字	zì	3
友	yǒu	20	自	zì	33
右	yòu	26	走	zǒu	35
鱼	yú	48	左	zuǒ	25
渔	yú	49	坐	zuò	36
羽	yǔ	47	做	zuò	181
语	yǔ	183			
雨	yǔ	41			
狱	yù	91			
玉	yù	130			
冤	yuān	102			
圆	yuán	179			
月	yuè	13			
云	yún	42			

Z

灾	zāi	53
旱	zǎo	16
斩	zhǎn	139
针	zhēn	73
争	zhēng	118
正	zhèng	34
政	zhèng	168
知	zhī	88
只	zhī	104
枝	zhī	162
纸	zhǐ	124
止	zhǐ	34
至	zhì	111
质	zhì	78
终	zhōng	126
中	zhōng	19
众	zhòng	181
帚	zhǒu	143
竹	zhú	55
主	zhǔ	132
住	zhù	133
装	zhuāng	151

ⓒ原版所有者(英文版)：Federal Publications (S) Pte Ltd 1998 出版

中文版权所有者：新世界出版社 1999 年出版

引进图书版权登记号：图字：01－1999－0662

图书在版编目（CIP）数据

趣味汉字/(新加坡)陈火平绘著.

－北京：新世界出版社，1999

ISBN 7－80005－515－9

Ⅰ.趣… Ⅱ.陈… Ⅲ.汉字－历史－汉、英 Ⅳ.H12

中国版本图书馆 CIP 数据核字(1999)第 35737 号

责任编辑：李淑娟

封面设计：唐少文

趣 味 汉 字

陈火平　绘著

＊

新世界出版社出版

（北京百万庄路 24 号　邮编：100037）

北京运乔宏源印刷厂印刷

新华书店北京发行所发行

新世界出版社发行部电话：(010)68994118

1999 年(16 开)第一版　2001 年北京第四次印刷

ISBN 7-80005-515-9／G·195

02800

9CE－3352P